The Complete Guide to Estate & Financial Planning In Turbulent Times

The Questions Consumers Are Asking,
with Answers from
America's Top Attorneys and Financial Advisors

Throughout this book, hypothetical examples are used to illustrate points. These are not representative of any specific situation. Your results will vary. The authors, editors, and publishers of this book are not engaged in rendering legal, tax, accounting, insurance, financial and investment planning, or similar professional services in the pages of this book. While legal, tax, accounting, insurance, and financial planning educational topics covered in this book have been checked with sources believed to be reliable, some material may be affected by changes in the laws or in the interpretations of such laws, since the manuscript for this book was completed. For that reason, the accuracy and completeness of such information and the opinions based thereon are not guaranteed. In addition, state or local tax laws or procedural rules may have a material impact on the general educational recommendations made by the authors, and the strategies outlined in this book may not be suitable for every individual or every situation. If legal, tax, accounting, insurance, investment, financial planning, or other expert advice is required, obtain the services of a competent licensed practitioner.

ISBN 978-1-4507-0384-0

Editor-in-Chief: Daniel P. Stuenzi, J.D.
Technical Editor: Scot W. Overdorf, J.D., C.P.A.
Marketing Services: Lydia Monchak
Dust Jacket Design Editor: Todd Richards
Website: Promising Sites, LLC

Printed in the United States of America

Collaborative Press, LLC
15606 Elm Street, Suite 105
Omaha, NE 68130
www.collpress.com

Table of Contents

Introduction

AT THE TIME OF THIS WRITING, THE AMERICAN ECONOMY IS IN THE MIDDLE of what is predicted to be several years of turbulence. We've been mired in what most consider the worst economy since the Great Depression. And since early 2009, we've experienced the greatest intervention of government into the private sector economy in the history of the country. Unprecedented foundational changes have been made in our system of free trade capitalism.

With bailouts in the banking and investment industries, the real estate and mortgage markets, and the automotive industries; and with continued attempts to take over the health care system—more and more of the economy is government-controlled. Couple that with a wildly unpredictable securities market, the general devaluation of the dollar, a growing tax burden, record-setting national debt and unemployment, insurmountable political division in Washington, and upcoming 2010 mid-term elections; and it's anybody's guess as to what lies ahead.

This is the environment that currently surrounds the contributing authors to this book. But with such a large and complex economy, we suspect that turbulence of one sort or another will always be with us—even if you pick up this book several years from now! With that in mind, our goal is to provide you with a reliable resource for answers regarding estate and financial planning in times like these.

The methodology for creating this book was fairly simple. First, we wanted input from more than one professional discipline. We've found that the best result for consumers comes when professional advisors work together; and it never hurts to have a second opinion!

Therefore, we contacted attorneys, financial and investment advisors, insurance professionals, and CPAs and asked them to apply to participate as a contributing author. We selected 24 of these professionals with extensive experience and expertise from different parts of the country. We provided them with an outline of topics within the estate and financial planning fields, and gave them one assignment. We asked them to submit the questions that clients were asking most frequently on these topics, along with the answers the professionals were providing to those questions.

The result is the volume you hold in your hand. It's written in a Question and Answer format which we believe makes it easier to use. And although you may decide to read it from cover to cover, it's designed primarily as a reference tool that you can use to find specific answers on topics in which you are interested.

Like most professional disciplines, estate and financial planning are both science and art. Two different professionals in the same discipline may approach a problem with two different strategies, and both may achieve successful results. And within the disciplines, attorneys tend to approach things one way and financial professionals another. So we are excited to provide you with a resource that includes the best of all worlds and approaches—a true collaboration of experts.

Remember, however, that these professionals are offering answers that they have given in actual client situations, and every client situation is unique. They and the editors are not intending to give you, the reader, specific legal, financial, investment, or accounting advice. That would be impossible to do without knowing you and your circumstances personally, and without comprehensive fact-finding and discussion.

Also keep in mind that tax laws and industry regulation change constantly. Indeed, we expect major changes in the estate, gift, and income tax laws during 2010. What appears in this book is believed to be accurate at the time of writing, but cannot be guaranteed to be so forever.

Throughout this book, hypothetical examples are used to illustrate points. These are not representative of any specific situation. Your results will vary. Therefore, we recommend that you visit with the professional who gave you this book; or another contributing author listed in the index; or a local attorney, financial advisor, insurance professional, or CPA in your community to find specific answers for your specific situation. We wish you prosperity and peace in these turbulent times—and those that lie ahead!

Daniel P. Stuenzi, JD
Editor-in-Chief

1 | Fundamentals of Estate Planning

Many people believe estate planning is only for the wealthy. But the authors believe that it's for anyone who cares about something or someone. Ultimately, it's about your family; not your financial statement. It's about your life and theirs; not about death. And it's a process; not an event.

What is estate planning?

In the most general sense, estate planning is a process that ensures that the people and things important to you are treated in a manner you would approve of, both while you are living and after you are gone. Planning isn't limited to financial assets, real estate, and personal possessions. It's much broader than simply creating a set of instructions to give away what you own at your death, or trying to minimize taxes and expenses in the future.

It also includes such things as naming someone to look after you if you become incapacitated, to look after your minor children if you're gone, and to protect adult children from lawsuits and divorces after they receive their inheritance. It's about planning for the future of a family business, or contributing to charitable and community causes. It might provide your children and grandchildren with a source of funding for their college education, or provide for the proper management and investment of assets for those in the family with special needs. For some, it includes an element of "legacy planning" incorporating your family values, beliefs, traditions, and stories.

In these ways and many others, estate planning is much more than simply planning for death and taxes. It's about sharing love and creating opportunities for you and the ones you care most about. Legal documents such as wills, revocable living trusts, and powers of attorney can be supplemented with journals, diaries, instructions, or recordings, which provide guidance and wisdom to those left behind.

Who needs estate planning?

There are a lot of misconceptions about estate planning. And part of the blame lies with professional advisors who speak a unique planning dialect. We talk about wills, so you may associate estate planning with death planning and distributing assets after you're gone. And since death usually happens when we're advanced in age, you may believe planning is for older, retired people. We talk about "wealth" so you may think planning is only for the wealthy. In fact, the word "estate" itself adds to the confusion. However, estate planning is concerned with much more than death, and is important for everyone; not just the wealthy.

Why should I care about planning?

Many people consider estate planning to be an act of stewardship. They spend their life maximizing the use of their "time, talents, treasure, and trust." They want to ensure that the benefits of this stewardship will continue even after the ability to control has ended. The control and benefit of everything we "own" will eventually be transferred. So planning helps control how, when, and to whom the transfer takes place, and anticipates the consequences of the transfer.

People plan in order to protect the people, causes, and things that are important to them, now and in the future. They do this by controlling whatever they can during life, and making sure that people they trust take their place when required.

I've heard that if I title my assets correctly, I don't really need a plan. For example, if all my property is in joint name with my spouse, isn't that sufficient?

First, the question seems to assume that planning is only about assets. As discussed above, plans are used for many other purposes beyond passing money and personal items to the next generation. Nevertheless, since assets are also involved, this is a good question.

There are several ways in which property can be titled. For example, property can be owned in one name by one person. It can also be owned by more than one person in joint names under one of four main structures:

1. As joint tenants with right of survivorship,

2. As tenants by the entireties (a form of joint tenants property between husband and wife that is available in certain states),

3. As tenants in common, and

4. As community property (a form of ownership between husband and wife that is mandatory in 9 states and optional in Alaska).

The type of ownership will determine how your interest in the property passes at your death. Title equals result. For example, a will controls only those assets owned by an individual in his or her own name. Your interest in joint tenancy property passes by operation of law at your death, to the surviving joint owner, even if you tried to leave your interest in the property to someone else through your will. Both wills and joint ownership are generally anticipating a death transfer. Ownership in a trust allows for lifetime planning as well, and includes specific transfer instructions that joint ownership cannot.

So, while joint ownership provides a method of transfer when the first spouse dies, it does nothing on the second death because the ownership has passed to one individual. And, in the event of a common disaster (husband and wife killed in a car accident for example) if property is owned jointly without an accompanying plan, the property would be subject to intestacy laws. That means the state would decide how the property will be distributed to the remaining heirs.

Do I have to give up control in order to accomplish this planning?

There is one common theme we hear from every person who begins the planning process. Everyone wants to maintain control. In fact, one of the most important things about a good estate plan is that it enables you to do exactly that. It protects your power to make decisions— during life, during periods of disability, and even after death.

Why do people fail to do estate planning?

People invariably fail to plan due to misconceptions about the process. As mentioned above, some people view estate planning as "death planning;" an event about which few people want to think. It's hard for most of us to face our mortality and the brevity of life.

Others believe that planning is complex and expensive. They fear they'll have to give up control, or that their lifestyle and income stream will be disrupted. Because they have busy schedules and lives, estate planning is simply not a priority.

Some fail to plan because they don't know about the benefits. They're unaware of all that can be accomplished with proper planning, or they just don't care what happens after they die, knowing they will not be around to witness any chaos that may result from the failure to plan.

Finally, there are many who understand the benefits of planning and know that they should plan, but who simply procrastinate. People fail to do estate planning for the same reason so many college term papers are written the night before they are due—it seems to be human nature to put "unpleasant" things off until the last minute. Of course, the problem is that no one really knows when "the last minute" will arrive.

What are the goals of estate planning?

Estate planning goals will, of course, vary from family to family, and depend on the things you find important. Generally speaking, estate planning is designed to allow you to give what you own to whom you want, when you want, and the way you want. In doing so, you are able to care for your loved ones in ways that are important to you. A good estate planning advisor team is able to help you clarify and define your goals, and then incorporate them into your plan. To do this, the advisors will need to gain a deep understanding of your core values and beliefs. They will need to understand the dynamics of your family.

You are likely to be asked such things as:

- What is important about planning to you?
- Do you desire to maintain control of your assets during life?
- How do you want to be cared for in the event of your disability?

- Who will care for you personally, and for your money in that event?

- Do you have minor children for whom a guardian must be appointed?

- What do you hope for your children's future? Are there family values and beliefs you want to pass to subsequent generations?

- What does money mean to you and what is its significance?

- Do you have a desire to make a difference in your community?

- What concerns, if any, do you have about the future of your loved ones? Are there those with special needs?

- Is it important for you to preserve family harmony?

- Would you like to provide positive incentives to motivate and inspire your heirs?

- What about negative incentives to discourage particular behavior?

- Do you have tax concerns?

- Is privacy important to you?

- Is asset protection important to you?

- How important is it that you are able to maintain your current lifestyle?

- Do you own a business?

- Do you want to encourage entrepreneurship in your children or grandchildren?

- Do you wish to provide for advanced education for anyone?

The answers to these questions can help clarify and define your basic goals which will form the foundation of your estate plan. Of course these questions will be followed by many others. The advisor team's first step is to listen carefully, so that you and they can design the specifics of how (and with whose help) those goals will be accomplished.

As you can see, a good estate plan can be much more than simple instructions to pass monetary wealth. You can lend purpose and meaning to a plan, and enhance the lives of your loved ones by connecting, motivating and inspiring them. Your estate plan should define who you are as a person and reflect your core values and beliefs.

Should I do my own estate planning?

Today there are limitless software programs and books that promote doing your own estate plan. Websites and self-help companies will sell forms claiming to help you create your own estate plan almost for free! Although it may be tempting to do so, you should think very carefully before undertaking the do-it-yourself approach.

Researching information on the Internet can be used as a means to provide various questions to the advisory team; however it will ultimately be the expert's experience that will make sure the strategies set forth apply to your plan. Advisors become experts not just by knowing the text book terminology, but by having in-depth experience handling and implementing the recommendations they have made.

Estate planning is a very complex area of the law that requires years of education and experience to master. Even among attorneys, a generalist may lack the skills necessary to competently assist you with proper estate planning. And it's even more difficult for a layman. The consequences of a poorly designed estate plan can be far-reaching. After all, you will be planning for the two things that most people find extremely important: everything you own and everyone you love.

Software packages and forms available on the Internet may not reflect each state's specific laws. In addition, most forms are very generic and lack the depth to handle most family complexities and unique planning situations. A generic form can never reflect your specific goals for your loved ones, nor can they incorporate your beliefs and values. These shortcomings are acknowledged by the companies that promote their use. That's why they include disclaimers that advise you to seek the help of an attorney prior to signing the documents. In short, using preprinted forms is likely to lead to poor results.

For example, it is not uncommon to find standard form trust documents that do not contain any provisions for removal or replacement of a Trustee when an acting Trustee dies or becomes disabled. You may prefer to grant to your adult children or others you trust, the power to remove a Trustee or to fill a Trustee vacancy. Using a form that lacks this specific provision, your children may be forced to bring a court action to replace a non-performing or unsatisfactory Trustee.

Do-it-yourself forms often leave the determination of your disability to one doctor, instead of seeking a second opinion or using a disability panel that may include family members. They often don't provide planning for estate taxes, and they usually call for outright distributions to heirs. You'll see in subsequent chapters that you can gain a lot of protections for your children and grandchildren that are forfeited with an outright distribution of funds.

Another problem with generic forms is that they may lack specific instructions related to document signing procedures, or may provide instructions that do not meet your state's requirements. For example, a standard will may have instructions that indicate two witnesses are required to witness and sign the will. However, if one of the persons acting as a witness is also receiving a benefit from the will, they would be considered an "interested witness" under most state laws. As an interested witness, it opens the door to disgruntled heirs to challenge the will on the belief that it might have been signed under duress, fraud, and/or undue influence.

Vendors of software programs and preprinted forms often advertise that the documents are "valid in all 50 states." The issue, though, is not whether the documents are valid. In fact, a will written and dated in your own handwriting in pencil on a page torn from a spiral-bound notebook may be valid in some states. The issue is whether the documents actually represent your specific wishes, achieve your specific goals, and take into consideration all the legal and financial issues that may have an impact. [A coupon for a free hamburger may be valid in all 50 states, but that doesn't mean that the hamburger is the best meal for you, or the meal that you want or need.]

Of course, not all things claimed to be valid are in fact valid. One example comes from one of the most advertised sites offering legal documents. In the section that provides pricing information for Louisiana documents, it notes: "In order for the county recorder to provide you with a copy of the new deed, two deeds must be recorded." Louisiana has parishes, not counties. Louisiana does not use deeds to transfer property. Documents are recorded at the clerk of court's office—there is no office called the "county recorder." If the form sellers make three mistakes in one sentence on such a simple matter on their website, one might wonder how many other mistakes lurk in the documents themselves.

Another service's website confidently assures its prospective customers: "This document is a statutory will codicil drafted in accordance with, and uses the attestation clause contained in, La. R.S. 9:2442B"—a specific Louisiana law. (They think it provides extra credibility when they cite a specific statute.) The only problem is that La. R.S. 9:2442 was repealed in 1999.

While it is possible for a layman to prepare an estate plan from Internet forms and instructions, it's equally possible to perform an appendectomy following Internet instructions. Neither act, however, is recommended.

How can I prepare for estate planning?

In most instances, your estate planning attorney will provide a questionnaire to help organize the data and provide the specific information needed for planning. The questionnaire will ask not only about your assets, but also about your citizenship, your family composition, your children and other beneficiaries, your wishes during a disability, a list of the people you might trust to serve as guardians and trustees, and much more. Every question is asked for an important reason, and bears directly on the plan that is designed for you.

You will usually need to gather documentation related to the things you own. For example, you should gather information from your bank and other financial statements, life insurance policies, stock certificates, deeds to real estate, and other titling documents. If you own a business, it will be helpful to have information such as appraised value and details on any business succession plans that are in place.

You may find it easier and faster to enlist the help of your accounting, insurance, and/or financial advisors to help you put together your asset information. The objective is to provide your estate planning attorney with enough information to gain a thorough understanding of what you own, its value, and how things are titled.

Also by way of preparation, you should give some thought to how you would like to dispose of your estate. If you are married, it's helpful to discuss these issues ahead of time with your spouse. When you know *who* you want to benefit, the attorney and other advisors can counsel you on *how* to best accomplish your goals.

You should also consider the individuals that you would trust to raise your minor children, to manage your finances and your personal care in the event of disability, and to make medical decisions if and when required. These helpers are critical to the success of your estate plan.

Do I really have to disclose everything I own to my attorney and/or financial planner?

In our experience, some clients are reluctant to reveal everything they own to any single advisor. They may have investment assets with more than one investment advisor or insurance policies with more than one insurance professional. However, when preparing for estate planning it is very important that the attorney (and any other professional advisors on the team) be informed of *all* assets you own. That is the only way to design a comprehensive plan that will preserve your whole estate.

Sometimes clients neglect to list assets because they simply don't think about them. Is there gold or silver in the safe deposit box at the bank? Are there valuable coins, jewelry, or heirlooms tucked away at home? What about the art collection that hangs on the walls? Are there life insurance policies from decades ago that you have forgotten about because they no longer require premium payments? It's easy to overlook these assets and to focus only on bank accounts, securities, real estate, and other obvious investments.

Anything you own, whether or not it actually has a recorded title, is part of your taxable estate. It is critical that when it comes to the estate planning process you fully disclose everything you own. The attorney's or advisor's questionnaire will typically provide a comprehensive check-list of assets to guide you.

What does estate planning cost?

Estate planning is as an investment in the future of you and your family. It is not a commodity that should be judged by price alone. By way of comparison, your local police department probably doesn't shop for the cheapest bullet-proof vests it can find for its officers. The emphasis rather is on quality and whether or not it will accomplish what it is intended to accomplish.

Your specific investment will depend on many factors including the nature and extent of your assets, your personal goals and objectives, and the experience and qualifications of the attorney you select. The investment in a good estate plan is money well spent. Most people don't think twice about spending several thousand dollars on an automobile. For the most part, that multi-thousand dollar automobile is not worth a lot after a few years.

Good estate planning, on the other hand, yields benefits beyond your lifetime, and through subsequent generations of your family. It allows you to protect yourself and everything you own for the benefit of everyone you love. In addition, it is not uncommon for a good estate plan to save millions of dollars in taxes and administrative expenses for clients and their families.

The fees you pay will vary according to the complexity of your affairs, and to some extent, your geographic location. Prices tend to be higher in big cities than rural areas. They tend to be higher with very large firms than with smaller boutique firms. At the time of this writing, if you are single and have no children, a simple will, durable power of attorney and healthcare directive might cost from $300 to $1500.

If you are married with minor children the cost for both spouses combined might be from $1000 to $4000. If you have a taxable estate, or own a business, you may need multiple trusts, a variety of entities, and gifting strategies, and the cost could be $10,000 to $50,000 or more. The only way to know for sure what your plan will cost is to consult with an estate planning attorney. Most will provide a fixed fee quote or a not-to-exceed cost established up front before any work begins, and many offer a free initial consultation so that you can get answers to your questions about cost and process before you spend any money.

There is one final thing to remember about costs. In every estate plan of every type and every level of sophistication, there are actually three costs:

1. The upfront costs of counseling and plan creation,

2. The cost to keep the plan up to date (or the larger cost of failing to do so), and

3. The cost of plan administration after your death.

Be sure to ask about ALL the costs involved!

What is the cost of failing to plan?

In failing to plan your estate, you risk your loved ones' futures. Much like the MasterCard advertisements, a well-designed estate plan is "priceless." After all, how do you put a value on protection and security for your children and grandchildren? What is the value of providing future generations with the opportunity to get a college education? How do you measure the value of contributing to your favorite charitable causes? A good estate plan is an investment in the things in life that are truly priceless.

Some specific costs of failing to plan can include:

- A chaotic search for what you own after you're gone
- Bickering and fighting among family members
- Extra administrative hassles and costs
- The involvement of a judge in probate court
- Additional taxes paid to the IRS
- Things going to the wrong people, or to the right people but in a manner that is unprotected from creditors and "predators"

What's the difference between estate planning and financial planning?

Financial planning tends to focus on the accumulation and preservation of wealth. It often encompasses such things as:

- Clarifying Financial Objectives
- Education Funding
- Retirement Funding
- Cash Flow Budgeting
- Risk Management
- Asset Protection
- Balance Sheet, Income Statements, and other financial measures

We will discuss financial planning in more detail in the next chapter.

Estate planning, on the other hand tends to focus less on accumulation and more on the protection and ultimate distribution of your assets, accompanied by specific instructions. Both financial and estate planning are ongoing processes—not events. It is inaccurate to say, "I did my financial plan" or "I did my estate plan." Nothing in life is more certain than change.

Depending on what type of professional you're talking to, you may hear financial planning described as part of estate planning, or you may hear that estate planning is a sub-set of financial planning. Nevertheless, both types of planning are crucial, and must be integrated to achieve the best results for you and your family.

2 | Fundamentals of Financial Planning

Like estate planning, financial planning is as much "art" as "science" and is performed on a custom basis for the individual needs and desires of each client. Whether you are just beginning to build wealth, are established and expanding your wealth, or are preserving wealth for the future; financial planning can provide a strategy and a guide to help you reach your goals.

What is financial planning?

Financial planning is probably one of the most future-oriented activities in which you will participate during your lifetime. Because it looks ahead to the unknown, it can also be an intimidating task. It requires you to determine where you want to be financially at different points in time in the years ahead; and then to set goals and establish strategies to get there.

In many cases the investment and insurance industries have created products to facilitate these goals and objectives. Because of this, the financial planning industry began primarily with sales professionals who distributed these products. As the profession matured, a more comprehensive financial planning process was created. Financial advisors became less sales-oriented, and more counseling-oriented.

Financial planning as a profession is relatively new, so the term can be confusing for consumers. There are no nationally prescribed standards defining what is meant by "financial planning." However, the CFP® Board of Standards, a self-regulatory organization for the financial planning industry uses the following steps in their planning process:

1. Establish and define the client/planner relationship,

2. Gather client data including goals,

3. Analyze and evaluate the client's financial status,

4. Develop and present financial planning recommendations and/or alternatives,

5. Implement the financial planning recommendations, and

6. Monitor the financial planning recommendations.

A comprehensive financial plan typically involves a review of at least the following broad areas of a client's finances:

1. Current financial position

2. Retirement planning

3. Investments

4. Income tax planning

5. Estate planning

6. Risk management (insurance planning)

7. Education planning

I often hear the term "wealth management." Is that the same as financial planning?

The term "wealth management" means different things to different advisors. However, in most cases it encompasses a broad approach to assisting individuals and families to accomplish their financial goals. Specific disciplines within the wealth management process may include financial planning, investment management, risk management, and estate and legacy planning.

Who needs financial planning?

Generally speaking, if a person has finances, they can benefit from financial planning. It is for anyone who is goal-oriented and organized in their approach to wealth management.

Financial planning involves a great many areas of technical expertise, so it is difficult for most of us to find the time and education to manage every aspect. Even if you were to become an expert in one area, it's possible that without professional guidance, planning decisions you make in one area will negate or be in conflict with decisions made in other dimensions of the plan. Ideally, it helps to have advisors involved that know something about each of the areas of planning. This allows for plan integration and the elimination of conflicts.

Why do people fail to do financial planning?

We have observed that many otherwise intelligent and responsible people fail to create a financial plan. Reasons include such things as:

1. Financial planning requires paying a professional in the present for something that is ultimately accomplished in the future. For many, paying for an intangible (such as advice and counsel) is a new thing. Not everyone is willing to spend money today for a future benefit that may be hard to calculate accurately, and that cannot be guaranteed.

2. Financial planning is not "required" so it is easy to ignore. Life is so busy and complex just dealing with what is required, that it's easy to ignore future planning until it's too late. Too often, the "urgent" replaces the "important." For example, everyone files a tax return because it is required by the government. But the majority of people do not do proactive tax planning to reduce their tax burden. It's similar to the way many people approach medical care. They react immediately to aches, pains, and injuries as they occur, but do very little with preventive strategies. In short, financial planning needs to be proactive rather than reactive.

3. There is no obvious pain to avoid. We as consumers tend to pay for things that help us avoid pain. However, the pain of not planning often does not occur until retirement, or even after death—and is suffered more by family members than by those who failed to plan.

4. Many families don't know where to begin the process. They are inundated daily with messages from professionals, mass media, family and friends on what they "should" be doing with their money. Unfortunately, many do not have a formal process to develop a personal vision and goals before they begin the planning process. Without a sufficient preliminary process many families end up with executed legal documents, investments, and insurance policies that do not integrate into the overall desired objective.

Why is it important to have a process to capture a personal family vision of wealth before beginning any estate or financial planning?

Having a formalized process allows you to reflect on what is most important to you and your family. It also affords the opportunity to break your vision into smaller goals and objectives so they can be prioritized and successfully completed.

Traditionally most professional advisors work only within their own education and skill set. There is a trend that is gaining strength, however, in which some advisors understand the value to the client and the professional's practice to be able to connect more meaningfully with their clients. Financial planners, attorneys, accountants, investment managers, and insurance professionals are beginning to take a more holistic approach to the client's needs. They are moving to areas of discussion that are not always directly related to the professional's discipline, and they are working as advisor teams to multiply their effectiveness.

Many professionals have developed processes that seek to understand and document the client's personal history and thoughts on several topics before formally engaging them. Generally this will include multiple meetings in which the client will share family history as well as their concerns about money with the advisor. Some advisors will use the information received during the discovery sessions to help the client draft a formal vision statement. This produces a much better result and greater satisfaction for the client.

How do I prepare for financial planning?

The most important part of a financial plan is deciding what matters most to you. Your financial planner should provide you with a comprehensive set of questions on a wide range of topics. Take the time to reflect on those questions before you meet with your advisor, so that you can begin that process of defining what matters most.

Your advisor should also give you a data and documents checklist to assist you in gathering all relevant information and documents. Be thorough in compiling everything the advisor asks for. Don't withhold something because you don't think it's important. Your financial planner has a reason for asking for that information. It is important to know all the pieces in order to develop an integrated and comprehensive plan.

Keep in mind that as you prepare for financial planning, all of your advisors need to be involved. In addition to the financial advisor, that may include your attorney, CPA, insurance professional, and others. Anyone that you rely upon to make decisions should be part of your team. If you are missing someone on that team let the others assist you in filling that position.

As you prepare, review the players on your team and ask yourself how you feel about each of them. If you find that you are not willing to involve each of them in the planning process, ask yourself why. Ultimately, you need to have an advisory team that you trust and respect to guide you through the implementation of your financial plan.

What are the costs of financial planning?

Financial planners can get paid in a variety of ways. None of these compensation methods are necessarily better than another. The important thing is to have a clear explanation and understanding about how your particular advisor is paid, including full disclosure of any potential conflicts of interest.

Fee-only financial planners may charge either an hourly or flat fee, or if investment advisory services are also provided, the fee may be asset-based (i.e. a percentage of the assets subject to the investment advisory services). Fee-only planners do not receive commission compensation and are not licensed to do so.

Fee-only is not to be confused with fee-based. Fee-based financial planners may also charge hourly or flat fees, and may also charge asset-based fees for investment advisory services. In addition, fee-based planners may be registered to receive commission compensation for things such as investment or insurance products. The potential for conflict of interest may exist if a financial planner charges a fee for planning advice that leads to product implementation upon which they also receive commission compensation.

Some planners are paid solely by commissions. They do not charge fees for their planning services and rely upon implementation using financial products that compensate them. Often these planners are not registered to provide financial planning on a fee basis.

Most CERTIFIED FINANCIAL PLANNERS™ (CFP®s) are compensated like any other consultant, CPA, or attorney. Although most CFP®s prefer to quote project fees, those fees are typically based upon their estimate of the time required to complete your project. Their goal is to provide the most benefit to you for the amount of time required. This is usually determined by an assessment during their discovery process of getting to know you, your affairs, your goals, and your expectations.

As a rough guide, a comprehensive review of your financial affairs and goals, development of strategies, delivery of recommendations, and assistance in implementing those recommendations may cost about ½ of 1% of your total net worth during your first year. So someone with a net worth of $5 million should expect fees to start at about $25,000. Someone with a net worth of $10 million should expect about $50,000 in first year fees. At every level, the cost of planning should result in substantial benefit from both basic and advanced estate planning strategies that have the potential to save significant amounts of income and estate taxes, as well as accomplishing other financial goals.

Some financial planning professionals include their financial planning fees within the Asset Management Fees that they charge to manage your investment portfolio. However, the trend is to move away from this type of billing as it is not always in the client's best interest. The complexity of providing ongoing comprehensive planning is not necessarily linked to the size of someone's investment portfolio.

What are the costs of failing to plan financially?

Failing to plan can result in both emotional and fiscal costs.

Emotional Costs

Financial planning is about being clear where you are going financially, and being confident that you have made the right decisions and have the best strategy in place. Lack of planning often leads to a lack of financial independence. The emotional cost is confidence.

Fiscal Costs

Financial planning is about increasing your net worth in the most effective way. If you were paddling down the river and could know that a waterfall with a 100 foot drop was ahead, when would you like to know? The sooner you know, the better your chances of saving your life. When it comes to financial planning, the sooner you know what might occur for you financially, the sooner you can make the decisions that will improve the growth or preservation of your net worth.

Much of the stock market news highlights information after the fact, and if we had acted on it before anyone else, it would have resulted in making a lot of money. The same is true for real estate. Millions have been earned by developers who had a vision of what could happen with a piece of real estate they discovered before everyone else. Personal financial planning is about applying the same concept to your own personal wealth planning in the areas of investments, income taxes, insurance, retirement planning, and estate planning.

How does your level of wealth impact your planning?

The greater your level of wealth, the less concern you have about meeting basic needs such as food and shelter, and the more freedom you have to pursue personal growth, achievement, and a personal legacy. Abraham Maslow developed a hierarchy of human needs that provides a corollary to a person's financial planning needs (see chart on next page).

Every person is first concerned with physiological needs including breathing, food, water, shelter, clothing, and sleep. The basic level of financial planning may include things like budgeting and medical insurance. Maslow's next level is for personal safety and security. The financial applications may include retirement and investment planning for the day you are no longer capable of working; as well as disability, long-term care, and life insurance planning.

Like Maslow's hierarchy, as your wealth increases you start to focus on intimacy, family, and the needs of others. Your financial planning may include education planning for your family, life insurance as income replacement for your spouse and children, and estate planning to provide for your family when you are gone. Finally, as you move to the top of Maslow's pyramid, and the final stages of your financial plan, you may start to focus on self-actualization: your search for purpose, meaning, and the development of a legacy. This focus may result in charitable work, community involvement, a focus on legacy planning, and a focus on spiritual matters.

Maslow and Financial Planning

The classic hierarchy of needs developed by Abraham Maslow can be overlaid onto a hierarchy of priorities to be addressed in planning personal finances.

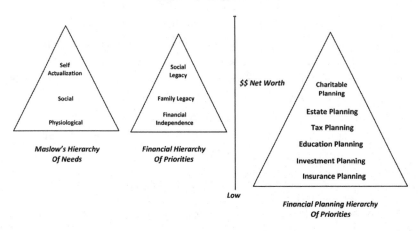

How can I find a qualified financial planner?

As mentioned earlier, the birth of the financial planning industry started with salesmen of financial products including specific investments, life insurance, and annuities. Sales professionals performed some planning on behalf of their customers in order to determine their needs and select suitable products. This planning was usually performed at no additional cost because the sales professional hoped to receive payment for their efforts from the commissions on their products.

The significant reduction in corporate pensions in the late 1970s caused many people to begin taking more responsibility for their own financial future. As people became more proactive in investing, and as the Internet provided ready access to information and products, people started to seek objective financial planning advice that was independent of the sales process. Many became less comfortable taking advice from someone who was compensated by a commission for the sale of a product. They wanted professionals who could help them coordinate planning in all of the major financial areas of their lives.

In the 1970s a new designation was created called the CERTIFIED FINANCIAL PLANNER™, or CFP®. Today there are over 120,000 CFP®s worldwide. To become a CFP® an individual must have three years of financial planning experience and have passed a challenging 2½ day exam covering multiple planning topics. In addition, CFP®s agree to adhere to a Code of Ethics including the principles of client first, integrity, objectivity, fairness, professionalism, competence, confidentiality, and diligence. Continuing education is also required.

The majority of financial planners have not yet completed all the requirements for the CFP® designation, but many follow the same ethical principles and have strong experience and expertise in their discipline. Some just haven't had time to pursue the rigorous training required for the designation. At any rate, the right financial planner for you is someone that demonstrates his or her expertise and professionalism, and is someone you trust and with whom you can relate. If you don't have this type of relationship, your planner will be of little help to you.

Other educational designations in the financial planning field include the ChFC (Chartered Financial Consultant), and in the insurance industry, the CLU (Chartered Life Underwriter). In addition, there are numerous other designations. The key to understanding designations is to find out what an advisor must do to qualify. A designation based on education and experience, and requiring some sort of testing, is considered stronger than those granted for simply belonging to a professional association.

In the end, the best place to find a qualified financial planner is often by asking your other professional advisors: your attorney, CPA, insurance advisor, and others. Then interview the recommended professional thoroughly to find out:

- how they earn their compensation,
- how long they have been in business,
- what special focus or expertise they might have,
- the planning process that they employ for their clients,
- how they keep up with new developments in their field,
- their methods of communication, and
- anything else you deem important.

In the process of interviewing, you should be able to determine if this is a person with whom you are comfortable from a personality standpoint, and who seems trustworthy and competent. You can also determine if the planner's processes and systems for working with clients meets your expectations.

LIFE COACHING AND FINANCIAL PLANNING

What is Life Coaching?

Coaching started in an organizational environment as a way of helping people advance in their careers. Business leaders saw the benefit of drawing out a person's gifts and strengths to be used to advance the needs and goals of the business. Coaching has evolved over time, and is now used outside the business setting as a way of drawing out those gifts and strengths to enable the individual to live a more proactive and productive life. Coaching has increased in importance as our society has moved from a centralized, hierarchical, or corporate society, to one that is more decentralized, flat, or entrepreneurial.

Coaching helps an individual see themselves objectively so that they can access where they are and develop a plan for where they need or want to go. An objective and trained coach can help you look in the mirror to see yourself: good and bad; strengths and weaknesses. Coaching is most effective when you desire a change in your life.

You probably experienced coaching through sports, or had great teachers, or mentors, who saw your potential, challenged you to be your best, and guided you in achieving your goals. They accessed your strengths, capabilities, and unique gifts. They listened to your passions, your goals, and your dreams. They helped you develop action plans to get there, and then provided objective monitoring and motivation to help you stay on course to achieve those goals. As life has become more complex, this same process helps individuals in different parts of their life make assessments, stay balanced, and stay motivated toward the goals that they believe define success in their lives.

Although life coaching is helpful to anyone who has set goals and wants guidance in achieving them, it is particularly helpful when trying to make significant change, like when an individual is going through a major life transition.

Major life transitions include:

1. A change in career,

2. The sale of a business,

3. The loss of a spouse through death, disability, or divorce,

4. Retirement,

5. A receipt of significant proceeds from a legal settlement, or

6. The receipt of a significant inheritance.

A relatively new trend is to combine life coaching and financial planning.

What is the difference between financial advice and financial coaching?

Most professionals that work on your financial and legal affairs are providing you with advice. The Webster Dictionary defines advice as: "recommendation regarding a decision or course of conduct." In this arrangement, most of the time you have already determined the problem or issues to which you would like a solution and you are coming to the professional to help you solve the problem. If you are paying them an hourly rate, you'd like the advice with as little of their time as possible. Advisors typically have the answers to your questions.

In coaching, everything is reversed. You have all the answers. The coach's job is to ask the right questions. The right questions are the ones that help you discover the answers that you can't articulate without the help of someone else.

What is the difference between the questions I ask and the questions a coach would ask me?

When you are seeking financial advice you typically want answers to the technical questions that involve investments, income taxes, estate taxes, insurance, etc. What should I invest in? How can I save taxes? How can I minimize the amount my heirs will have to pay the government when I die?

When you are seeking financial coaching you are looking for the questions that will guide you to finding the answers that only you know. You may want to know: What is enough money for me to be happy? What do I want to do when I stop working? What do I want to leave behind when I'm gone? These are difficult questions. Finding honest answers to them may require the help of someone who can guide you through a discovery or discussion of your values and beliefs.

Why integrate life coaching and financial planning?

One of the first steps in financial planning is being very clear about your goals in life. If you want to take this deeper you can also search for your purpose in life. It is a waste of time and money to plan or develop strategies unless you are very clear about what you are truly committed to achieving. Most people have some idea of the general direction that they would like to go; they know that they would like to be happy. However, they may not know how to get there. More profoundly, they may not know their purpose or have a clear mental picture of what they really want in life. Coaching helps you articulate your direction and write it down into a life plan.

What does the financial life planning process look like?

You should create your life plan before you create your financial plan. Where life plans are created to help clients achieve their dreams, financial plans are developed to help clients achieve their life plans.

One approach to integrating financial planning and life planning might follow this 4 step process:

1. Purpose—Clarify where you want to go

2. Vision—Paint a mental picture of what it looks like

3. Plan—Determine the steps to achieve your Vision

4. Implementation—Execute the steps

Let's look at each of these in greater detail.

Purpose   How much money is enough? What is success? What are the top priorities and values that should be fulfilled first at the sacrifice of others? Clarifying purpose, values and priorities is the single most important step in the financial planning process. Spending the time to determine what is most important to you is the best investment you can make in your life. Without it all the darts you throw in your life (spending and investing) will miss your bull's eye. Without it the end of the game will be disappointing. Time will be wasted on acquiring money misdirected. However, it is so difficult that most people avoid it. Most people are embarrassed that they don't know what they really want that they avoid having this conversation with their financial advisors.

Vision   Exploring your possibilities through scenario building stimulates awareness of new opportunities, helping to identify what is financially feasible. This is a trial and error process.

Plan   This is the traditional financial plan. Sometimes this document is an inch thick. It includes documentation of the planning process, goals, financial strategies (tax investment, estate planning, etc.), to pursue and maximize your cash flow around your chosen scenario. It includes action steps to work toward goals with dates and assignments of responsibility for you and your advisors.

Implementation   Many financial plans are put on a shelf and never implemented. However, a coach or financial life planning advisor can help you stay motivated, clear, grounded, and moving toward your vision so that you are energized to implement your planning. This is where the coaching expectation of accountability provides you with the motivating confidence that you have a path and that you are not alone on the journey—that you can do it. This stage will involve revising the path to the vision a number of times due to changes occurring in the global environment or other obstacles discovered during implementation.

How do you integrate life planning and financial planning?

Life plans are based on the client integrating a number of life areas into their plans for a desired future, prioritizing and balancing them with one another. Financial plans also include the integration of a number of financial areas into the plan to efficiently manage your life plan.

Areas integrated into a balanced life plan may include:

1. Personal Growth
2. Significant Other/Romance
3. Friends and Family
4. Health
5. Career

6. Money

7. Physical Environment

8. Fun and Recreation

Areas integrated into an efficient financial plan may include:

1. Investment strategies

2. Tax planning

3. Estate planning

4. Insurance planning

5. Retirement planning

6. Education planning

7. Charitable planning

What is Scenario Development?

The most profound contribution financial planning can make to life planning is in the creation of financial scenarios to support the client's review of what approach makes sense for developing a life change agenda. It is here that a number of possible scenarios, or life paths and contemplated decisions can be tested for their financial feasibility. Technology has made it easy for us to simplify the complex areas of financial planning. With the help of high-speed computers and sophisticated integrated software programs, we can convert the components that make up a strategic financial plan into an easily understood single concept: Cash.

Investments   Aside from the liquidity aspects of investments (how fast they can be sold for cash), investments are cash, they grow to produce more cash, and they may pay interest or dividends in cash.

Taxes   Taxes reduce cash and proactive planning strategies can miti-gate this reduction.

Estate Planning   Estate planning is about the net property valued in cash being distributed at death with the objective of increasing amounts going to heirs (bequests), and possibly charities, and controlling the amount going to the government (estate taxes) and termination costs (probate fees, trust administration, etc.)

Insurance Planning   Insurance planning (life and disability) is concerned with calculating the amount of cash needed to fulfill an individual's responsibilities, needs, and desired legacy in the event of death or disability of a breadwinner or caretaker.

Retirement Planning   Retirement planning is projecting the amount of cash that will be available to spend after income-producing activities slow or terminate. Will the amount last beyond life expectancy or fall short, requiring a reduction in current spending, increase in savings, or revision of retirement date?

Education Planning   Education planning is the computation of cash required today or to be deposited over the next number of years to fund a future payment for educational expenses.

Charitable Planning   Charitable planning is the calculation of cash left over after projecting cash requirements for financial independence and a desired family legacy.

After converting all of the above to cash, financial scenarios can be developed to help you determine the feasible paths to your dreams.

Can you give me an example of Scenario Development?

Suppose that you are age 55 and have accumulated a net worth of over $3 million from a life of hard work. Your children have all graduated from college, have jobs, and are no longer dependent on you. You want to explore some of the possible opportunities available for the rest of your life.

After a few coaching meetings with a financial life planner you remember that you always wanted to teach law. However, you never thought you could afford to do it because it only paid about ⅓ of your current income, and that would not have been enough to support your family's goals when they were younger.

Your wife always hoped that you would stop working a little earlier in life. When you first met you spent summers in Europe and she would like to return to that lifestyle. You mentioned to your advisor that if you could afford it, you've always wanted to help families with disabled children that were not as fortunate as you and your family.

Your advisor runs these scenarios for you to consider with the following results:

Scenario 1:   Continue working in your current career until age 65. Result: Leave an estate worth over $20 million to your children and charities.

Scenario 2:   Stop current career and take a teaching position. Result: Leave an estate worth over $10 million to your children and charities.

Scenario 3:   Same as Scenario 2, but spend summers in Europe. Result: Leave an estate worth over $5 million to your children and charities.

Scenario 4:   Same as Scenario 3, but give all your excess funds to charity while you are alive. Result: Spend all your net worth in your life time.

Discussing the potential financial outcomes of these alternatives can help you proactively refine what you value most at this stage in your life, and help you choose a path with passion and confidence. It will also expand your thinking to new possibilities that you may have never considered.

What are some common applications of coaching to financial planning?

The following are a few of the potential coaching applications that can be addressed in a financial planning setting:

Money vs. Meaning   The trade-off between money and meaning is one that has been going on for centuries. A few issues include:

1. If you don't have money, you need to accumulate it. If you have to accumulate it, it will usually require that you trade your time for it.

What is the right amount of time away from your other fulfilling roles and how much is enough money?

2. Saving and sacrificing to accumulate money without any purpose for the money. Just to have more money for something. Greed? Power?

3. Out of balance lifestyle: staying in meaningless jobs for the money, yet spending the extra money to try to replace the lack of fulfillment.

Couples   Money can create power imbalances and friction. The priority to spend versus save may be different for each. The definition of "enough" may be different for each spouse. Coaches can act as facilitators to help clients make joint decisions around money.

Money History   Most of our attitudes with money are based on early childhood experiences. Working for an allowance taught us the value of money. If your family did not have it when you were growing up, that may have made you an over-accumulator or workaholic, impacting the rest of your life and preventing you from making healthy decisions regarding money.

Retirement   Most financial planning is focused on retirement. There are a number of coaching issues around this important transition. For example:

1. *Coaching the primary bread winner.* This is often a workaholic requiring coaching about what to do at the traditional retirement age of 65. Many clients were raised to work and provide as their primary purpose and goal in life. They wake up the day after age 65 and ask now what? They have tremendous anxiety.

2. *Coaching the couple about retirement.* He worked during the day. She took care of the house, family and spent time with her friends during the day. Now they are together fulltime. What do they both want to do and what are the new ground rules? New habits need to be formed. They need to revise and share their individual purposes, goals, and ideal retirement scenarios. These individual scenarios need to be reconciled. This is hard as the submissive partner in the

relationship (gender is not relevant) has habitually subordinated his or her wishes and may do so in the planning stage, later resenting it. A coach/facilitator can add value by making sure the less dominant partner gets an equal say and asserts his or her ideas in the planning stages.

Inheritances   Money received from your parents as an inheritance. Sometimes this money seems to be blood money. There appears to be some guilt attached to it. It gets invested with no evidence of intent of ever spending it. This may be a coaching issue, a money history issue, and/or a psychotherapy issue. Other professionals can be brought into the process if desired.

Divorce   The non-working spouse handling her own money for the first time. She usually requires a substantial amount of education about money and how to work with professional advisors. She may also need to be educated and supported in how to make confident financial decisions.

Spouse Death or Disability   This requires that the other spouse handle money and make his or her own decisions in a number of areas for the first time. This situation can require education and coaching for years before the spouse can make intelligent decisions with confidence.

Would coaching help the estate planning process?

Absolutely! Many people procrastinate in going to their estate planner. Many who start the process never complete it. Many who complete the process do not keep it current by revisiting it periodically, leaving wishes and people in their documents that are no longer relevant in their lives. Why? One reason may be because "doing your estate planning" is treated as a necessary legal step that a responsible person should complete. It is treated as an obligation.

However, what it really should be is a deep purposeful conversation, or maybe several conversations. Conversations about how you want to be remembered when you are gone. Who should get what, when and why? How much should you give to charities, which ones and why?

A coach can help you move the estate planning process from an obligation to an opportunity. An opportunity to discover the legacy that is buried within the way you have lived your life and the values you hold important. A coach can help you tell your story and discover who you have been throughout your life.

Would coaching help me with my philanthropic planning?

Yes. Our observation in working with clients is that many people are reactive in their giving to charities. They respond to solicitations received in the mail, the year-end appeal from charitable organizations to give for tax deductions, and the call from a friend to help with an organization where the friend is on the board. We believe that everyone has the power to make a difference in their community, country, and world. However, few people ponder what's really important to them and many are embarrassed to admit that they really don't know what they care about, want to change, or help maintain.

This problem is more profound the more money you have to direct to charities. It is a burden for many of the affluent. However, we have found that this is an area where coaching helps clients connect with their values and the legacies that they want their lives to represent. If you are stuck on how to allocate your charitable funds, you may be able to express your purpose and discover your legacy with the help of the reflective listening and thoughtful guidance of a coach.

3 | The Team Approach to Planning

When it comes to estate and financial planning, the team approach works best. Nothing is more frustrating than getting contradictory advice from your attorney, financial advisor, insurance advisor, or CPA. Who are you to believe? The authors know that the best results are achieved when all the professionals are working together to craft and implement a comprehensive and integrated plan that truly meets your needs and goals.

What do you look for in an advisory team?

Connection   One of the primary attributes a team can have is the ability to connect with you and your objectives. Teams that immediately go into "problem solving" mode typically are not good listeners. In planning there is no such thing as one size fits all.

Experience   There are many professional generalists. The right team will have the experience to guide you in the area of expertise in which they are proficient, and rely on other team members in the areas they are not.

Collaboration   An effective team is one that has a seamless collaborative process. All the experts know their roles, and provide accountability to the other advisors on the team.

I already have an advisor. Why should I use a team?

The planning process has many areas of engagement such as Risk Management, Investment Analysis, Education, Retirement, Charitable, and Trust and Estate Planning. Your advisor may have expertise in one or two of these areas, but all the topics need to be considered when planning properly. Therefore, it is typically the team approach that works best to achieve your desired results.

Who are the members of a typical advisory team?

Attorney, CPA, Financial Advisor, and Insurance Specialist.

What role does the attorney have?

The attorney will participate with your financial advisor and CPA in the discovery of information and clarification of those objectives you wish to accomplish. Once plan design is agreed upon, the attorney will draft the proper documents to make them legal and binding.

How can I find a good attorney?

Most likely somebody will refer you to an attorney. How was their experience? Do you have similar circumstances and goals as they? Was the attorney responsive when asked questions? Are they known for practicing Estate Planning? If not they can refer you to an attorney that does. Are they a member of any professional organizations such as one of the national associations of estate planning attorneys, or a local estate planning council?

Many attorneys claim to be qualified in estate planning. Since drafting a simple will is often considered estate planning, the claim can be misleading. Many plans require more sophisticated and complex strategies. A useful screening mechanism is to ask the attorney what percentage of the practice is spent in estate planning, and on what other areas he or she focuses. An experienced estate planning specialist will typically spend at least 50% of his or her time in estate planning. The more numerous the areas of practice, the less specialized the practitioner, and the less time he or she will have to keep up with constant change.

Surprisingly, one indicator may be the fees that are being charged. Those who treat estate planning as "selling wills and trusts" tend to be peddling one-size-fits-all plans at high volume and low prices. The experts have high fees for a reason. They are counseling-oriented rather than document-oriented, and will spend considerable time in getting to know and understand your situation. Their approach will be to design a plan customized for your specific needs and desires. There are few things more costly than the negative results provided by a low fee attorney who neglects counseling.

What questions should I ask an attorney when I interview him or her?

1. Do they have expertise in the area for which you would like to plan?
2. What percentage of their practice is dedicated to estate planning?
3. What is the typical client profile of the attorney?
4. Are they a solo practitioner? If so, what is their succession plan if something happens to them unexpectedly?
5. How much time do they need to complete your estate plan? What steps are involved in the planning process?
6. What will be needed to be provided for them to make the appropriate recommendations?
7. How are their fees determined? Do they charge a flat fee or bill hourly? Can they give you a specific quote or "not to exceed" amount? Does the fee include re-titling of assets as required by the plan?
8. What are the ongoing costs for updating and maintenance of the plan? What costs are involved with the eventual settlement of the estate and implementation of the plan?
9. Do they belong to any professional organizations or have any special credentials in the field?

What role does the accountant or CPA have in Estate Planning?

For many people, the accountant is one of their most trusted advisors. This seems to be especially true for people who own businesses. They have utilized the advice of the accountant in many diverse situations. Estate planning is no exception. The accountant can provide clarity as to registration of assets, financial statements and net worth determination, asset valuation, and current and future tax issues. Additionally, as strategies are implemented the accountant can provide tax expertise to the team and tax return preparation as needed.

What questions do I ask the accountant when I interview them?

1. What credentials do they have? Are they a CPA (Certified Public Accountant)?

2. How much experience do they have regarding trust and estate planning administration and tax preparation?

3. For how many clients are they currently preparing Trust and Estate returns?

4. How do they get compensated? Hourly or flat fee?

What is the role an Insurance Specialist?

Many advisors use life and long term care insurance as tools in an estate plan. Life insurance may be used for income replacement at the death or disability of a breadwinner, as a way to create an inheritance, to replace assets that are given to charity, or to pay estate taxes. Long term care insurance is used to offset the high costs of medical care during long illnesses that can lead to wealth erosion.

With the many choices of insurance plans available, an insurance specialist is necessary to make sure you obtain the most appropriate coverage based on your personalized needs and purposes.

What questions do I ask the insurance specialist when I interview them?

1. How much experience do you have in the use of insurance for estate and financial planning?

2. Have you ever worked with a team of advisors before?

3. What is your typical case and client profile?

4. Are you captive to one insurance company or can you represent several?

5. What are the industry ratings of the companies you are recommending?

6. How do you get compensated?

7. Do you have a CLU or ChFC designation?

What is the difference between an insurance agent and an insurance broker?

An insurance agent is typically a representative of the insurance company. Agents must be licensed in the states in which they do business and licensed with the various companies they represent. Captive agents typically do the vast majority of their insurance business with one company and may be contractually prohibited from selling other companies' products. Some agents can be licensed with multiple carriers and make products from all of those companies available to their clients.

Insurance brokers differ in that they represent the client. Brokers typically have additional tests they must pass as well as bonding requirements that may be determined by the state in which they are licensed. Most often a broker will represent many companies and offer multiple alternatives to their clients.

When contemplating an insurance purchase consider asking the person you are working with whether they are an agent or a broker, or both. Also ask them for a list of all of the companies they have done business with in recent years and what percent of their business has gone to each. There are a wide array of choices, prices, products, and financial strength of companies, which should all be taken into account during the insurance acquisition process. Generally, the more options you have, the better.

What role does a Financial Advisor have in estate planning?

The financial advisor/planner spends time clarifying goals and objectives, and then assists in the development of your personalized vision. Additionally, the financial advisor spends time guiding the planning process. He or she may assist in the gathering of information, and organize that information in a format that is useful to all the team members.

Once data is verified, the advisor will seek to find inconsistencies within the existing plan and begin discovering the "gaps" of those problem areas that are not consistent with your vision.

Once areas of concern are identified, the financial advisor will collaborate with the advisory team to verify the appropriateness of the suggested recommendations. Upon agreement, the financial advisor will often guide the implementation process with the other advisors until the areas of concern are satisfied. (Sometimes the process is guided by the attorney.)

Thereafter, the financial advisor will help monitor the plan and make appropriate recommendations to make sure the plan is meeting the goals set forth during discovery and implementation.

What questions should I ask a financial advisor when I interview him or her?

1. What are their credentials and experience in financial planning?

    Do they or anybody in their organization hold the CFP® or other designation? Are they licensed to sell securities? How many years have they been practicing financial planning?

2. Does the financial advisor follow a process when developing a financial or estate plan?

    Financial and estate planning is a process of gathering information, reviewing the data, finding potential weaknesses, implementing the recommended changes, and providing ongoing monitoring of your progress. It is essential that your advisor has a process in place.

3. How is the financial advisor compensated?

4. What is the advisor's investment philosophy?

How do I find a qualified financial planner or investment advisor?

Ideally, you would be referred to someone that a trusted advisor recommends. A trusted advisor could be a member of your family, your CPA or attorney, or a friend or colleague. Next, you might want to locate those advisors in your area that have achieved a higher level of education in planning or investments. These certifications are granted by various organizations and you can search for advisors in your area on their websites. Some of the more recognized certifications are CERTIFIED FINANCIAL PLANNER™ (CFP®), Certified Investment Management Analyst (CIMA), Chartered Financial Consultant (ChFC), and Chartered Life Underwriter (CLU). If the advisor in question also has a securities license, you can search the SEC's website to find out how to check the record of the advisor and their company.

Once you've narrowed your list, it's best to schedule an introductory appointment to interview each of them. Come with the questions you want answered, and try to determine the advisor and firm's personality and experience, and whether or not they're a good fit for you and your circumstances.

A good practice when engaging the services of *any* of your professional advisors is to ask for two or three references of clients that are similar to you, and that would be willing to discuss their relationship with the advisor. However, be aware the professional ethics imposed on certain advisors, such as an attorney, may prevent the disclosure of references due to the client privilege.

How does the planning team work together?

Imagine that you are going to build your dream home. You have the perfect piece of property and money is no object. You are free to hire the very best to construct every facet of your new home. You locate a phenomenal theater expert to design and install your ultimate home theater. You have the best custom cabinetmaker do all of the built-ins throughout the house. The top of the line granite and marble workers are available with the best products and processes. This excellence carries through every aspect of your project and every craftsman involved.

But then you inform them that they are expected to build your dream home without a blueprint, and without ever speaking to one another. How do you think your home will turn out?

This is a common occurrence in estate and financial planning. Clients begin without a blueprint. They have typically hired an attorney to handle business and estate planning issues. They usually have a CPA who takes care of all the tax issues. Other advisors often include insurance agents, investment professionals, bankers, realtors, and others they rely on to make important decisions. But there is typically very little communication between members of the client's advisory team.

The problem with this scenario is that the client is left in the role of coordinating all of the advisory team members and determining whose advice is correct if there are contradictions between the advisors. Clients usually hire advisors because the advisors have a higher level of expertise than their own. So it's virtually impossible to determine whether all of the pieces of advice are fitting together correctly.

For example, have you properly coordinated the beneficiary designations on your life insurance, retirement plan accounts, IRAs, and annuities with your estate plan? Do you realize that these things do not pass according to your will, but according to the named beneficiaries? The estate planning attorney may not have spoken to the insurance agent, investment professional, and other team members to ensure all of these details are properly coordinated.

What about the blueprint? Make certain that at least one of your advisory team members is in the business of helping you construct that master financial blueprint. It is best that one team member be responsible for the overall coordination of the team, to ensure proper communication and maximize your chance of building that financial dream home.

Do I have to meet with every advisory team member separately?

In a well-coordinated team, you should be able to tell your story once. You typically begin with one of the advisory team members by identifying your goals and objectives. The other team members are brought in, and the coordinating team member will assist in directing and obtaining a consensus of recommendations made from the other team members. Once the implementation process begins, you may continue to meet with one or two team members at a time to review the strategic component of the plan for which each is responsible.

What is the best way to communicate with my advisory team?

It is recommended that you and the team members agree on a communication plan with which you are comfortable. The communication with various team members will differ. You may need quarterly communications with your financial advisor, and possibly annual communication with the attorney, accountant, and insurance advisor. The rule of thumb is if your lifestyle needs, goals, and objectives change, you must contact your advisory team so they may update your plan.

Some advisors are using technology that allows you and each member of your advisory team to access planning notes, forms, documents, and project tasks electronically so that everyone involved has all the information in one place.

With so many advisors, will I maintain control of my finances?

When you are working with qualified and experienced advisors, you remain in the driver's seat. Once you communicate your objectives and vision to them, it is their responsibility to perform the services necessary to accomplish your wishes. As your circumstances change, so should your plan. You will be responsible to keep your advisory team updated as to various modifications you would like as time passes and/or your lifestyle changes.

How often will I need to update my plan?

Depending on the complexity of your plan, typically, you should review your plan each year to make sure the details of the plan have not changed. Details include such things as: asset rate of return, business growth, lifestyle income need, retirement date, and so forth. As financial or family circumstances change, your plan needs to be updated. You will need to communicate these changes to your advisory team.

What happens if one of my team members retires, or closes their business?

This is one of the primary benefits in working with a team. Most likely, the other team members have worked with several specialists in the area. They will introduce you to several of the new advisors from which you can choose the one with whom you are most comfortable.

My financial situation is very basic. Do I still need a team of advisors?

Most likely you may already have one or two advisors you trust to handle most of the areas of your financial and estate plan. Typically, people have a tax preparer, an attorney, and perhaps a financial planner. It is your responsibility to ask them if they feel comfortable giving advice in all these areas and if not, have them refer you to additional experts.

4 | Planning for Gift, Estate, and Generation-Skipping Taxes

Everyone who has had a job knows about income taxes, and every investor knows about the capital gains tax. In fact, whole books have been written on how to plan for, reduce, or even avoid these taxes. This chapter, however, focuses on the taxes that most often impact estate planning: the federal estate and gift taxes, and the generation-skipping transfer tax. These are often referred to as "death taxes," but they must be planned for during life!

Is it wrong or somehow unpatriotic to want to reduce my taxes?

Some believe it is illegal and possibly immoral to use estate planning strategies to reduce one's taxes. Judge Learned Hand stated more than a century ago that:

"Anyone may arrange his affairs so that his taxes shall be as low as possible; he is not bound to choose that pattern which best pays the treasury. There is not even a patriotic duty to increase one's taxes. Over and over again the Courts have said that there is nothing sinister in so arranging affairs as to keep taxes as low as possible. Everyone does it, rich and poor alike and all do right, for nobody owes any public duty to pay more than the law demands."

What is the gift tax and why do we have one?

The gift tax is imposed by the federal government on an individual for gifts made during lifetime. The gift tax will apply to an outright gift or a gift to a trust.

Each individual may give away up to $1 million over his lifetime without incurring any gift tax. The $1 million limit is known as the gift tax exemption. This amount is cumulative and applies to all gifts made during one's lifetime. Any gifts in excess of the gift tax exemption will be subject to a gift tax at the then prevailing gift tax rates. However, there are certain tax-free gifts that you may make beyond the $1 million gift tax exemption as described in the following question and answer.

The reason we have a gift tax is to prevent individuals from giving away everything during their lifetime in an effort to avoid an estate tax at death. Thus, if you give everything away during life in excess of the gift tax exemption, you will pay a gift tax. However, if you hold onto your assets until you die, you will pay an estate tax at your death to the extent your estate exceeded the estate tax exemption.

The gift tax was taxed at the same rate as the estate tax until 2010. The *gift tax* rate was 45% in 2009. The *estate tax* is repealed during 2010, and the *gift tax* is 35% during 2010. Unless Congress makes changes, the gift tax and estate tax rates are scheduled to increase to 55% in 2011.

I heard that I can make gifts during my lifetime to avoid the estate tax, and avoid the gift tax as well. Is this true?

Gifts can be categorized as present interest or future interest gifts. A present interest gift means the person receiving it has immediate possession or enjoyment of the gift. A future interest gift is the opposite of the present interest gift, meaning no immediate possession or enjoyment of the gift. Most future interest gifts involve transfers to a trust where the beneficiary does not have the immediate use or possession of the trust property.

A present interest gift may or may not be taxable. Currently, you may make present interest gifts up to $13,000 per person per year (known as "annual exclusion gifts"). This is a tax-free gift to the person receiving the gift. A future interest gift is always taxable.

However, for present interest gifts beyond the $13,000 per person limit, and for all future interest gifts, there is a lifetime exemption of $1,000,000 to use against those taxable gifts. The giver, not the receiver, normally pays the gift tax.

For example, assume that the size of your estate is such that estate taxes will be due at your death, and that you have six children. You might want to reduce the size of your estate (and therefore the estate taxes) by making a tax-free gift to each of your children every year. The annual tax-free (present interest) gift is $13,000 per person or a total of $78,000 per year ($13,000 × 6 children).

Also, please note that the $13,000 amount under the law is indexed for inflation and periodically increases.

What is the federal estate tax?

The federal estate tax is a tax on everything you own at the time of your death. On June 7, 2001, President Bush signed into law the Economic Growth and Tax Relief Reconciliation Act of 2001 (the "Act"). Under the Act, individuals were not subject to estate tax unless their estates exceed the applicable exclusion amount of $3.5 Million in 2009. Under the Act, the estate tax was repealed in 2010. Beginning in 2011, the estate tax applicable exclusion is scheduled to revert back to $1 Million, the amount under the law that existed before the Act. The federal government may decide to change the law before December 31, 2010.

At death, the estate tax applies to the transfer of property to another person. The personal representative (executor or Trustee) is required to take an inventory of all property owned by the decedent at death to determine the gross estate before any deductions, exclusions or credits. The executor must determine the fair market value of all properties, which means an independent qualified appraiser for certain assets, may be required.

The date of valuation for assets may be the date the decedent died or an alternate valuation date (six months after the date of the decedents' death). After the gross estate value has been determined, funeral, administration expenses, marital/charitable deductions, state death tax deductions are subtracted to determine the Taxable estate. The tax is due and payable within 9 months after death.

Also, depending on the state in which the decedent resides, the state inheritance tax may take up to 16% after exemptions in some states—again payable within 9 months after death. For example, if the taxable estate (federal and state) is $5 million, the executor may have to raise $3 million to pay all taxes within 9 months after death. This puts undue pressure on the executor to sell assets (or borrow money) under possibly unfavorable market conditions.

You mean there are state death taxes too?

That depends. Some states have a separate death tax and some do not. Historically, for those states that have a state death tax, the tax is either independent of the federal estate tax system or tied to the federal estate tax system. In those states that have an independent death tax, it is usually known as an "inheritance tax" and the tax is based upon the relationship of the beneficiaries to the deceased.

Prior to 2004, most states had a death tax that was tied to the federal estate tax system. Congress used to provide a federal estate tax credit for state death taxes paid by an estate (known as the "state death tax credit"). Those states would then impose a state tax in an amount equal to the federal state death tax credit. This was known as a "pick-up" or "sponge" tax. Under a "pick-up" or "sponge tax" state, the state would impose a state death tax only when federal estate tax was due. In 2004, the federal government repealed the state death tax credit.

With the repeal of the federal state death tax credit and the increases in the federal estate tax exemption amounts, many states that were tied to the federal estate tax system experienced a significant drop in state revenue. Therefore, many of those states have enacted their own state death tax with a lower exclusion amount than the federal estate tax exclusion. This means an individual who is not subject to the federal estate tax may still end up paying a state death tax. Residents of these states will have to deal with planning for two different death tax systems, the federal and the state systems.

What is the "unlimited marital deduction?"

The federal unlimited marital deduction allows an individual to leave unlimited amounts of assets to his or her surviving spouse, free of federal estate tax. Likewise, most states exempt transfers to a surviving spouse from state death tax.

Under current law, since there is no federal estate tax in 2010, the unlimited marital deduction is irrelevant. However, beginning again in 2011 married couples will be able to pass unlimited sums to each other, and the couple together will be able to pass up to $2 million in assets to children or other beneficiaries free from federal estate tax. In 2011 and beyond, an unmarried person will be able to leave no more than

$1 million to a surviving partner free of federal estate tax. All sums in excess of that amount are subject to federal estate tax upon the first partner's death.

Is it possible to reduce my federal estate taxes to zero?

Yes, the estate tax is a voluntary tax! You can choose to pay it by not planning ahead, or you can reduce or even eliminate it with planning. The easiest and simplest way to eliminate the Federal estate tax at death is to not allow your estate to be valued more than the Federal Estate Tax exemption.

On the other hand, if your estate considerably exceeds the Federal Estate Tax exemption, then there are several steps you can take to reduce or eliminate the estate tax altogether. The simplest step is to leave your excess estate (over the Federal Estate Tax exemption) to a qualified charity. This may be suitable if you're charitably inclined. If not, this will take property away from your heirs who would have received at least part of that amount after paying the estate tax.

Other possible plans to avoid or eliminate estate taxes and provide flexibility in overall planning include: revocable trusts with bypass trusts; property transfers during life to discounted entities; charitable trusts established during life and/or at death; and life insurance policies to pay the taxes on behalf of the estate. It is beyond the scope of this book to discuss the details of these strategies, but your advisor will be happy to discuss them with you.

Unfortunately, the government requires a taxpayer to jump through certain legal hoops and undertake some fairly sophisticated planning to avoid or eliminate estate taxes, but it can be done.

What is the Generation Skipping Transfer Tax?

The Generation Skipping Transfer (GST) Tax is designed to ensure that a transfer tax is paid at each generational level. In the early days of the federal estate tax, the wealthiest families devised a method to effectively be taxed every other generation. Your parents would leave their estate to your children (instead of you), thereby avoiding tax on their estate upon your death. In turn, you would leave your estate to your grandchildren instead of your children, thereby allowing the transfer to escape estate tax when your children die. This became known as a generation-skipping transfer. Over time, wealthy clients then began leaving their assets in long term trusts to benefit multiple generations, and thereby escaping taxation at each generational level.

In order to make up for this lost revenue and assure taxation at each generational level, Congress enacted the GST Tax. For 2009, the GST Tax rate was a flat rate of 45%. Like the estate tax, under current law, there is no GST Tax in year 2010. However, in 2011, the law will revert to the levels in existence before the 2001 Tax Act, which means there will be a 55% GST Tax rate. As with the estate tax, Congress may decide to change the law before December 31, 2010 so it pays to stay in touch with your advisors.

Any transfers you make to your grandchildren or subsequent generations, whether during your lifetime or at your death, may be subject to the generation skipping transfer tax ("GST Tax"). The GST Tax differs from the estate and gift tax in that the GST Tax is taxed at a flat rate (the highest marginal estate and gift tax rate). The estate and gift tax are taxed at graduating rates. Therefore, it is almost always more favorable to pay an estate tax than it is to pay a GST Tax. Moreover, a transfer to your grandchildren will not escape any gift tax that may apply to the transfer as described above. Thus, you could end up paying both a GST Tax and a gift tax on the same transfer!

5 | Revocable Living Trust Planning

There was a time (a couple of decades ago) when planning with a trust was thought to be only for "rich people." Trust planning was perceived to be complex and costly, and something that the "average" American didn't really need. Today, revocable living trusts serve as the center of most comprehensive plans. But it's not really about the documents at all—it's about the results! This chapter explores the benefits of trust planning for every family and every estate size.

What is the difference between a Will and a Trust?

A will is a document that tells the world where you want your assets to go when you die. It becomes effective only upon death. Unfortunately, your will controls only the property you own in your own name at the date of death. It does not control joint tenancy property or property that you leave through beneficiary designations such as retirement plans and life insurance unless the named beneficiary is your estate.

The problem with a will is that even though it states where you want certain assets to go upon death, those assets remain titled in your name. As a result, when you die, your loved ones cannot just step in and start handling those assets. Because those assets are titled in your name, your loved ones are forced into the probate court. The assets cannot usually be transferred into the beneficiaries named under your will without an order from the probate court.

Because a will becomes effective only upon death, it does not address what happens in the event you become mentally incapacitated and can no longer handle your financial affairs. With a Will-based estate plan, attorneys typically utilize a Durable Power of Attorney in which one or more persons are designated as the Agent for the Principal who is granting the authority. If there is no Durable Power of Attorney, or in the event the Power of Attorney is not accepted by one or more financial institutions, a disabled person's loved ones might have no alternative but to file a petition with a court to be appointed as a Guardian and/ or Conservator for the disabled person. If approved by the court, the Guardian will be granted specific powers to administer the disabled person's assets, and often further authorized to handle the disabled person's daily personal needs.

A trust is a legal contract in which property is held by one or more trustees for the benefit of one or more beneficiaries. There are a number of different types of trusts. *Testamentary trusts* are trusts created by a person within his or her Will. A testamentary trust might be established to preserve the estate tax exemption; to provide for creditor protection of a spouse, children or other beneficiaries; to provide for a special needs beneficiary; or for a variety of other purposes.

The *revocable living trust* acts as a will substitute and contains instructions for managing your assets during your life and also upon death. A living trust is created during your lifetime and becomes effective immediately when you sign it. After a trust is created, your assets should be transferred into the name of your trust. You can transfer property to the trust, and still maintain control and use of all the property while living. You can revoke or change the trust at any time. You can be the trustee of your trust while living, and because these transfers are made ahead of time, upon your mental incapacity or death, your successor trustees can step into your shoes and start handling your financial affairs without a court order or the need to establish a conservatorship.

Another type of trust is the *irrevocable trust*, discussed in Chapter 6 of this book.

Upon your death, a will becomes a public document through the probate system. Your financial data and list of beneficiaries is on display for all who care to see. A trust, on the other hand, generally remains a private document.

Although a trust needs to be administered upon your death, the cost is normally lower than going through the probate process. The counseling and design of a trust-centered plan is often more extensive and expensive to initially create, but it is more cost effective in the long run.

Who needs a revocable living trust?

When revocable living trusts first became popular in the 1980s, most thought that they were only for the wealthy. Over time, trusts have become a popular planning tool for any size estate. Revocable living trusts are amazingly flexible legal tools that can help the creator of the trust— referred to in legal terms as the "trustmaker", "grantor" or "settlor"— achieve a variety of goals and objectives.

For example, revocable living trusts may be used to avoid the probate process upon death. But to achieve that objective, the trust must be fully "funded" with your assets during lifetime, since assets left in your own name will most likely have to go through probate. As mentioned above, revocable living trusts can provide a set of instructions for taking care of you and your loved ones if you become disabled.

If you are married, the revocable living trust may provide for the creation of a marital trust and family trust upon the death of the first spouse. You'll sometimes hear these referred to as "A and B Trusts." These "subtrusts" are designed to both maximize a married couple's total estate tax exemptions, and to protect the trust assets against the surviving spouse's "creditors and predators"—which may include a new spouse should the surviving spouse remarry.

After both spouses have died, assets may be distributed to the couple's children or other beneficiaries in a variety of ways—including

- immediate outright distributions,
- staggered distributions at various ages,
- lifetime trusts with liberal standards,
- lifetime trusts with conservative standards, or
- special needs trusts.

In summary, anyone who would like to accomplish any of these things in their estate plan would benefit from trust planning.

One of my professional advisors says I don't need a revocable living trust

It's not uncommon for professional advisors (attorneys, financial and insurance advisors, CPAs) to think of estate planning as pertaining only to finances, avoiding probate, or reducing taxes. That is the focus of the training most have experienced. Therefore if you have jointly held or beneficiary assets (thereby avoiding probate), or a smaller estate (thereby avoiding estate taxes) the professional may conclude that you don't need trust planning.

However, knowledgeable advisors know that trusts are also used for disability planning, creditor protection for your spouse and children after death, passing along family values, and many other purposes beyond probate and taxes.

I've been told that even if I plan with a revocable living trust, I'll still need something called a Pour-Over Will. What is that?

The Pour-Over Will serves as a safeguard in case an asset gets left outside of your trust. It's not uncommon to find that in the process of funding a trust (changing title of assets to the trust name), an asset has been overlooked. Sometimes clients acquire new assets in their own name or joint ownership, forgetting that they must be owned by their trust in order for the trust instructions to be effective.

Under a "Pour-Over" will, the only beneficiary is your trust. Therefore, your Pour-Over Will catches the overlooked asset, and "pours it over" to your trust after your death. Once titled in your trust, the trust instructions will now apply to the distribution of that asset. However, that transfer will usually still have to go through probate to be put into your trust, because it's in probate court that the instructions of a will are carried out. This, of course, is not the preferred way to get assets into your trust. It is much more efficient and effective to ensure that all assets are re-titled when your trust is created, and then have in place a system to add new assets to your trust as they are acquired.

Under many state laws, guardians for minor children can be appointed only through a will (not a trust). Therefore, the Pour-Over Will is also used for this purpose.

TRUSTEES

Who are trustees, and what do they do?

Trustees are those individuals or entities (such as a bank trust department) named in a trust agreement to administer the trust. Trustees are required to manage and invest trust property and to distribute the trust property to certain individuals (the beneficiaries) based upon the instructions contained in the trust. Because trusts often last for years or even decades, a well-designed and drafted living trust agreement should include different trustees for different phases of your life, and the lives of your beneficiaries.

In a typical Revocable Living Trust, you will serve as your own *Trustee* as long as you remain "alive and well." When a joint Living Trust is used (a trust created by both), the couple will usually serve as *co-trustees* of the trust while they are both "alive and well." When each spouse has their own Trust, it is customary that both spouses will serve as co-trustees of each spouse's individual Living Trust.

Because of longer life spans and medical advances, more people will suffer periods of disability prior to death; requiring the assistance of others to manage the Living Trust and its assets. One or more *Disability Trustees* should be named in the Trust document to take care of your personal affairs and assets in the event of disability or mental incapacity. It is critical that the Trust document include detailed instructions for the care of both you and your loved ones in the event you become disabled.

The trust should specifically state who is a permitted Trust beneficiary during your disability, and whether there is any priority for distributions (e.g., "provide for me, then my spouse, then my children, in that order of priority"). The Trust should also include your preferences for gifting of assets during a period of disability. For example, if you are using a gifting program to reduce the size of your estate, you may want that to continue during a period of disability. But a Trustee can do that only if the trust includes those instructions.

You will also name one or more *Death Trustees* who will assume management of the Trust upon your death. The death trustees are responsible for all phases of Trust administration, including identifying assets, working with professional advisors (e.g., attorney, accountant and financial advisor) to prepare tax returns, and distributing the trust assets to the named beneficiaries. If assets are to remain in trust for one or more beneficiaries, the death trustees may be appointed as trustees of the beneficiary's trust share, or other trustees may be named for that role.

If you create a "protective trust" for a child that will be funded at your death, or the death of you and your spouse if you are married, your attorney may suggest that a responsible adult child serve as a trustee of their own trust share along with a "friendly" co-trustee. This technique would allow for your child to have access to their trust assets for their needs, but can help insulate those assets against attacks by your child's creditors, including a divorcing spouse.

What are the primary duties of my Trustee?

A Trustee has the legal duty to carry out the directions set forth in your trust. As a fiduciary, the Trustee cannot derive personal benefit from the assets he or she is entrusted with. If the Trustee does not follow the directions set forth in your trust, they can be subject to personal liability. Some of the duties of the Trustee include taking a complete inventory of the assets when they begin to act as Trustee; obtaining a tax identification number for the trust; determining values of the assets in the trust, if necessary; investing the money in the trust for the benefit of the beneficiaries of that trust; paying expenses of the trust; preparing accountings for the beneficiaries of the trust; preparing tax returns for the trust; and distributing the assets in accordance with the terms of the trust.

What happens if my Trustee fails to follow the terms of my trust?

A Trustee is required to abide by the terms of a trust. If that Trustee fails to do so, a beneficiary of the trust is not without recourse. One of the benefits of naming co-trustees is that they tend to hold one another accountable. In addition, most trusts will provide a way for the beneficiaries to remove a Trustee, and replace them with the next successor trustee on the list. If no specific provision is made for replacement, a beneficiary may generally petition the Probate Court, and the Probate Court may review the acts of the Trustee.

Who should I select as Trustee of my trust?

You can select an individual as a Trustee, such as a close friend or family member; or a professional Trustee can be selected, such as a financial institution or a bank. A good Trustee should be someone who is honest and trustworthy, because they will have a lot of power under your trust document. The person you choose to act as a Trustee should also be financially responsible, because they will be handling the investments for the benefit of your beneficiaries. The Trustee should be someone who can get along and have a good relationship with the beneficiaries of your trust. They should also possess good record-keeping abilities.

Is the Successor Trustee important?

Yes. It is wise to name not only your immediate successor, but subsequent successor trustees as well. An individual trustee may refuse to accept the position, or may resign from the position due to any number of reasons. The trustee may become disabled or die. Most clients tend to want other family members or close friends to act as successor trustees. But since all individuals eventually pass away, it is good practice to name a bank trust department or other corporate trustee as the final successor trustee on the list. Some clients with very high net worth, or very complex assets, may name an institutional trustee from the very beginning—either as a co-trustee with a trusted family member, or serving as the sole trustee.

What are the advantages of using a corporate trustee?

A corporate fiduciary manages trusts professionally every day. They have experience in the area, and they know what they are doing. They act very objectively to follow the instructions set forth in the trust document. They have investment experience and record-keeping skills. They know the law, and follow the prudent investor rule. If they make a mistake, they have errors and omissions insurance, so the trust beneficiaries have a source to recover any potential damages.

The primary disadvantages of a corporate trustee are cost and the fact that they may not have a personal relationship with the beneficiaries. A family member acting as trustee may better understand the family dynamic, and make better discretionary decisions when it comes to your loved ones.

Wouldn't it be best if I named a family member as my Trustee?

Although family members will usually serve for little or no compensation, they may not be the best choice for a trustee. While the trust may allow for some discretion, some family members are prone to make decisions on an emotional basis. Most times, the family member is not an experienced trustee and does not know what is required of him or her under the law. If they make mistakes, they may face the wrath (and legal action) of the beneficiaries, or the beneficiaries may be unwilling to take action, and your plans and goals for the beneficiaries are not fulfilled. If you do choose a family member as a Trustee, it is best to train them for the responsibility before you die. Perhaps your attorney or advisor provides successor trustee training, or you can spend time educating them now, before they are called upon to act.

Can I have a corporate trustee and family member trustee act together?

Yes. A corporate trustee and family member trustee can act as co-trustees. In fact, this is sometimes a way to get the best of both worlds. The family member brings knowledge of the family situation, and the corporate trustee knows how to invest and maintain records.

PLANNING FOR DISABILITY

How can I use a living trust to plan for my possible disability?

One of the most important reasons for having a revocable living trust is to plan for a possible incapacity. With improvements in health care and lifestyle, more people are living longer. With this increase in lifespan, the likelihood of becoming incapacitated some time before death is greater than ever.

The most important part of estate planning for many people is the ability to keep control. Rather than have a judge appoint a conservator and/or guardian to care for you and your possessions, a good estate plan will allow you to name people you choose to see to your personal care and manage your finances.

An important consideration in a living trust design is the mechanism for determining *when* you are in fact disabled. Many "boilerplate" trust documents provide that you are deemed disabled when a doctor, or maybe two doctors, make such a determination. You may choose to broaden that to specifically include a medical specialist in the area of your disability. Given the option, however, many people prefer having their spouse, adult children, or other loved ones participate in such a critical determination. After all, certain symptoms of incapacity are noticed first by family members, not by your doctors

A living trust can include a "disability panel" comprised of medical professionals as well as a combination of family members or friends. The disability panel may be given authority to make a determination of your disability by unanimous vote, by a majority, or any other method you choose. The disability panel combines clinical medical advice with input from people who love you and understand what you would want if you could speak for yourself. That allows your affairs to be handled privately among the individuals you trust the most.

You can also provide detailed instructions in your living trust providing for your ongoing care when you are incapacitated. For example, you may wish to remain in your home with private duty in-home care for as long as possible. Or, you may wish to provide detailed instructions to provide for your daily routines so that you can continue them during your incapacity.

In addition to your preference on where to live, these instructions may also include such things as the types of foods you prefer to eat, your daily grooming habits, your favorite hobbies and activities, care of your pets, your preference for religious or spiritual practices, and a description of other beneficiaries whom the trustees are authorized to provide for from the trust assets. Taking the time to consider all of these personal wishes and preferences is part of a well-designed estate plan.

PLANNING FOR WHEN I'M GONE

What are some of the things my estate plan should provide for after my death?

The goals that we hear most often from clients for "after I'm gone" include:

- I want to give what I have to the people I care about, with timing and protections that will benefit them the most.

- I want those in charge of my affairs to be the people I pick, based on trust and my belief that they are best able to act for the benefit of everyone involved.

- I want to minimize the expenses of identifying, determining the value of, and transferring what I own.

- I want to make sure my family has the most flexibility in dealing with my debts.

- I want to avoid taxes as much as possible.

- I want everything finished as quickly as possible.

- I want my family to continue to rely upon my trusted advisors.

- I want to keep information about me, my assets, and my plans (such as "who gets what") private.

- I want to know that the cost of administration is not "open-ended" but instead is controlled and limited.

- I want my loved ones to know what to expect. I want them to be brought together through my planning, not driven apart.

- I want my wisdom to be passed along with my wealth.

PLANNING FOR MY SPOUSE

What are some of the things my estate plan should include for my spouse?

The goals that we hear most often from clients regarding a spouse include:

- I want my spouse to be able to maintain the lifestyle that we currently enjoy after I'm gone.

- I want to protect what I leave my spouse from people who might otherwise take advantage; whether family members or strangers.

- I am in a second marriage, and I want my spouse cared for after I'm gone. But I also want to ensure that my estate goes to my children after my spouse passes away.

- I have handled most of our investments throughout our married life, and my spouse has not been involved. I would like my spouse to maintain control, but I'd also like to provide investment help.

- I want to be sure my spouse can, while still benefiting only my bloodline, make adjustments in my bequests in order to address changes in the circumstances of my children and descendants that occur after I'm gone.

- I want to maximize any tax protections available to my spouse.

What if my spouse remarries?

Most people want to know that if their spouse remarries, the plan for children or loved ones is protected, and not lost to a new spouse. One of the ways this can be accomplished is to have the estate plan require the surviving spouse to sign a prenuptial agreement if they want to maintain control of the assets when they remarry. The plan can make this a recommendation, or it can be as severe as removing the spouse as successor trustee or even as a beneficiary of the trust. This is obviously a counseling discussion with your advisors, and typically works best when both spouses have the identical provision for the other.

How else can I use a living trust to plan for my spouse?

Living trusts can be used to plan for a spouse's well-being in a variety of ways. During any period that you are disabled, the trust language may authorize the successor trustee—who will often be the surviving spouse either serving alone or serving with a co-trustee—to provide for the spouse's needs out of the trust assets. Upon your death, the trust may specify that the trust assets are to be funded into one or more new "subtrusts" that may include the surviving spouse as a beneficiary. These subtrusts are often used for estate tax planning, to protect the spouse and other beneficiaries from creditors, and to provide you with some control of the assets after your death.

Typically a portion of your living trust assets equal to the Federal estate tax exemption would be transferred to a "Family Trust." This is usually designed so that the surviving spouse, children, or other descendants are beneficiaries of the principal and income. Your trust assets in "excess" of the Federal estate tax exemption would be funded into a "Marital Trust" that by its terms must distribute its income to your surviving spouse.

You have the option to authorize the Marital Trust trustee to make distributions of principal from the Marital Trust to the surviving spouse. Upon the surviving spouse's death, the assets remaining in the Family

Trust—including any growth of those assets—will pass to your children or other beneficiaries free of Federal estate tax. Assets in the Marital Trust will be included in the surviving spouse's estate for estate tax purposes. Any portion of the Marital Trust assets not needed for payment of taxes will be available to pass to the next generation.

Can my spouse be a trustee of the family or marital trusts?

Yes, but naming the surviving spouse as a Trustee should be done only after reviewing all the facts and counseling with your advisors. In a "first time" marriage where both spouses have great confidence in each other, it is common for the surviving spouse to be designated as a Trustee of the Family and Marital Trusts. To maximize the creditor protection aspects of these subtrusts, it is recommended that a "friendly" co-trustee be named to serve along with the surviving spouse. The Trustees can be provided broad authority to distribute income and principal from the Family Trust to beneficiaries that may include the surviving spouse. The Marital Trust may also provide for principal distributions, but only to the surviving spouse.

There are some circumstances where it may not be preferred to have the surviving spouse serve as a Trustee of the Family and/or Marital Trusts. Perhaps a spouse has not had experience dealing with finances, maybe they have poor spending habits, or perhaps the couple is in a second or subsequent marriage. In such circumstances, the couple may prefer that an independent third party serve as Trustee. It is not advised to name a child to serve as the sole Trustee of these Trusts, since such an arrangement would likely lead to conflict if the child denies their parent's request for a distribution from the Family or Marital Trust.

SPECIAL CONSIDERATIONS FOR SECOND MARRIAGES AND BLENDED FAMILIES

What are the concerns of blended families in second marriages?

Generally the concern and conflict in planning occurs in those situations where someone with children from a prior marriage has entered into a second or subsequent marriage. The conflict arises out of the client's desire to provide for the current spouse and yet not disinherit the children from the prior marriage. This can create a challenge if the various estate planning techniques that are available are not understood or properly implemented.

The goal is generally to provide sufficient access and income for your surviving spouse so that he or she may continue to live comfortably after your death. Attitudes and consequences regarding remarriage of your surviving spouse following your death need to be addressed. An open and frank discussion of the potential for friction and conflict between your surviving spouse and your children from a prior marriage needs to occur. The emotional needs of all those involved will need to be anticipated and considered.

Generally speaking, the pure tax technique employed in estate planning is to transfer taxable assets, such as those owned and included in the decedent's estate, to beneficiaries who are not subject to estate tax. As a result of the unlimited marital deduction, the surviving spouse is typically not subject to tax at the first death. The corollary is to provide for the transfer of non-taxable assets, such as life insurance proceeds contained in an irrevocable life insurance trust, to taxable beneficiaries. The goal, from a pure tax planning perspective is to transfer assets that would be excluded from the gross estate of the deceased, for tax purposes, to beneficiaries who would otherwise be taxable, such as children.

That goal is not always achieved due to the desires and dynamics of each family. Beneficiaries may place significant emotional value on assets that may have little or no intrinsic value. On the other hand, beneficiaries may place significant emotional value on fungible assets such as investments and retirement accounts and attribute little value to personal property of the decedent.

The typical plan utilized for first marriages, where at the death of the first spouse all of the property passes to or is held for the use and benefit of the surviving spouse and at the surviving spouse's death the property passes to the children will not normally be satisfactory in blended family and second marriage situations. Part of the concern with blended families and second marriages is that your surviving spouse is placed between your children and their ultimate inheritance from you and the potential for hard feelings between your surviving spouse and your children can be created. In this situation the inheritance of your children is dependent upon the spending habits of your surviving spouse.

Your children may view each expenditure by your surviving spouse as a reduction in their inheritance. Their vigilant scrutiny of your surviving spouse in and of itself can create conflict and foster resentment. Your children may believe that your surviving spouse is living too extravagantly, is taking too many luxurious vacations, is squandering their prospective inheritance; or is intentionally spending their inheritance in order to preserve your surviving spouse's assets for her children. The surviving spouse, on the other hand, may feel that he or she has not been treated properly by your children and may retaliate in a manner that would reduce or eliminate your children's inheritance. Ideally you should provide for your surviving spouse and your children entirely separately. As a consequence, it makes sense to segregate your children's inheritance from your surviving spouse's inheritance.

Should I leave my estate to my spouse or to my children?

Most people want to benefit their spouse in a blended family or second marriage situation and yet still provide for their children. Experience teaches that the potential for conflict is so great that to follow traditional estate planning patterns could be a mistake that could create problems, legal fees, and conflicts between your surviving spouse and your children.

There is a technique that can be employed if that is not a concern. That is the establishment of a trust for the benefit of your surviving spouse that requires that all of the income of the trust be distributed to your surviving spouse. Principal distributions can be prohibited, permitted for your surviving spouse's health, education and maintenance during her lifetime, or permitted in the total discretion of the trustee. Upon your spouse's death, the proceeds pass to your children.

The conflicts using this technique, while somewhat diminished remain substantial. However, this technique may be necessary to eliminate the estate tax by utilizing the marital deduction for amounts in excess of your estate tax exemption amount. If your surviving spouse is adequately taken care of, or has wealth of her own and the marital deduction is required to reduce the estate tax, a form of the marital deduction trust can be employed that would minimize the income distributions from the marital trust and prohibit principal distributions. The trust may be subject to estate tax at the second death, which your surviving spouse's federal estate tax exemption may be available to shelter.

This type of trust called a Qualified Terminal Interest Property Trust or often referred to as a QTIP trust. This trust differs from the standard marital trust in that your surviving spouse lacks the ability to alter the distribution scheme established by your estate plan. This can be effective in sheltering from tax, delaying the tax, and perhaps avoiding the tax.

The irrevocable life insurance trust (discussed in more detail in the next chapter) is another technique that should be considered. The life insurance trust could be established for the benefit of your children with life insurance in an amount equal to the value of your entire estate or equal to the amount passing from you to your surviving spouse. This is a classic example of taking taxable assets, passing them to a non-taxable beneficiary (your surviving spouse) while distributing non-taxable assets (the death proceeds in the life insurance trust) to taxable beneficiaries (your children).

Monetarily this can be equalized and the parties can be segregated in use and benefit from your estate. However, if your children have emotional attachment to your actual assets, then this particular planning technique would not be effective. As an alternative, the life insurance trust could be established for the benefit of your surviving spouse and your children could receive your other assets, less any estate tax due.

PLANNING FOR MINOR CHILDREN

Do I have to create a living trust if my only asset is a life insurance policy and I name my minor child as the beneficiary?

A life insurance policy will pass to a designated beneficiary without going through the probate process. However, if you have minor children who are the beneficiaries of that life insurance policy, the life insurance company will generally not distribute those policy proceeds to a minor. Instead, someone usually has to go to court and set up a guardianship on behalf of that minor. If you fail to plan properly, you may end up with a guardian appointed by the court, and that guardian may be someone you would rather not have controlling that minor's money. Once the guardianship is set up, the court will often try to protect the money in a closed account that can only be accessed by court order. Whenever that minor needs that money for things like braces or medical care or education, the Guardian must petition the court to access the money. Plus, there is a cost for ongoing attorney's fees and court costs. Then when the minor reaches the age of majority (18 in most states), the law goes to the other extreme. The money is then given outright to the minor with no instructions and no control.

When you have a living trust, you can name the trust as the beneficiary of the insurance policy. The trustee then uses the money to provide for the beneficiaries of the trust according to your instructions. No guardianship or court intervention is required.

Who will raise my children if I die while they are still minors?

Some people think that estate planning is for millionaires. In fact, if you have any assets at all, or if you have minor children, estate planning is just as important for you. Not only does the process deal with how assets are distributed at your death, but perhaps more importantly who will raise your children and watch out for their financial well-being.

There are two types of guardianships for minors. The first is a guardianship over the minor, and the second is a guardianship over the minor's property. Under the law, a minor is legally unable to care for herself and is legally unable to deal with her property.

A guardian over your minor children is named in your Will. If you are using a revocable living trust as the center of your estate plan, it will include a pour-over will as discussed above. In that case, the guardian is named in the pour-over will. A guardian over your minor children's property is usually not necessary, since your living trust will allow the Trustee to care for and manage your minor children's property.

The person you name as the guardian of your minor children will be responsible for taking care of your children until each child reaches the age of majority (18 in most states). If you die without a valid will naming the guardian for your minor children, the decision will be made by the court. The court will often name a close family member, but it may not be the family member you would have chosen.

What qualities should I look for when choosing a Guardian for my minor children?

When you are nominating the Guardian of your minor children, the goal is to provide each child as little disruption to his or her life as possible. To accomplish that, you want to choose someone who will raise your children the same way you would raise them if you were still alive. The Guardian should have similar philosophies to yours about raising children, about education, about discipline, and about religious or spiritual matters. A good indicator of how someone might raise your children is how they are raising their own children.

If you are choosing a married person, you will need to decide whether to name just one individual (perhaps your relative) or if you are naming the couple. You should consider what will happen if the guardians you appoint get divorced after your children have moved in with them.

You'll also want to consider the economic wherewithal of the guardian so that you don't saddle them with responsibility that will overwhelm them financially. If you have more than one child, and want to keep your children together, you'll have to name a guardian that is willing and able to take all of them.

All of this assumes that the person you name agrees to take your children. You should always check with them ahead of time to be sure they are willing, and then name back-up guardians in case circumstances change and the person who agreed in advance, is unable to take the children at the actual time of your death.

Should the same person who is raising my children also be in charge of the financial assets?

Sometimes the people who are the most nurturing are not necessarily the best at handling money. Although the person you name as Guardian of your minor children can also serve as Trustee of your trust that may not be the best solution.

It's easy to see that filling the dual role of Guardian and Trustee presents the potential for a conflict of interest. For example, imagine you leave your four children to your sister as guardian, and you also make her the trustee of your children's trust. Would it be reasonable for her to use $100,000 from the trust to add two bedrooms and a bath to her home? Many people would say that is reasonable. But what if she wants to use $750,000 from the kids' trust to buy a larger home when her current home is valued at $300,000? In that case, it might be good to have a second opinion.

These types of scenarios can be avoided when you appoint one person to raise the children, and another to manage the finances. When the Guardian needs funds to help take care of your children, he or she simply contacts the Trustee, and explains the need.

But since the trustee has a measure of discretion in these matters, it's also important to give clear guidance to the trustee so that your children are cared for in the way you want them to be. Some things to consider for the trustee instructions:

- Can my guardian expand the size of their current house (or buy a new house) in order to house my children?
- Can my guardian buy new appliances (such as bigger washers and dryers)?
- Can my guardian use the funds in the trust to pay for private school?
- Can my guardian use some of the funds to benefit the guardian's own children so that there isn't a perception of "special treatment" that will cause resentment between my children and the guardian's children?
- Can money from the trust be used to take the whole family (including the guardian's children and mine) on vacation?
- Do I want the trustee to generally be conservative or liberal when allocating funds to the guardian to care for my children?

Do I need to set up a separate trust for each of my minor children?

Many clients set up individual trusts for their adult children to maximize protections. But for minor children, a useful tool is the Common Trust. A common trust is a trust that benefits all the minor children together, as their needs dictate. Each of the children are treated fairly, but not necessarily equally.

For example, imagine a common trust set up for three minors: Sally (age 12), Billy (age 10), and Mary (age 4). Sally may need braces this year at a cost of $3000, but the trustee does not have to give $3000 to Bill and Mary to keep things equal. Billy may be constantly outgrowing his clothes and requiring new ones, but Sally and Mary do not need to receive a dollar for dollar payout to match Billy's. Money is spent from the trust the same way you would spend it if you were still alive and taking care of your children's individual needs.

When does the common trust end and what happens then?

Most common trusts are designed to terminate when the youngest child reaches a certain age or completes college. At that time, the funds that are left in the trust are divided among all the children, equally or unequally, according to the trust instructions. Instead of outright distributions at that time, you may specify that the funds will pass from the common trust into an individual trust for each child. This preserves a level of protection throughout the child's lifetime as discussed below.

There are many years between the oldest and the youngest of my 10 children. I don't want my oldest child to have to wait until they're 40 to receive their share of the proceeds from the common trust. What can I do?

Once again, you can accomplish almost anything by providing the trustee with clear instructions on what types of things the money in the trust can be spent. For example:

- Can the money be used for medical care for one child, even if it wipes out the whole common trust?
- Are there annual spending limits per child in any category of spending?
- Can the money be used for higher education? If so, what happens if some of the children decide to go to college, and others don't?
- If the funds in the common trust can be used for advanced education, does that include Masters' and Doctoral studies or only a Bachelor's degree?

- Can the trustee advance funds to an older child to buy their first home, to start a business, or to pay the expenses of a wedding?

- If so, are those funds accounted for like every other expenditure in the common trust—or do those advances count against that child's eventual share?

These and many other questions will be the subject of discussion when you meet with your estate planning attorney to design the trust(s) for your minor children.

PLANNING FOR ADULT CHILDREN

What things should I consider as I plan for my adult children?

Like every other part of your plan, you should start by determining your children's needs and your specific goals for their future. "Fair is not always equal and equal is not always fair," is a common estate planning quote. You probably have a desire to be fair with your children, but you also recognize that children are unique in their personality, their needs, how they handle money, their marital situation, etc. Therefore, while treating each child fairly, you may decide you also need to treat them differently.

In your estate plan you have the freedom to do what you believe is right, based on your understanding of the individual uniqueness of each child. One may need protection from creditors. Another may have a drug or alcohol problem. Another may have won the lottery, and therefore has little need for an inheritance. One may be married to someone you don't particularly trust.

The beauty of estate planning is that you can customize your plan to fit each individual set of circumstances.

What is the best way to leave an inheritance to my adult children?

Many clients begin the estate planning process assuming that upon their death they will leave assets to their children as an "outright" distribution. Parents are often reluctant to leave assets in trust for adult children because they don't want to be seen as overly controlling. In addition, relatively few professional advisors promote the many advantages that a protective trust may provide to an adult child.

But leaving assets in trust for an adult child doesn't necessarily mean that the child will lose control of the assets. To the contrary, if the child is appointed as a trustee over their own trust, that child will have both control over the trust assets, *and* can receive critical protections.

There are many ways to leave an inheritance to your children. For instance, you can provide for assets to be held in a trust with staggered distributions based on your best guess of when your child will be mature enough to make good financial decisions. As an example, you could provide for a distribution of one-third of the trust assets upon the child attaining the age of 35, one-half of the remaining trust assets upon the child attaining age 45, and the balance upon the child attaining the age of 55. This would provide the child with protection of undistributed assets while allowing a portion of the trust to terminate at given age intervals. Of course, that would still result in outright distributions at each of those times, and that portion of the inheritance would no longer be protected.

Alternatively, you could provide for your assets to be distributed to your children in continuing lifetime trusts. These trusts will last for the duration of the child's lifetime. A lifetime trust provides ongoing protection of the child's inheritance from lawsuits, divorces, and immature or fiscally irresponsible behavior. Within each child's trust, you can carve out individual distribution guidelines that provide for the manner of distributions in accordance with your values, goals and beliefs. For example if you wish to encourage entrepreneurship, you can provide that the Trustee will distribute funds to provide for the start-up costs of a new business or professional practice. By doing so, you will encourage an entrepreneurial spirit while also providing opportunities otherwise unavailable to your child.

You may also wish to divide your property based on the individual needs and wants of each child. For example, a child who has been employed in a family business for years may be the most suitable person to take over the business. The estate plan can provide for this child to receive the family business while making an equalizing distribution of other assets to other children, who may have no interest in the family business.

Depending on state law, you can also give your child the power to determine who will inherit any remaining trust property upon the child's death. The ability of a beneficiary (your child) to determine who ultimately gets any remaining trust property is called a "power of appointment." This power to "rewrite" your estate plan can be very limited (i.e., your child can leave the property only to your descendants), or can very broad (allowing your child to leave the property to any person, whether inside or outside of your bloodline). Granting a power of appointment to a beneficiary may have estate tax consequences, so you always want to receive advice from your professional advisors on this strategy.

PROTECTING YOUR ADULT CHILDREN'S INHERITANCE

How can a trust protect my children's inheritance?

One of the main reasons to do Estate Planning is to provide loved ones with protection from claims of future creditors and divorcing spouses or lawsuits ("Predators"). If you leave your property to your child as an outright distribution, the property will not be protected.

There is a longstanding concept in trust law known as "spendthrift" protection. These are provisions which provide that the Trustee will have sole control to make distributions from the Trust without interference from others. The spendthrift clause prevents a third party (i.e., a creditor or "predator") from being able to compel the Trustee into making distributions of trust property for the benefit of the third party.

Under the spendthrift rules of most states, a person is free to leave assets in trust for another person, with specific language in the trust specifying who, besides a trust beneficiary, can have access to the trust assets. If the trust includes a "spendthrift" clause that specifically states that trust income and principal is *not* to be available for payment to a trust beneficiary's creditors, then as a general rule the trust would be immune from attack by a beneficiary's creditor. This sweeping protection would apply regardless of the amount or nature of a beneficiary's liabilities, and would include protection of the trust assets if the child were to go through a divorce.

However, the extent of protection offered by a trust with a spendthrift clause will depend upon state law. Under some states, certain creditors are still allowed access to a trust. This could include a beneficiary's obligations for alimony or child support, or payments to creditors who have provided certain "necessities of life" to the beneficiary.

Can my child serve as the trustee of her trust share and still have protections?

Yes. Note, however, that the general rule is that a creditor or "predator" may be able to "step into the shoes" of a child in order to enforce a judgment or claim. Once in the shoes of the child, the creditor or "predator" can compel the child to exercise any rights held by the child over the trust assets. For example, if the trust permits the trustee to make distributions of trust income or principal to the trust beneficiary in the trustee's "sole and absolute discretion," and the child is the sole trustee and sole beneficiary, in many states such broad language might make those assets available to the child's creditors.

More protective provisions would limit distributions to the certain things, such as "health, education, support or maintenance." But even the more seemingly restrictive language is quite broad, as "maintenance" means a distribution necessary to help maintain your child's standard of living. Distributions for a house, a car, travel could all be included as distributions for your child's "maintenance." Also, if your child is named as the sole Trustee of his trust and the trust allows the Trustee to make distributions of income and principal for your child's support, a creditor who has furnished goods or services that may be classified as "support' may be able to "step into the shoes" of your child and make a distribution to satisfy the judgment or claim. Generally, if under state law a beneficiary has a right to compel the Trustee to make a distribution, then the creditor will be able to enforce that right.

To keep this from happening, you may want to name an independent party as co-trustee of your child's trust. In a serious situation, your child could even resign as Trustee, leaving management in the hands of the co-trustee.

Since the independent Trustee has no connection to the creditor or predator, the creditor or predator is generally unable to "step into the shoes" of the independent Trustee and exercise the right of the Trustee to make a distribution. The reason is because the spendthrift clause will prevent anyone from interfering with the independent Trustee's discretion in making distributions of trust property from the trust. You can choose to give your child "indirect control" over his trust by allowing him to remove and change the co-trustee whenever he wants.

In conclusion, the degree of protection will depend upon the wording in the trust regarding the Trustee's discretion to make distributions, who the Trustee is, and the rights of beneficiaries and creditors under state law.

I don't expect my children to have problems with creditors or predators, so shouldn't I just leave my property to them outright?

Even if an adult child is debt free and will never divorce, leaving their assets in a protective trust can still be beneficial. For one thing, life is uncertain, and you have no way of knowing what the future holds for your child. Your son, the doctor, may be sued for malpractice. Your daughter, the entrepreneur, may experience a business failure due to the turbulent economy. Your other daughter, the business executive, could be "downsized." The bottom could fall out of the market, and wipe out the investments of all three of your children. And any of their marriage relationships, that now seem so strong, can be turned upside down through one lapse of judgment. Assets within the reach of creditors *include* any assets that the person had inherited as an "outright" distribution.

In addition, millions of Americans become severely disabled at some point during their lifetimes, sometimes as a result of accidents, and sometimes as a result of physical or mental illness. Federal and state governments have a myriad of entitlement programs available to support the disabled, but the majority of these programs are "means tested"— that is, you qualify for aid only if you don't have too many assets or too much income.

For example, to qualify for Supplemental Security Income benefits, a single applicant today can have no more than $2,000 in assets, plus a house. Income limits vary among the states, but as a rule of thumb you will be ineligible for SSI benefits if your non-exempt income exceeds approximately $1,500 per month.

If assets are passed to a child through an outright inheritance, the inherited assets would be counted in determining the child's eligibility for governmental aid. That would typically disqualify the child from receiving that benefit, and would use up his inheritance instead.

However, those assets can be passed to the child in a spendthrift trust containing a "trigger" provision that converts the child's trust to a "special needs" trust should the child become seriously disabled or otherwise eligible for governmental assistance. In that circumstance, the trust assets and its income should be excluded from the calculation in determining the child's eligibility for assistance.

Are there other times a "special needs" trust would be helpful besides a future disability?

Yes. Special needs trusts are used for a wide variety of situations. The most common are for chronic physical or mental health issues. There is little sense in leaving an inheritance to a child or grandchild just to have it taken to reimburse an insurance company or government program.

A special needs trust is also valuable to protect a loved one who is trapped in a drug or alcohol addiction. The money can be managed by a trustee (other than the beneficiary) to provide for basic physical needs and rehabilitation expenses, while preventing its confiscation for reimbursement to government programs, and preventing its use for harmful substances.

But I don't want to "control from the grave"!

There is a continuum that balances control and protection. You can give up all control over your assets at death, and pass them outright to your beneficiaries. That gives the beneficiaries complete control, and therefore provides no protections.

On the other end of the continuum, you can maintain complete control of your assets after death, provide no control to the beneficiaries, and provide fairly ironclad protections.

Most clients end up planning for something toward the middle of the continuum. They maintain limited control after death, and give the beneficiaries as much control as they can without sacrificing the protections from the beneficiaries' creditors and "predators."

DISINHERITING A CHILD

I have a child who has led a lifestyle with which I disagree.
I don't want to provide for that child upon my death.
Can I disinherit that child by providing that he is
only to receive $1.00?

Your children do not have a legal right to your estate. You can leave it to anyone you desire, and disinherit anyone you want to. You do not have to leave them $1.00 to disinherit them. If you want to disinherit someone, it is important to make that clear in your plan documents. This is done by acknowledging the existence of that child, and then affirmatively stating that you have intentionally decided not to provide an inheritance for this child.

If you fail to do an estate plan, your child may inherit by intestate succession under state law. If you create an estate plan but simply fail to name your child as a beneficiary, the child could go into court and claim you just forgot about them. They could then inherit under a statute that protects forgotten children. Therefore, if you are going to disinherit a child, you should make sure you do so clearly and affirmatively.

NOTE: An important exception is found in Louisiana law. In Louisiana, children age 23 or younger, or who are permanently incapable of taking care of their persons or administering their estates, are entitled to a portion of their parents' estates.

If I affirmatively disinherit a child in my estate planning
documents, can my child contest it?

Anyone can file an action to contest a Will or Trust. However, that doesn't mean they will prevail. If an action is filed, that child will have to prove that you either lacked capacity to make the decisions you made in that plan document, or will have to prove that you were under some sort of undue influence when you created your plan.

If you anticipate that someone will claim you lacked capacity to sign your estate planning documents, you may want to have your physician provide you with written documentation that you still have the ability to make your own financial decisions. You can have your estate planning attorney document his or her file with this doctor's declaration of your capacity. You can also have the signing of your estate planning documents videotaped to show that you were interacting with the attorney about your wishes and confirming your decisions.

Another defense against a claim of incapacity is to specifically state the reasons for the disinheritance such as addiction, trouble with the law, the fact that you gave her money during life, the fact he never visited you or acknowledged your existence during life, or any other rational reason. However, if the reason you state is later found to be incorrect or irrational, your child might be able to successfully avoid disinheritance.

You can also create a financial disincentive for the disinherited relative to challenge the plan. Trusts are more useful for this purpose than wills. For example, a beneficiary that would expect to inherit $100,000 may be left $5,000 as a bequest, with the provision that if the plan is challenged by the individual, he gets nothing at all. Whether or not this works is dependent on state law. Again, a qualified estate planning attorney needs to deal with issues related to disinheriting family members or beneficiaries in general.

I love my child very much and do not want to disinherit him; however, he has a drug problem, and I don't want to leave him money to use for drugs. Should I disinherit that child?

You could disinherit that child if that is what you wish to do. However, you have other options. As mentioned above, this might be a situation that can be solved with a "special needs" trust. The trustee evaluates the needs of that child, and can do things such as:

- make sure the child has medical insurance in place
- provide food or shelter for that child
- provide distributions based on drug testing
- provide for the costs of rehabilitation or counseling
- disinherit at a later date, if the child doesn't change his behavior

Through a trust you can control when and how that child receives money through careful planning and clear instructions.

I have two minor children and I have several older children who are all married and well taken care of. I feel my minor children need to be provided for if something happens to me. Is it wrong for me to disinherit my older children?

It is not wrong for you to disinherit your older children if that's your desire. However, if you are going to make the decision to disinherit them, you may want to consider the psychological effects it can have on those older children. Assuming that you love all your children equally, it would be important to sit down with them and explain why you are taking this action—and then reiterate your reasons in writing within the plan. This will certainly make things much easier than learning of this decision after your death.

In addition, disinheritance can still be worded in a way that removes the sting. For example, you could state that you love and value each of your children equally, but since your older children are already self-sufficient, you have decided to pass the bulk of your inheritance to the younger children.

FUNDING YOUR TRUST

What is trust "funding" and why is it important?

Funding is the act of transferring your assets to your Living Trust. Think of a Living Trust as a bucket. Just as an empty bucket is of little value, even a well-drafted Trust is of little use unless it is "filled" with your assets. If you create a Living Trust but never get around to funding the Trust, then your unfunded assets will not be controlled by the Trust provisions. At best, the unfunded assets will be transferred to your Trust after you death by use of a "Pour-Over Will." But such after-death funding generally requires that your Will be probated so that your executor will have legal authority to transfer your assets to your Living Trust. Since many people establish Living Trusts with the expectation that their estate will not require probate, relying upon the pour-over will to fund a Living Trust should be only as a last resort.

And even with a pour-over will you can't be sure that all of your assets will make it into your trust after death. Most married people own the majority of their assets with a spouse as joint owners with rights of survivorship. Such joint ownership means that the assets will pass auto-matically upon one owner's death to the surviving owner.

Likewise, assets such as retirement plans, annuities, and life insur-ance are contractual assets that pass to persons named on a beneficiary designation form. While such assets will not be subject to probate upon an owner's death, the assets that pass to individual co-owners or suc-cessor beneficiaries will receive none of the valuable tax and personal planning protections that are available for assets passing under the terms of a trust.

Filling your trust "bucket" is accomplished by the process known as *trust funding*. Trust funding involves transferring title to the assets from your name (or from you and your spouse in the case of a joint account) into the name of the trustees of the trust. Funding is not a difficult task, but it requires attention to detail and persistence. It requires you to no-tify all of your financial institutions in writing of the proposed change. Most of the time, at least one follow-up communication is required to ensure that proper titling takes place.

The new name on the account is not listed as the "John Doe Living Trust." Instead, title should be held by the trustee(s) in their fiduciary capacity, as follows: "John and Mary Doe, Trustees, or their successors in trust, under the John Doe Living Trust, dated June 1, 2010, and any amendments thereto." A shorter version that will work in most cases would be "John and Mary Doe, Trustees, under the John Doe Living Trust dated June 1, 2010."

Special care must be given for funding certain assets such as real estate, life insurance policies, IRA's and other retirement assets. Retirement account ownership should never be transferred to a revocable trust, since a change of ownership will be deemed a distribution of the assets and cause the retirement account to be fully taxable. Instead, the trust may be named as either a primary or contingent beneficiary of the retirement account to provide maximum after-death flexibility.

If you have an existing trust, you should periodically review whether the trust is properly funded. And when you buy new assets, keep the titling issue in mind. If you are thinking of establishing a trust for the first time, be sure to work with advisors who are committed to the funding process so that all of your planning goals can be achieved.

Do I have to fund all of my assets into my trust?

Most estate planning attorneys would encourage you to fund all of your assets into your trust, either by change of ownership, or by change of beneficiary as mentioned above with retirement plans. A revocable living trust can control only those assets which are titled into your trust name.

There are exceptions however, and they may vary from state to state. Your professional advisors can provide counsel on assets that may need to be handled outside the trust process.

Can I do the funding of my trust myself?

Yes, you can take the steps to fund your trust yourself. However, most clients that start out with good intentions end up never completing their funding. When an advisor checks on the funding process a month or two later, they typically hear the client say one of two things: Either "Remind me what funding is again," or "We've been meaning to get started on that, and haven't had a chance to."

The process of funding the trust can be tedious and time-consuming depending on the nature and quantity of your assets. The biggest enemies of proper funding are procrastination and frustration. Most attorneys who specialize in estate planning will have processes in place to get funding completed efficiently, and to verify that the re-titling has been completed correctly.

You should normally expect to pay your attorney for providing this service. However, you will have the comfort of knowing that the assets are funded and they have been funded correctly. Also, the charges for funding assets into a trust are nominal compared to the costs that would be incurred if unfunded assets had to be transferred through a probate after death.

Your financial advisor who maintains the records on your financial assets can be of great assistance to the attorney because he or she will have records on most accounts, and the means with which to change ownership.

Will I have to amend my trust every time I acquire a new asset?

You do not have to amend your trust every time that you acquire a new asset. The trust instructions control the eventual disposition of the assets, but those instructions don't change each time an asset is included. Instead, acquiring new assets is part of the ongoing funding process, and you will want to take title to the asset in your trust's name.

If a change occurs that is so big that I need to create a new trust, will I have to fund my assets into my trust all over again?

No. Your attorney can "restate" your trust. A restatement acknowledges the creation of your trust on the date you originally created it, and states that you wish to restate that trust in its entirety. The restated contents of the trust will take the place of the contents of your old trust, but the trust name doesn't change. It's still the "John Doe Living Trust, created June 1, 2010" or whatever it was originally called. Think of it as the same book cover, but with changes in the text within.

MAINTENANCE OF MY TRUST

I've created and funded my living trust—what do I need to do to maintain it?

It is simply not enough to create a living trust, no matter how well designed and drafted. Changes in your personal and financial circumstances, changes in the law, and changes in your attorney's knowledge and experience, affect the long-term viability of your estate plan. It is important that you periodically meet with your attorney and other professional advisors to review and update your estate plan.

Of course, you are the expert on your family, so you need to keep your lawyer informed on any changes in your family situation. That would include marriages, divorces, new children, a change of beneficiaries, a change of the distribution split, and so forth. Your attorney is the expert on changes in the laws which would affect your trust. And, as your attorney continues to gain experience and participate in continuing education, he or she may develop new planning techniques that you might want to adopt.

The best type of estate plan maintenance is a *formal* updating program that provides for regular periodic meetings, often annually or semi-annually, between the client and estate planning attorney. A formal estate planning maintenance program will ensure that your documents remain "state-of-the-art," will provide for a funding review to verify that all your assets are properly titled to match your estate planning objectives, and will alert you regarding changes in the law that might impact your estate planning objectives.

MISCELLANEOUS QUESTIONS ABOUT TRUST PLANNING

What is a Convenience Trust?

A Convenience Trust is a trust that permits the beneficiary to withdraw the assets at any time for any reason without restriction. It gives almost as much control of the inheritance to a beneficiary as an outright distribution. However, it may provide some protections, provided that he or she leaves the assets in the trust, and there is a way for another trustee to take over to protect the trust in the event of an attack by a creditor or predator. This is generally the least protective type of trust.

What is a Lifetime Trust?

A Lifetime Trust keeps the assets within the trust for the lifetime of the beneficiary. This trust avoids probate and has asset protection features. The majority of lifetime trusts distribute income and principal as needed for health, education, lifestyle maintenance, and support. This is typically the most protective type of trust, especially when co-trustees are appointed.

Is it possible to establish a trust for my pets?

Perhaps nothing better illustrates the importance of pets in people's lives, and the affection that they feel for them, than the events which followed Hurricane Katrina in 2005, and the failure of the levees in New Orleans. When rescuers arrived, some people who had been trapped for days by the flood waters refused to leave their homes unless they were allowed to bring their pets with them.

Laws on the subject of pet trusts vary from state to state. Since animals are not allowed to be beneficiaries of a trust, various legislative devices have been employed in the past. Some states authorized the creation of "honorary trusts" which could be used to provide for the care of a pet, but were not enforceable by a court. The Uniform

Probate Code recognized "pet trusts" in 1990, and the Uniform Trust Code added a pet trust provision in 2000. However, the Uniform Codes are only recommendations, and each state chooses whether or not to adopt any of their provisions. As of the end of 2009, 42 states and the District of Columbia have adopted some type of provision which allows creation of a pet trust, some based on the Uniform Probate Code provisions, some based on the Uniform Trust Code provisions, and some on neither, including some remaining "honorary trust" provisions.

The law has traditionally regarded pets as "property" and thus not possessing any rights. In the past, individuals had to do such things as leaving money to a person with instructions to care for their animals, and hope that their wishes would be carried out, since there was no legal way to enforce such a provision. However, a growing recognition of the importance of companion animals to people has led to several advancements in legislative establishment of means to protect animals left behind.

What do unmarried or same-sex couples need to consider in preparing an estate plan?

Unmarried couples face special estate planning challenges. For those with larger estates, the "unlimited marital deduction" described in Chapter 4 is not available as a planning tool.

What if an unmarried couple, like the majority of Americans, never gets around to doing any estate planning? If one partner were to become incapacitated, the healthy partner would have no legal authority to handle the personal, financial or medical affairs of the ill partner. The healthy partner might have to file a court petition to be appointed as the ill partner's legal guardian. If there is opposition from any of the ill partner's children or other family members, the healthy partner's lack of legal standing might prevent him or her from gaining appointment as guardian, thereby losing all control.

If one partner dies without a plan, the surviving partner retains no statutory rights to any of the deceased partner's property. The laws of intestacy (those that control when someone doesn't plan) usually provide for a spouse, children, and then other blood relatives. A non-married partner would not be in that line of succession.

Unmarried couples should first ensure that they have well-drafted estate planning documents, which typically include wills or trusts, living wills, health care powers of attorney, and financial powers of attorney. These documents must clearly spell out the role that the surviving partner is to play as health care agent, executor, trustee, and agent under the power of attorney. Just as important, if the couple wishes that the surviving partner receive some or all of the first partner's retirement accounts and life insurance proceeds upon the first partner's death, it is important that the beneficiary designations for these types of assets name the partner as the primary beneficiary.

When it comes to Medicaid planning, if one partner seeks Medicaid coverage for long-term care costs, the assets and income of the healthy partner are *not* counted in determining the Medicaid eligibility of the ill partner. However, unmarried couples cannot freely shift assets between themselves without financial penalty, nor can they utilize the "spousal refusal" technique that is available in some states to married couples to help protect a greater amount of the ill spouse's assets while allowing the ill spouse to qualify for Medicaid benefits.

What happens to my assets if none of the beneficiaries named in my living trust survive me?

Your living trust should include an "ultimate distribution" provision that addresses the unlikely scenario that all of your beneficiaries—typically your spouse, children or grandchildren—do not survive you. What is sometimes referred to as a the "family disaster" provision might specify that your assets would pass to designated "contingent" beneficiaries such as your siblings, nieces or nephews, charities, friends, or some combination of these people or entities. Or, the ultimate distribution provision might simply provide that your assets would be distributed to your "intestate" heirs—that is, those persons who would receive your assets under the laws of your state had you died without a plan.

My husband did not have a revocable living trust. He only had a will and there were no big problems when he passed away, so why do I need a revocable living trust?

This specific situation would need to be reviewed by your professional advisors, of course, but one reason you may have experienced no problems is because you and your husband owned everything jointly (like your house, bank accounts, investments, etc); or it passed to you by way of a beneficiary designation (like insurance and IRAs). If the assets were held in these ways, there would have been no probate at your husband's death, and all would have been fairly simple.

Now, however, all those assets are now in your name individually, and things won't be so simple upon your death. And when things pass from you to your children and other beneficiaries, you may now want to take advantage of all the benefits of trust planning mentioned earlier in this chapter.

I heard that I could put assets into a revocable trust, retain control, and then apply for Medicaid benefits, and the assets in the trust would be protected from Medicaid?

No. The assets in a revocable trust are not protected from Medicaid. If the transfer had been to an irrevocable trust or gifted away, the technique may allow the assets to be excluded from Medicaid, subject to the applicable rules regarding the time of the transfer.

What is a community property agreement and how does it interact with my trust?

If you live in one of the ten community property states, your state law may allow for a community property agreement. This is an agreement between spouses that acknowledges that all assets are community property. In addition, it stipulates that in the event of the death of one of the spouses, all of the assets are immediately transferred to the surviving spouse.

Some practitioners use this agreement in lieu of other planning for spouses in community property states. Be careful when entering into more sophisticated estate planning such as trust planning, that you make your estate planning team aware of any previous community property agreements. A previously signed community property agreement could negate the effectiveness and planning benefits of that trust planning by passing everything to the surviving spouse outright, thereby causing the trust to be unfunded.

Historically, the nine community property states have been: Arizona, California, Idaho, Louisiana, Nevada, New Mexico, Texas, Washington, and Wisconsin. In 1998 Alaska passed the Alaska Community Property Act which allows a married couple to elect for all or part of their property to be treated as community property.

How is my personal property handled in a trust?

Personal property such as jewelry, antiques, artwork, family heirlooms, and household effects can be passed on to your beneficiaries through a specific bequest: "I leave my Ming Vase to my sister Betty." But for most people, it would be overwhelming to try to inventory and choose a beneficiary for every last item you own. Instead, it is common to use a separate "Personal Property Memorandum" that is attached to, and incorporated by reference into the trust.

The memo is generally a handwritten or typed list of your wishes of bequests to family or charities, which is signed and dated by you. They can cover each personal item that you own, but typically include only those items of financial value or of strong sentimental value—the types of things that lead to disagreements among the heirs.

The benefit of a memo is that it can be easily changed if you sell something, give it away during life, or change your mind about who should receive it after you're gone. You simply throw it away and replace it with a new memo. Each personal property memorandum should be dated, and the trust should contain instructions that if more than one memo is discovered after your death, the one with the most recent date is binding.

Of course, you should also provide for personal property that is not specifically listed on the personal property memorandum. Most trusts will state that the trustee can dispose of it equitably to the beneficiaries, and if they can't agree on the disposition, the trustee can sell the items and split the proceeds of the sale according to the trust distribution plan.

DISCLAIMERS

What is a disclaimer?

A disclaimer is an irrevocable refusal to accept an interest in property. In other words, it is the legal way of saying "no thank you." The effect of a disclaimer is that the disclaimed property will be treated as if it had never been transferred to the person making the disclaimer. Most states have statutes that allow for disclaimers and describe the method for making a valid disclaimer.

What is a qualified disclaimer?

A disclaimer is qualified if it meets certain requirements under the Internal Revenue Code. If these requirements are not met, the person attempting to disclaim the property will be treated as having received the property, and then as having made a gift to the person to whom the property passes as a result of the disclaimer. The disclaimer must meet the following requirements:

- it is irrevocable;
- it is unqualified;
- it is in writing, specifically identifying the disclaimed interest and signed by the person making the disclaimer;
- the written disclaimer is delivered to the person who is attempting to transfer the property, his legal representative, or the holder of legal title;
- the written disclaimer must be delivered no more than nine months after the date on which the transfer creating the interest is made, or nine months after the date on which the person making the disclaimer reaches age 21;
- the person making the disclaimer must not have previously accepted the disclaimed interest or any of its benefits prior to the disclaimer; and
- the disclaimed interest must pass to a person other than the person making the disclaimer without any direction from the person making the disclaimer. However, a surviving spouse of the person making the transfer may remain as a beneficiary of a trust which receives the disclaimed property.

Why would I use a qualified disclaimer?

A qualified disclaimer is a very useful estate planning tool that gives a beneficiary the ability to redirect assets after the death of the person making the bequest to another person for tax planning purposes or for nontax purposes. If the qualified disclaimer is considered as part of the estate plan, it allows you to give the beneficiaries the flexibility to determine when and where the assets are most needed after the estate plan is written when circumstances may have changed.

I don't need the money from my father, and I'd like to pass it to my children instead, without any adverse tax consequences. Is that when a disclaimer might be used?

Yes. A qualified disclaimer could be the perfect tool to accomplish this goal. If you disclaim your interest in the inheritance after your father is deceased, but before you accept any benefit from the inheritance, the inheritance will pass as though you predeceased your father. In that case we would look to the terms of your father's estate plan to determine who would be the beneficiary or beneficiaries to receive the disclaimed portion of that inheritance.

If the document provides that should you predecease your father your share of the inheritance is to be distributed to your children equally, then your children would receive the assets you disclaimed. Since you made the qualified disclaimer, you will not be deemed to have made a gift to your children and thus you won't suffer any adverse tax consequences. Plus, those disclaimed assets will not be included in your estate at your death, thus avoiding additional estate taxes. However, there may be generation-skipping transfer taxes due from your father's estate if the amount transferred to your children exceeds your father's generation-skipping transfer tax exemption as discussed in Chapter 4.

6 | Irrevocable Trust Planning

Another tool in the estate planning toolbox is the irrevocable trust. As the name implies, unlike the trusts discussed in the last chapter, the irrevocable trust cannot be changed once established. Therefore it's a tool that should be used only under the guidance of a professional advisor. However, when used correctly, these trusts can provide outstanding protection and tax savings.

What is an Irrevocable Trust?

An irrevocable trust is a trust that may not be altered, amended or revoked by the creator of the trust. The reason you may consider creating an irrevocable trust is because all gifts you make to the trust are treated like gifts made to a "third party," which means the gifts are excluded from your estate for estate tax purposes. This also means any gifts you make to the trust are generally subject to gift tax if the value exceeds the lifetime gift tax exemption discussed in Chapter 4. However, the benefit is that any growth and appreciation of the assets gifted will escape estate taxation at your death.

You can name the beneficiaries of the trust and provide them with protection from the reach of creditors and "predators" (those who would take advantage of them). You can also carve out distribution guidelines stating the rules on how the gifts may be used for the benefit of your beneficiaries.

Although an irrevocable trust may not be amended or altered by the creator of the trust, a Trust Protector, an unrelated independent third party who is not the creator or a beneficiary of the trust, may be given a power to amend the trust for limited purposes. For example, a Trust Protector may be given the power to amend a trust for drafting errors or changes in the tax law, which necessitates a change to continue the trust's objectives. In this way, there is some flexibility in dealing with future changes in the law and unforeseen circumstances.

Most states allow an irrevocable trust to be amended by court action. Most courts will allow an irrevocable trust to be amended if to do so would further the trust's intent and purpose, and if all of the beneficiaries of the trust agree to the modification.

Are irrevocable trusts somehow more "powerful" than revocable trusts?

In general, the only way to obtain tax advantages using a trust is to give up ownership. Irrevocable Trusts require you to give up legal title (ownership) to any property and that can never be changed. Revocable trusts, on the other hand, do not require giving up ownership and may be changed. But, there are no tax advantages to revocable trusts.

Revocable trusts are primarily used for control and management of assets. The revocable trust usually becomes irrevocable upon your death.

THE IRREVOCABLE LIFE INSURANCE TRUST (ILIT)

What is an Irrevocable Life Insurance Trust?

An Irrevocable Life Insurance Trust ("ILIT") is probably the most frequently used type of irrevocable trust. It's an irrevocable trust that you can establish to own a life insurance policy on your life. If you personally own a life insurance policy, the policy proceeds will be includable in your taxable estate and subject to estate tax at your death. However, if someone other than you owns the policy, the policy proceeds will be excluded from your taxable estate.

For federal death tax purposes, you are treated as the owner of a life insurance policy if you have any "Incidents of Ownership" in the policy. Incidents of Ownership include, among other rights, the right to borrow the cash value, surrender the policy, or change the beneficiaries of the policy. If an ILIT is created to own a policy on your life, the ILIT, not you will possess all incidents of ownership. Therefore, the death benefits will not be includable in your estate. The ILIT is usually also named as the beneficiary of the death proceeds at your death, and you can provide distribution guidelines and asset protection for the policy proceeds.

Life insurance policies may be subject to substantial fees and charges. Guarantees are subject to the claims paying ability of the insurer. Loans will reduce the policy's death benefit and cash surrender value, and will have tax consequences if the policy lapses.

I thought my insurance agent told me that insurance proceeds are tax-free. Did I miss something?

Life insurance is NOT always tax-free. One of the most common misconceptions about life insurance has to do with its tax status. In virtually all circumstances life insurance is *income* tax free. The premiums were paid with after-tax dollars and the death benefit is not subject to income tax.

However, life insurance is not necessarily estate tax free. Any assets owned in your estate are potentially subject to estate tax. Most life insurance policies are owned by the insured and therefore included in the estate of the insured. One of the biggest errors by clients in estimating the size of their estate is failing to include the death benefit of life insurance they own.

One of the easiest ways to reduce the size of your estate is to have an irrevocable life insurance trust (ILIT) own the policy rather than yourself. Existing policies can be gifted to that trust, or new life insurance can be acquired by the trust. Life insurance that is gifted to an irrevocable trust is subject to being included in your estate for three years after the date of the gift. Insurance that is initially acquired by the trust can be immediately excluded from your taxable estate.

How does an ILIT work?

The steps to successfully establishing an ILIT include the following:

1. Your advisors, including your attorney, help to design and create the ILIT.

2. The trustee of the ILIT applies for an insurance policy on your life, or the lives of you and your spouse.

3. You make a gift of the premium amount to the ILIT.

4. The trustee notifies the beneficiaries of their "demand right."

5. The trustee pays the premium for the insurance.

It's important that you and your advisors follow the steps slowly and carefully to prevent mistakes. If any of these steps are skipped or rushed, you run the risk of having the insurance proceeds brought back into the estate for tax purposes.

The design of the ILIT will depend upon its purpose. An ILIT doesn't exist until it is drafted and signed, and the ILIT must be in existence before the life insurance application is submitted to the insurance company. If you apply for the insurance personally, and then immediately move the policy to the ILIT after it's purchased, it will be 3 years before that policy is considered out of your estate. The same result occurs if you transfer the ownership of an already existing policy on your life to the trust. Many times it is more advantageous to have the trustee of the ILIT buy a *new* policy on your life.

Once the trustee has applied for the insurance policy, underwriting has been completed, and you are approved as the person to be insured, it's time for the Trustee to pay for that policy.

The next step is for you to make a gift of cash to the Trustee of the ILIT to pay for the policy premiums. Whether your gift to the ILIT will be considered a taxable gift will depend upon the terms of the ILIT, including the right of your beneficiaries to access (withdraw) the gift. As a general rule, if no beneficiary has a right to withdraw your gift, then you have made a taxable gift that will reduce your lifetime federal gift tax exemption of $1,000,000 (2010). If the gift exceeds this amount, then you will owe federal gift tax. Your gift may also be subject to state gift tax. However, if your beneficiaries have the right to withdraw the gift, then it will not be considered a taxable gift for federal gift tax purposes if it meets the requirements discussed below.

A beneficiary's right of withdrawal is necessary to avoid the taxation of the contribution to the ILIT as a taxable gift. As discussed in Chapter 4, each person can give a present interest gift of a certain amount each year (up to $13,000 per beneficiary in 2010) to any number of beneficiaries without the gifts being subject to gift tax. But to qualify, the gift must be a "present interest" (as opposed to a future interest) gift.

Only gifts where the recipient has the immediate right to the use and enjoyment are "present interest" gifts. The problem is that gifts to a trust are normally future interest gifts, and thus do not qualify for the annual gift tax exclusion. That is, the beneficiaries do not normally have the immediate right to the contributions to the trust. They will only receive the trust proceeds sometime in the future.

However, if the ILIT gives the beneficiaries the right to withdraw those funds for a limited period of time (usually 30 days), they are then entitled to the present use and enjoyment for that period of time. That right is enough to cause what is otherwise a future interest gift to be considered a present interest gift. This right of withdrawal technique is sometimes called a "Crummey demand right," or "demand right" and this type of trust is often referred to as a "Crummey Trust." That name is not a commentary on the quality of the trust.

The term "Crummey trust" originated with the 1968 case, <u>D. Clifford Crummey v. Commissioner of Internal Revenue</u>. In that case, Mr. Crummey had established an irrevocable trust for the benefit of his four children. He and his wife funded the trust with cash transfers each year, allowing the children to withdraw the amount of the contribution (not to exceed $4,000) any time prior to December 31 of the year of the contribution. The Ninth Circuit Court of Appeals ruled that the withdrawal right made the transfers gifts of a "present interest," and therefore eligible for the annual exclusion from the Federal gift tax. The decision paved the way for establishment of similar trusts, which became known as "Crummey trusts" or "demand trusts."

This right of withdrawal qualifies the gift for the annual exclusion from gift tax, *whether or not the beneficiaries actually withdraw anything*. If the beneficiaries do not exercise their right of withdrawal within the time limit provided in the trust, that right expires and the trustee is then free to pay the life insurance premium. When the beneficiaries understand why you have established the ILIT, they will not normally exercise their demand right.

The annual gift tax exclusion limit applies to each beneficiary of the trust. So if you have an insurance policy premium of $50,000 per year, and you have five beneficiaries, the maximum gift ($13,000 per beneficiary in 2010) to each beneficiary would more than cover the premium cost.

Is the ILIT useful for anything else besides keeping insurance proceeds out of the estate?

Another benefit of an ILIT is to place the cash value and death benefit of the life insurance policy beyond the reach of lawsuits and claims against the insured.

If the purpose of the insurance is to replace the income that would be lost upon the death of the insured, the ILIT provides a viable tool to fully protect those funds. By placing the death proceeds in a properly designed ILIT, the proceeds can be placed out of the reach of a beneficiary's creditors. Thus, if the beneficiary is sued, suffers a business failure or is the cause of a terrible accident for which the beneficiary is responsible, the funds held by the ILIT are protected from those creditors, yet can be used to provide for all of the beneficiary's needs. If the beneficiary is married or might marry someday, the insurance proceeds can be protected from the spouse of the beneficiary in the event of divorce or upon the death of the beneficiary.

If the purpose of the insurance is to replace wealth, the same protections can be designed into the ILIT. Wealth replacement ILITs are many times used in conjunction with a charitable remainder trust (CRT) to replace the amount passing to the charity at the end of the term of the charitable remainder trust. We explore CRTs in much greater detail in Chapter 9 of this book, but we'll provide a brief summary of the strategy here as it relates to the use of an ILIT.

A charitable remainder trust offers great advantage to the trustmaker, but at the end of its term (usually when the trustmaker dies), the trust proceeds pass to a charity. This effectively disinherits the trustmaker's beneficiaries; at least from that portion of the estate. By purchasing a life insurance policy on the life of the trustmaker, however, and holding ownership of that policy in an ILIT, the beneficiaries can still enjoy a full inheritance. The insurance can be purchased in an amount equal to the value of the property passing to the charity at the end of the term of the CRT, thus replacing the funds going to charity for the beneficiaries, estate tax free.

ILITs can also be used in conjunction with buy-sell agreements to protect the ownership of a business in the event of the death of the owner. The insurance on the life of the business owner is owned by the

ILIT. At the owner's death, the ILIT purchases his or her ownership interest in the company with the life insurance death proceeds received from the insurance company.

Another use for the ILIT is to enable business owners to equalize their estates between those children who are active in the business and those who are not. The insurance proceeds in the ILIT can be left to the non-involved children, while the business is passed to those children who have been active in the business, and have demonstrated a desire to own the business in the future.

Who may serve as trustee of the ILIT?

To avoid "incidents of ownership," and thereby pull the insurance proceeds back into your estate for federal estate tax purposes, the Trustee should be someone other than you.

A family member may be named as the sole Trustee of the ILIT, but it is usually better to name a professional Trustee, such as an accountant or institutional Trustee familiar with the administration of ILITs. The corporate trustee can act as a sole trustee, or as a co-trustee with the family member.

Professional trustees are accustomed to maintaining adequate records, handling notifications of demand rights to beneficiaries, filing any necessary tax returns, reviewing insurance policies for performance, and furnishing periodic accountings and information to the beneficiaries. All of these operational steps in the ILIT are crucial to maintain its federal estate tax-exempt status. Moreover, when the Trustee collects the death benefits from the insurance policy, a professional Trustee may be able to provide better asset protection from the beneficiaries' creditors or "predators" who would seek to take advantage of them.

Can I put something other than life insurance in the trust?

Yes. Any asset can be placed in the ILIT. Sometimes an income producing asset is placed inside of an ILIT to provide an income stream from which to pay the premiums on the life insurance. This technique eliminates any further gifts by the trustmaker/insured to the ILIT for the purpose of paying the life insurance premiums.

What if I want to access the cash value of an ILIT?

Generally speaking, you cannot directly access the cash value of an insurance policy owned by your ILIT. However, if the trust document permits, you can borrow funds from the life insurance trust, provided it is fully documented, interest is paid at an appropriate rate, and the loan is repaid over time. ILITs can also be designed to provide access to the cash value of the life insurance policy for the needs of your spouse or your child.

What happens to the ILIT when I die?

At your death, the death benefits are payable to the ILIT, because the ILIT is not only the owner of the policy, it is also the beneficiary. The death benefits are then held and administered by the Trustee according to the ILIT's specific terms.

The trustee can use those funds to provide liquidity to your estate or to pay your estate taxes. In most cases, those funds cannot be paid directly to the creditor, nor paid directly to the IRS in satisfaction of your estate taxes. To do so, would cause those proceeds to be taxable in your estate. One of the ways to avoid this result is to include a provision in the ILIT that it may lend your estate such amounts as are necessary to pay the estate tax or other debts or claims.

In that scenario, the cash goes to your estate (probably being managed under the terms of a revocable living trust). Your estate now has a "note payable," and the ILIT has a "note receivable." An integrated estate plan will often provide that if one or more trusts have virtually the same distribution instructions, they may be merged after your death. So after the taxes are paid, and the debts are settled, your RLT and your ILIT can merge, cancelling out the notes payable and receivable, and making distributions to your beneficiaries.

Another option is for the ILIT to purchase property at full market value from your estate, so your estate can use those proceeds to satisfy debts or to pay estate tax. When this strategy is used, it is again important that your estate plan be integrated so that whether money is coming from the revocable living trust or the ILIT, the result for the beneficiaries is the same—both in the distribution patterns and the protections.

Can the ILIT last forever?

Depending upon state law, a life insurance trust can last as long as any other trust, including dynasty trusts. If the ILIT is a dynasty-type ILIT, it will be subject to generation-skipping transfer taxes as discussed in Chapter 4. However, your generation skipping transfer tax exemption can be applied against the amount contributed to the ILIT, not against the death proceeds of the insurance policy purchased by the ILIT. The ability to purchase life insurance inside of a dynasty ILIT provides significant leverage for the use of the generation skipping transfer tax exemption.

I've created an Irrevocable Trust and am interested in gifting annual exclusion amounts to decrease my taxable estate, but I am gifting in disproportional amounts for each of the children's families. Isn't this giving unequal amounts to my children?

No, contributions into an Irrevocable Trust do not determine the ultimate ownership of the property contributed. The distribution clause in the Trust controls the ultimate disposition.

For example, you have two children, and you intend for them to be equal beneficiaries of your trust after your death. One child has two children and the other child has no children. Structured properly, you could make a gift to your ILIT of up to the annual exclusion for each of the four of them. Say you contributed $48,000 to the trust. However, after your death, each child will receive ½ of the assets of the trust, or in this example (ignoring potential growth) $24,000.

THE GRANTOR DEEMED OWNER TRUST

What is a Grantor Deemed Owner Trust?

A Grantor Deemed Owner Trust (GDOT) is an irrevocable trust that is treated differently for federal income tax purposes than for federal estate tax purposes. For estate tax purposes, any gifts you make to the GDOT will be treated as completed gifts, meaning the gifts are excluded from your taxable estate (just like the ILIT). However, for income tax purposes, you are treated as the owner of the GDOT assets. As a result, you are responsible for the income taxes. Paying the income taxes on assets that you gift to the GDOT is the equivalent of making additional tax free gifts to the beneficiaries of the GDOT. This is because the GDOT funds will not be depleted by payment of income taxes generated by the income of the GDOT. As a result, the beneficiaries will receive more assets in trust than if the GDOT was required to pay its own income taxes. This additional gift does not count against your lifetime gift tax exemption or the annual exclusion for gift tax.

A common planning technique is to sell your assets to the GDOT. The sale may be in exchange for a promissory note payable to you. For income tax purposes, the sale is not recognized (since you are treated as the owner of the GDOT assets for income tax purposes) and there will be no taxable gain on sale, thus avoiding income or capital gains tax. However, for estate tax purposes, any assets sold to the GDOT would be excluded from your estate.

Your estate will own the promissory note and receive periodic payments of interest and principal as provided in the note. Although the promissory note is included in your taxable estate at your death, the value of the note is fixed at the time of the sale. Therefore, if the assets sold appreciate in value from the time of sale to your date of death, the appreciation is excluded from your taxable estate. The assets of the GDOT, including all of the appreciation, will pass estate tax free to the GDOT's beneficiaries, according to the GDOT's terms.

For this strategy to work, the transaction must be a commercially reasonable transaction. The mechanics are as follows:

- You establish the GDOT and name a Trustee other than yourself or a beneficiary of the GDOT.

- You make a gift of cash or property to the GDOT (called "seed money").

- The amount of the seed money must be commercially reasonable, say, for example, ten percent of the assets to be sold. The seed money must be sufficient to assure that the GDOT will have enough funds to pay off the note. That's what makes it commercially reasonable.

- The note must bear an adequate rate of interest. Many times the note requires the payment of annual interest with a balloon payment of principal at a later point in time.

- The GDOT Trustee will then negotiate for the purchase of the assets from you.

- You enter into an agreement for the sale and purchase of the assets with the Trustee.

- You should sell income-producing assets that are expected to appreciate in value to the GDOT. This way, the GDOT will have sufficient funds to pay off the note. The Trustee will use the income produced by the assets sold to the GDOT to pay the note's interest.

- When the note matures, a final balloon payment will be made to you (or your estate) and the assets that are sold, including all of the appreciation in value, will be distributed or held in the GDOT for the benefit of the beneficiaries.

THE DYNASTY TRUST

What is a Dynasty Trust?

You can utilize your Generation Skipping Transfer (GST) Tax exemption to plan for several generations and build enormous wealth. This type of planning is known as dynasty planning. One of the reasons Congress enacted the GST Tax is to curb the wealth-building effects of dynasty planning. The concept of dynasty planning is to pass the maximum amount of wealth you can to your grandchildren (and subsequent generations) in a dynasty trust without subjecting the transfer to the GST Tax. In so doing, you can exempt the trust property from future GST and Estate taxation.

Allocating your maximum GST Tax exemption to the dynasty trust for your grandchildren (and subsequent generations) will cause the trust to be exempt from GST Tax. Since wealth that is not subject to death tax has the potential to grow much faster than wealth that is taxed, the property transferred to a dynasty trust may accumulate and grow more rapidly than wealth transferred outright.

For example, assume you have $1 Million and that you leave it to your child. For ease of illustration, assume a $1 Million estate tax exemption, a $1 Million GST Tax exemption and a 50% estate and GST Tax rate. At your death, you can leave the full $1 Million estate tax free to your child. Assuming your child is able to double her inheritance to $2 Million over her lifetime, at her death, there would be an estate tax on $1 Million, so that your child's estate would pay $500,000 in estate tax. This would leave an inheritance of $1.5 Million to you grandchild. Assuming your grandchild is able to double her inheritance over her lifetime, she would have an estate of $3 Million at her death. After estate taxes, she would be able to leave a $2 Million inheritance to your great-grandchild.

In the alternative, what if you had funded a dynasty trust with your $1 million and allocated your estate and GST Tax exemptions to make the trust exempt from estate and GST Tax? Assume that the trust value doubles at every generational level just like the above Scenario. Upon your child's death there would be $2 million in the trust with no death tax due. Upon your grandchild's death there would be $4 million in the trust for the benefit of your great-grandchild, with no death tax due.

Notice the amount left to the great-grandchild under the first scenario was $2 million and under the second scenario was $4 million.

Once property is exempted from the GST Tax, all future appreciation and growth potential of the underlying assets in the trust also remains exempt from GST Tax.

As you can see, Dynasty Planning can account for growth in wealth over several generations. And, it is logical to most families that any benefits given to their children through their estate plan should be extended to their grandchildren and beyond.

Are there non-tax reasons to use a Dynasty Trust?

The non-tax reasons for creating the dynasty trust vary depending upon the needs and desires of the trustmaker. Dynasty trusts can be created to provide creditor and "predator" protection for the beneficiaries of the trust, generation after generation. They can shield against divorce proceedings initiated against a beneficiary of the trust, or creditors of a beneficiary arising out of a business failure.

The dynasty trust can also provide a pool of assets to be managed by a trustee for the benefit of all of the beneficiaries, thus preventing individual beneficiaries from squandering their inheritance by misusing the funds or investing poorly.

The Dynasty Trust can also be used to encourage participation in certain worthwhile causes or discourage behavior that is unacceptable.

One of the greatest ways Dynasty Trusts are used by families who value education is to establish a fund that will pay for the secondary and graduate education of many future generations. When you ask most people to name their great-great grandparents, they are unable to do so. But when you provide full college and graduate school tuition and other education costs for your great-great grandchildren through a dynasty trust, you can be sure you'll be remembered!

THE QUALIFIED PERSONAL RESIDENCE TRUST (QPRT)

What is a Qualified Personal Residence Trust?

A QPRT is a trust that holds a personal residence for a term of years, allowing you, in effect, to give away your residence at a discount and "freeze" its value for federal estate tax purposes—all while continuing to live in it.

How does it work?

A Qualified Personal Residence Trust takes advantage of certain provisions of federal law that allow you to make a gift to the trust of your personal residence, for the ultimate benefit of the remainder beneficiaries at a discounted value. Assume that the remainder beneficiaries are your children—the most common situation for most QPRT planning. Either your principal residence or a vacation home can be transferred into a QPRT. This, in turn, removes the asset from your estate, reducing potential estate taxes at your death.

For gift tax purposes, the original transfer will be treated as a gift to the children, but not a gift of the current fair market value. Instead, it's a gift of the value of your children's *future* right to the residence at the end of the QPRT term (called the "remainder interest"). You must file a gift tax return at the time the residence is transferred to the trust.

The value of the remainder interest is derived by first determining the fair market value of the entire property, and then subtracting the value of the right you retain to live in the residence (your "retained interest"). In general, the longer the term of the trust, the longer you get to live in the property and the larger the value of your *retained* interest.

As the value of your retained interest increases, the value of your children's *remainder* interest decreases. This results in a smaller taxable gift by you.

If you haven't previously used your lifetime federal gift tax exemption amount ($1,000,000 in 2010), the amount of gift tax due may be offset by that amount, thus possibly eliminating the need to pay any gift tax on the transfer of the residence to the QPRT. Of course, if the residence is appreciating quickly, the potential savings can be even greater in a shorter period of time.

Are there any disadvantages to a QPRT?

If you live to the end of the specified period, the residence, including all post-gift appreciation, passes to the children free of any additional federal estate or gift taxes. However, one disadvantage is that if you die before the end of the period, the value of the residence, as of the date of death, will still be includible in your estate for federal estate tax purposes. The result in that case is the same as if you had never created the QPRT. Therefore, for maximum benefit and results, you need to outlive the term of the trust.

A second disadvantage of the QPRT is that if the house continues to be a part of the trust after the initial term ends, it will pass to the remainder beneficiaries with your original income tax basis.

What is the disadvantage of passing the house to my children with my original income tax basis?

For the sake of illustration, let's say that you bought your house for $50,000 and lived in it for 30 years without putting any more money into it. After 30 years, you decide to sell it, and you are paid $350,000 at today's market prices. For income tax purposes, the IRS would say that you had a "basis" in the house of $50,000 and a taxable gain on that house of $300,000. You would have to pay capital gains tax on that $300,000 of "profit." At 15%, for example, the tax would be $45,000— leaving $305,000 for the children. However, if the house is your primary residence, you may be able to avoid taxation on all gain (up to $250,000, or $500,000 for a married couple).

Let's say, however, that you never sell the house, but rather live in it until your death, and then leave it to your children as part of their inheritance. In that case, the house gets a "step up" in basis to the date of death fair market value. If the fair market value on the day of your death is $350,000, the "basis" is adjusted to that level. And if your children sell the house a month later for $350,000 there is no capital gains tax due. They were able to get the full value of the $350,000 inheritance. (Please note that the current 2010 law does not allow an unlimited "step-up" in basis for your assets. Absent legislation, beginning in 2011, an unlimited "step-up" will return.)

When you gift your house to a QPRT, the remainder beneficiaries do not get a step-up in basis to your date of death value. The likely result is payment of capital gains tax when the children eventually sell the house.

What if I survive the trust term?

If you are still living at the end of the term, you will have accomplished the goals of this planning strategy. Your children in our example (or trusts for their benefit), are now the owners of the house. However, you do not have to move out.

To assure that you have a place to live, the terms of the QPRT can permit you to enter into a lease or rental agreement of the house with the remainder beneficiaries when the trust ends. The terms of the lease must be at fair market value. An additional benefit is that each payment of rent to the remainder beneficiaries will effectively transfer additional funds to them, free of gift or estate tax consequences.

The QPRT can also be written so that after the initial term of the trust, if you are survived by a spouse, your spouse can be permitted to occupy the residence rent free for his or her life.

Can I buy the house back from the trust after it ends so that my kids can still get the capital gains benefit?

A QPRT may allow for the sale of the residence during its term. In addition, the trustee of the QPRT may hold the sales proceeds as long as the proceeds are held in a separate account. However, the residence may not be sold to the grantor, the grantor's spouse, or any entity controlled by the grantor or the grantor's spouse.

Properly drafted QPRTs specifically prohibit the sale of the personal residence back to the grantor. The law specifically is intended to prevent you from buying the house back from the trust after it ends, owning it until death, and passing it to your children at the date-of-death income tax basis (thereby reducing the potential capital gains).

Because of this rule, it is important to compare the potential estate tax savings of the QPRT with the increased capital gains tax potential, assuming the remainder beneficiaries of the residence will sell the house.

Who pays the real estate taxes and maintenance expenses?

The grantor pays for all repairs to the house, utilities, lawn care and other basic maintenance, homeowner's insurance premiums, and real estate taxes. Such payments are for the benefit of you, the grantor, as the tenant during the trust term, and do not constitute taxable gifts.

As a "grantor trust," you are treated as the owner of the property for federal income tax purposes. Therefore, all income, deductions, and credits associated with the property pass through the trust to you. For the same reason, if your primary residence is the property of a QPRT, then you will qualify for the $250,000 ($500,000 for married couples) capital gain exclusion.

How many QPRTs can I set up?

Each person can set up no more than two QPRTs: one for the primary residence and one for a vacation home or condominium.

7 | Cabin and Recreational Property Planning

Your family cabin, cottage, or vacation home may be one of your most significant financial assets. It is also likely to be the one with the most enduring memories and emotional ties. Therefore, it makes sense to give it special attention in your planning, and not treat it as just "another piece of real estate." This chapter provides guidance for how to do that. You'll learn how to ensure that future generations of your family can continue to enjoy their time "at the cabin."

Why plan for a cabin?

Your family cabin, cottage, or vacation home may be one of your most significant financial assets. It is also likely to be the one with the most enduring memories and emotional ties. The property may have been in your family for decades with your children and grandchildren growing up there and having spent their summers there. Because of this, you probably have a strong desire to keep the property in your family, to protect it, to pass it down to your children, grandchildren, and maybe even your great grandchildren. *This isn't stocks and bonds; it's your legacy!*

Unfortunately, without proper planning, those inheriting the interests of long-time cabin owners may have too many divergent interests, financial and otherwise, to be workable. These new tenants in common (TIC) owners have often never discussed who gets to use the property and when, how to share expenses, handle the maintenance and upon what terms they can be bought out. Disputes can easily occur in these situations. Such family fights are often talked about among cabin owners. Most know at least one family story where after the death of the senior generation the property ended up having to be sold outside the family because the heirs could not work out their differences. By applying some of the strategies in this chapter you can avoid these pitfalls, and plan properly for your special family property.

How do most people inherit cabin property?

Most people who inherit cabin property do so in a form of ownership known as tenants in common (TIC). Less common is to inherit or receive as a gift property owned in joint tenancy with right of survivorship. In practice we also see property held in a life estate by the owner with the remainder interest passing at death to their heirs who then become TIC owners. These forms of ownership create too many problems for cabin owners and their families.

What's the problem with deeding the property to my kids and keeping a life estate?

Creating a life estate is often short sighted; not only because of the eventual TIC ownership problems, but also where the owner wants to do something different with the property. For instance, if they decide they want to sell the property or do some other kind of distribution (such as creating a cabin trust or LLC discussed below), each person holding a remainder interest will normally need to sign the deed granting the remainder interests back to the owner. Under some state laws, the spouses of the remainder interest owners may also have to consent.

If one of the owners is in the middle of a divorce and their spouse refuses to sign, the desired transactions become stalled. There are also gift tax implications in creating or reversing a life estate. For these reasons, before you deed your cabin to others and reserve a life estate, you should carefully look at how one or more of these issues may affect you.

What's the problem with leaving the cabin to my kids as joint tenants with right of survivorship?

When something is owned in joint tenancy with right of survivorship, the basic rule is "whoever lives the longest gets the whole thing." Imagine you have 3 children and 15 grandchildren, and you leave the property to your children as joint tenants with right of survivorship. When one of the children dies, the other two then own the whole property. When the second child dies, the surviving child then owns the whole property—and can do with it whatever they please. That includes leaving it just to their children, thereby excluding all your other grandchildren—not the result you were looking for!

Also, 100% of the property is available to a creditor of a Joint Tenant; not just their proportionate share. This means the financial troubles of one Joint Tenant, in this example, would jeopardize the entire cabin, not just ⅓.

What are some of the problems associated with tenants in common (TIC) ownership of cabin property?

The problems associated with co-tenancy ownership are many and varied. Part of this has to with it being very old law. TIC arose out of the English common law over 600 years ago when life was much different. Many attributes of TIC property seem unfair or illogical when applied to today's world. For example, disproportionate ownership does not mean disproportionate rights to use. If your brother owns 10% and you own 90%, he has to pay only 10% of the expenses yet he has the same rights to use the property as you do. Does that seem fair?

Another example is that the majority does not rule. If all co-tenants but one agree to a schedule of use or to make certain repairs, nothing in TIC property law requires the dissenting co-tenant to follow along. Let's look closer at the common right to use and the problems it presents for owners of cabins and recreational property.

1. *The common right to use.* All co-tenants have the same common rights to use the property. If July 4th rolls around and all owners enjoy getting together and space is no issue, great; but what if the relations among the owners have changed due to inheritances and the family gathering dynamics are different? If people do not get along or the cabin is simply too small to accommodate everyone, this aspect of TIC ownership becomes a huge and often unworkable issue. Enter the phrase "cabin hog" into the family lexicon.

2. *Non paying TIC owners.* This is where the trouble can really start, because even if a co-tenant does not pay their share, as a TIC owner,

they still have the same common right to use the property as the others. TIC property law does not impose a penalty, such as forfeiting the right to use the property. During this time, other owners essentially have to subsidize the non-paying TIC owners because, if they don't, it affects their own interests.

For example, if they don't make up the shortfall for property taxes, a lien would be placed against the property and eventually the property would be put up for tax sale. If they don't cover the insurance premium, the policy would be canceled and the cabin uninsured. The other TIC owners usually pay more than their share to avoid these occurrences. They silently (and sometimes not so silently) see the over this. Eventually, when the inequity feels too big and they are mad enough, they may see an attorney about their rights. They are often surprised to learn that they may not be able to recover their extra payments. If the non-paying TIC owners won't voluntarily pay, those who paid extra will have to file a lawsuit, often against their siblings, if they want to recover.

Furthermore, it is not at all clear whether they would win such a lawsuit, although recovery for property taxes would probably be ordered. For other expenses including mortgage payments, a judge might simply conclude that their payment was a protection of that owner's TIC interest and the fact that it benefited others is of no legal significance. If the property is sold, it is also unlikely that the TIC owners who paid more can collect extra from the proceeds of the sale. In many cases the ones who pay more are simply stuck with their unintended generosity.

3. *Legal and financial problems of other owners.* If a co-tenant is getting a divorce or files for bankruptcy, those problems can quickly become the problems of the other TIC owners. They may be forced to transfer their TIC interest to a successful judgment creditor including an ex-spouse. Similarly, one co-tenant may have to file an action to partition the real estate to get the money to pay his or her divorcing spouse. This may be a very inopportune time for the other TIC owners to buy out the TIC owner with legal problems, but unless they do, a judge is likely to order the property sold and the proceeds split.

4. *Divergent interests.* This is the most fundamental of all the TIC ownership problems. Some new TIC owners want to sell; some do not. Some need the money and some do not. Some can go to the cabin often while others are too far away to enjoy it. The list goes on and on. The more owners there are, and the more divergent their interests, the greater potential there is for problems and the greater the need to plan to avoid them.

5. *Disproportionate physical work, property management, or improvements.* It's not easy to keep up lake homes, beach front properties, or cabins in the woods. Things need to be cleaned, fixed, bills paid, etc. Most owners cannot afford to hire out all this work so it often falls upon the owner who lives closest to the property. Is this you? Have you been managing the property and doing most of the work to keep the property up? While you might enjoy doing this, many times this extra burden is no longer desired and you would like to be compensated for it or just want some help!

Unless the other TIC owners voluntarily agree to help out or pay you for your extra work, you are unlikely to be able to collect money for your services. You can't force them to come to a work weekend to maintain the property either. We have seen numerous situations where one TIC owner does nearly all the physical work and has paid thousands more than the other owners. Unless the other owners "do the right thing," the people, who put in a disproportionate amount of work, money, or both, are again stuck with their unintended generosity. The others reap the rewards without the cost.

Cabin trusts, cabin LLCs, and TIC property agreements will deal with this issue and set forth either formally or informally what work is required of the cabin trust beneficiaries, cabin LLC members, or TIC owners who have written agreements covering their ownership. These plans can set forth mandatory work weekends that if missed, require some type of penalty—either in making up the work another time, or paying the trust, LLC, or other owners some amount to offset what they contributed. The trustee or manager is usually allowed compensation for their duties.

These legal maxims also apply to capital improvements as well. Let's assume I own our farmhouse with my sister as TIC and I want to put in a rock fireplace. I think it would be great to sit by the fire in the winter and read and maybe do some writing. Let's assume she does not want to do this, does not want the added expense, feels she will never go there in the winter, etc.

As a co-tenant, I'm free to put in the fireplace despite her objections, but does she have to pay for half of it? If we sell the place later do I get a higher amount of the proceeds for improving the property with the fireplace? Absent an agreement to the contrary, the answer under most TIC property laws is that I would not be allowed to recover the costs for these capital improvements now or to receive a larger share from the sale proceeds if we sell the property.

6. *Unintended and unwanted heirs.* Assume Bob and Pat die and leave their cabin to their three children, John, Peter and Susan as equal TIC owners. Assume that their son John dies a few years later and leaves his ⅓ TIC interest to his spouse, Jane. Jane remarries and names her new husband Ted as a joint tenant with her on her ⅓ TIC interest. She does not need to consult with Peter and Susan and is free to do this. Now, even though Peter and Susan never liked Jane and have never even met Ted, they now share the same common rights to use the property as they do. Ted shows up each weekend "to check on things." Even though Peter and Susan have told Ted they want their privacy, he continues to do this. Jane and Ted also don't pay. Peter and Susan have to make up the shortfall and have to continue to deal with Ted stopping in all the time. Since Peter and Susan can't force Ted and Jane to abide by a schedule for using the property or to pay expenses on time, they may have to bring an action to partition the real estate to end the undesired co-ownership with their former in-law and her new husband.

What is an "action to partition?"

An action to partition is a legal action where one co-tenant asks a judge to divide the property if possible (if it is land for instance) or if it is not feasible, then to order the property sold, with the proceeds split between the co-tenants. These actions are much more likely to occur when there are new multiple owners with divergent financial and other interests. For example, you may have new owners who very much like the property and can easily afford their share of the ownership expenses; and also have heirs who would prefer the cash and are not as attached to the property. If one of the parties really wants out, and the others do not agree to buy them out, the action to partition may be the only way to settle the matter between them.

Absent an agreement to waive the right of partition, it exists and the other owners can't stop it. What's also surprising to the other TIC owners is that the cost of bringing an action to partition usually does not have to be paid up front by the person bringing the action. Rather, the attorney fees and other expenses of sale will get paid later out of the proceeds of sale. This spreads the cost of the lawsuit and sale (brokerage commissions, appraisals, inspections, closing costs, etc.) among all owners and not just the ones who wanted out. When we look more closely at what is occurring in these situations, what we see is that one person's personal financial needs and wishes are being placed above the others. The will of the majority should be paramount in cabin planning, not the will of one. Unfortunately that is how TIC ownership works.

I have a living trust. How would a cabin trust work with my existing living trust or will?

You can create a cabin trust as a sub-trust within your existing living trust. This is probably the most common way of setting up a cabin trust for single or married cabin owners. It is done by simply amending your existing living trust so that upon your death the cabin passes into a separate trust designed specifically for the cabin. The language to create the cabin trust activates only upon the death of the revocable trust creator. Until that time the language lies dormant and can be easily changed as the circumstances may warrant. Because such cabin trusts take effect only upon death of the trustmaker owner, they are often referred to as *springing cabin trusts*. They "spring" into existence when you die.

While cabin trusts can just as easily be created by placing similar language in your will, such testamentary cabin trusts eventually will require a probate to be legally established. Transfer upon Death Deed

(TODD) laws have been adopted in a growing number of states, including Arizona, Arkansas, Colorado, Indiana, Kansas, Missouri, Minnesota, Montana, Nevada, New Mexico, Ohio, Oklahoma and Wisconsin. In those states, at least the probate of the cabin itself can be avoided. Because we get the same results without probate if we create the cabin trust as part of the owner's revocable living trust, such trusts are preferred over testamentary cabin trusts created under a will.

Cabin trusts can also be completely separate from your will or living trust and many families prefer this approach. There also may be other reasons to do the cabin planning separate and apart from the person's revocable living trust or will. Examples include where there are already multiple owners of the property, or when gifts for estate tax planning are being considered. In these situations separate trusts or limited liability companies (LLCs) may have more utility. This is easily done, but stand-alone cabin trusts or cabin LLCs still require a review of and integration with the main estate plan and the rest of the owner's assets.

How can I keep the cabin in just my family if one of my children divorces?

This is the most common question raised by clients with children. Even though divorce rates have been declining, the latest statistics still indicate that many marriages will end in divorce. When coupled with the fact that only a small fraction of married couples enter into pre-nuptial agreements, there is plenty of room for trouble if a child gets divorced.

It depends a great deal on the state's marital property laws, but even in states where inheritances are considered the separate property of the one who inherited, it does not necessarily stop a divorcing spouse from laying claim to a family cabin. Fortunately, a cabin LLC or cabin trust can provide a significant level of protection in the event one of the future owners of the cabin divorces. Asset protection planning techniques are discussed more thoroughly in Chapter 11 of this book. You can utilize some of those techniques in formulating your cabin planning so in the event of a divorce or some other lawsuit, the family cabin is protected. This is of significant importance to someone who has owned a family cabin for 50 years and does not want the divorce or legal problems of one owner to impact the others.

What is a TIC agreement?

A TIC agreement is a contract between tenants in common owners to use the property a certain way. When using this type of agreement, the, property is not conveyed to an entity as with cabin trusts and LLCs. Rather, the owners continue as tenants in common owners, but now have an agreement to govern the property. These agreements can be simpler plans than cabin trusts and cabin LLCs, but that is not always the case. Their main limitation is their ability to effectively handle issues through several generations.

Cabin trusts and LLCs tend to accomplish more of what people want over a longer period of time and so they tend to be more comprehensive plans. Nevertheless, a tenant in common agreement is better than no agreement at all between co-tenants.

TIC agreements will waive the right to partition the property and spell out how expenses are to be shared and paid. The agreements can provide a method for dividing the time at the cabin fairly among the owners, establish majority rule, create rights of first refusal, and address other important issues about which bare TIC ownership is silent.

TIC agreements can be formed as "executory contracts" meaning they will take effect based upon some occurrence in the future, usually the death of the present owners. Provided it has been properly executed by its intended parties, the contract will become binding on the prior owner's death and will govern the rights of the new owners.

What are some of the similarities and differences between a cabin trust and a cabin LLC?

A limited liability company is a business entity like a corporation. Trusts are also legal entities similar to corporations but they are governed under a different and much older body of law. The first LLC statute was adopted in Wyoming in 1977. Since that time each state has adopted its own statutes allowing for the creation of LLCs, including single member LLCs. These laws vary from state to state, as do the filing fees charged by state authorities (secretary of state's office or its state equivalent).

Trust law is older and tends to be more uniform throughout the country. In most cases, there is no need to file a trust with a state regulatory board to bring it into existence and no need to file an annual report as with cabin LLCs. In most cases they are simply signed before a notary public although at least one state (Florida) has the additional requirement that they be witnessed like a will.

Managers of LLCs are generally held to a "business judgment" standard toward the non-managing members whereas the trustee of a trust owes a higher "fiduciary duty" to the beneficiaries. This is the highest duty that the law imposes.

One of the most significant differences between LLCs and trusts is that LLCs can last forever whereas trusts are often governed by what is called the "rule against perpetuities." These laws seek to restrict how long a person can control their property after they are gone. The theory is that people should not be able to control their property from the grave indefinitely and that at some point (usually a considerable period in most states, 90 years for example) the trust should be required to end, so that the assets can be distributed to the beneficiaries who can then put them to work in society unimpeded by instructions left long ago by a deceased ancestor. Many states, however, have greatly extended the time period that trusts can last or have eliminated the rule against perpetuities altogether.

For instance, Florida has a 360 year rule and Wyoming has a 1,000 year rule. South Dakota has no rule against perpetuities so a cabin trust established there can last forever. South Dakota also has very progressive trust laws, and no state income or estate tax. For someone who wants to keep their cabin in their family forever, it is an excellent state to consider as the situs (controlling law) of the trust.

Which is better, a cabin trust or a cabin LLC?

This question cannot, in our experience, be readily answered without first looking at a family's particular situation, how they own their property, how many own it, and what they want to do with it after they are gone. For some purposes an LLC might be better and, in others, a trust will better accomplish the family goals. However, we do favor LLCs in several situations. One example is for out of state owners who own cabins in states that have "decoupled" from the federal estate tax system, and have a state-level estate tax exemption lower than the federal ($3,500,000 in 2009). These states include Connecticut, Illinois, Kansas, Maine, Maryland, Massachusetts, Minnesota, New Jersey, New

York, Ohio, Oregon, Rhode Island, Washington, and the District of Columbia. If you live elsewhere, but own property in these states, a cabin LLC might be preferred over a cabin trust because of the potential for state estate tax savings.

We also favor cabin LLCs over cabin trusts where there are already multiple owners of the property, and/or the property is rented out on a regular basis or has a business operating from it. These may be factors making a cabin LLC a better choice; but again, this depends on the individual situation and goals of each owner.

This seems too complicated, why don't I just give my cabin away to my children now?

In some situations this may be worthwhile from an estate tax standpoint, an asset protection standpoint, or both. However, there are many traps for the unwary and so caution is in order. Before making such a transfer it is extremely important to look at the tax implications of the sale, both gift and capital gain taxes. If the property has appreciated considerably since you bought it, (common with lake and beach front property) it may be a tax mistake to gift it to your heirs if they are likely to later sell it. This is because, in tax parlance, your gift recipients get "carry over basis" whereas if they inherit from you through your living trust or will they receive a new income tax basis to the date of death value. This is what's known as a "step-up in basis" and allows your children or other heirs to sell the property without capital gains tax (as described above in the discussion of QPRTs).

In many situations, however, your children have no intentions of selling the property and in fact want to keep it as much as you do. If this is the case, then you will no doubt be freer to consider making a gift of your cabin during your lifetime. Since gifts during life can remove the property from the gift giver's taxable estate and potentially make it unavailable to pay for a catastrophic medical bill or other creditor, many people are interested in doing this. It just needs to be done carefully so that you do not inadvertently lose your step-up-in basis and are never in the situation of having to say "Hey kids, can we get that cabin back now?"

If I implement a cabin trust, or cabin LLC, can I still use the cabin like I do now?

In most cases the answer is yes. This is because many cabin trusts are created within your main revocable living trust. As such, the cabin trust is not legally established until you die and the terms set out in your revocable trust become activated. Until that time you continue to have total control over all assets in the trust including your cabin. You continue to use the property the same as before the transfer to the revocable trust. If you want to sell it, mortgage it, lease it, fix it up, or leave it as is, you can.

Many cabin LLCs would work the same way, and the person setting it up continues to use the property the same as they did before transferring it to the LLC. This is because they may own all of the LLC ownership interests (sometimes called "units") and they are the manager of the LLC. Managers of LLCs control all aspects of the property itself.

If you transfer your cabin to an irrevocable cabin trust, however, your use of the property is likely to be significantly changed; however, this depends on the type of trust. With the QPRT cabin trust discussed in more detail below, even though it is an irrevocable trust, the trustmaker typically continues to use the property the same as before the transfer to the QPRT, at least for the initial term of the trust. With a more typical irrevocable trust no rights are reserved, as for example, with a GDOT cabin trust (see Chapter 6).

We can use the same type of trust to hold a cabin and possibly also to receive gifts of cash or marketable securities. While some small permissive use by the trustmaker is probably alright, it should not be ongoing. If any ongoing use occurs, it should be done under a valid fair market value (FMV) lease with the trustee. Such lease-back arrangements, even if done at FMV, will likely be heavily scrutinized by the IRS.

The IRS may conclude the lease gives too much control over the gifted property and include its value in the trustmaker's estate anyway. Lease-backs should be avoided or entered into with an understanding of the audit risks. The FMV of any such lease should be established by a qualified appraiser. The lease should be in writing and for a short term. Even with these safeguards, the risk of estate inclusion is real, and all things considered, it is better for the trustmaker to avoid retained interests in irrevocable cabin trusts.

In what situations might it be a good idea for a cabin trust to be formed as an irrevocable trust?

- *Creditor protection.* Many clients are concerned about a catastrophic medical bill late in life and what impact that would have on their cabin. Would it have to be sold to pay for those bills? Many people certainly want to pay their share of medical costs, but if they suffer from a debilitating long term medical problem, or simply grow so old that they are in need of expensive medical care during the last chapter in their life, they feel strongly that their assets should be protected for the benefit of their heirs. This is especially true for cabin property that has been in the family a long time.

   The planning needs to be done far in advance of the medical bills, usually five years or more, and the transfer cannot render you insolvent. If you meet those requirements, cabin property placed into an irrevocable trust for the benefit of your children or other selected heirs would generally be considered unavailable for purposes of paying for long term medical bills.

   Likewise, many clients are concerned about a predatory lawsuit against the property either now or after they are gone. They recognize the risk factor associated with the occupations of the present or future owners and the potential for divorce litigation as well. Irrevocable trusts (as well as cabin LLCs) can be designed to create a significant barrier between the cabin and frivolous civil claims and divorce actions.

- *Estate tax reduction.* If your estate size is larger than the exemption to federal estate tax or state estate taxes, you might be a candidate for an irrevocable cabin trust plan. See broader discussion about the use of cabin LLCs and the QPRT cabin trust for estate tax reduction on page 116.

- *Spendthrift or minor beneficiaries.* Minors cannot legally manage property in their own name. People who want to give assets to minors often do so in custodial accounts and under the uniform gift to minors act. Assets held in such custodial accounts must usually be paid outright to the minor when they reach adulthood. Just because they have reached the age of majority does not mean that they have reached the age of maturity. They may not be capable of managing an interest in real estate or other assets.

For these reasons, transfers to trusts that are irrevocable as to the minor beneficiary are very useful. The trustee manages the property for them subject to the instructions that the trustmaker left for those beneficiaries, such as "All my Grandchildren." This way the beneficiaries, even after they turn 18, cannot demand that the trustee give them the property outright in their own name. If they are divorced or in a lawsuit, the property held in the trust can be unreachable by the divorcing spouse or judgment creditor.

How can cabin LLCs and cabin trusts help reduce estate taxes?

Cabin LLC interests can be gifted to children at a discount from the value of the underlying assets. For example, if the underlying cabin property was worth $400,000, a 25% interest in the LLC would not normally be valued at $100,000. Instead, it might be valued at $70,000 for example. The ability to value these gifts at a lower level with these discounting techniques can allow more wealth to transfer to the next generation and at a quicker pace than otherwise possible. A major benefit to these types of plans is that the giver often retains the ability to manage the property because they are the manager of the LLC.

Gifting property to an irrevocable trust, such as a GDOT cabin trust, can remove the property from your taxable estate. However, in order for this to be effective, you generally must give up your rights to use and control the property. Irrevocable trusts can't be easily amended so they are inherently less flexible plans.

Some states have a lower threshold for estate taxes than the federal estate tax, such as Minnesota. If a Minnesota resident has a 1.5 million dollar estate with $500,000 of that comprising their cabin, they would owe $64,400 in state estate taxes. However, if they gift that cabin away <u>during their life</u>, even if it is the day before they die, the asset will be excluded from their taxable estate. Since in this example the gift-giver is well under the federal estate tax exemption, their estate would pay no federal estate taxes on the cabin and also no state estate taxes.

In addition to saving $64,400, their estate can dispense with having to file the Minnesota estate tax return which is fairly complex, and often requires the preparation of a federal estate tax return to complete the state estate tax return.

Why would someone who is over the threshold for state estate taxes not do this? The owners in this situation may not feel comfortable giving away their valuable cabin, thinking, perhaps correctly, that they may need to tap into its equity for a rainy day. Or, they might just not get around to making the gifts before they die.

Because state estate tax rates are usually lower than the capital gains rate, it can be a tax mistake to gift the cabin to children if they are more likely to sell the property during their lives rather than pass it to their children at their death. While gifting the asset would avoid state estate tax, because of the carryover basis rules mentioned above, the gift recipients would likely pay more in capital gains tax than they would save in estate taxes.

For these reasons, people who are contemplating gifting their property away to avoid state estate taxes should take a realistic look at how likely it is that their heirs will sell the property after they are gone. If they are more likely than not to sell, then gifting during life should be reconsidered.

I have heard that I am going to be subject to death tax in the state where my cabin is located even though my state has no death tax. How can I eliminate these taxes?

Some cabin owners may owe no state death taxes in their home state but the fact that they own their cabin in a state that *does* levy such a death tax will mean not only having to pay the tax, but also having to file a fairly complicated out-of-state death tax return. This adds to the complexity of settling an estate and should be avoided if possible. Let's look at a California resident who has a total estate of $1.6 million with $600,000 of that being their Minnesota lake cabin. This person owes no California death tax and no federal estate tax; however, they are subject to Minnesota death tax on their cabin and any other real or personal property such as bank accounts owned *in Minnesota*. Here the key phrase is "owned in Minnesota."

By transferring such property into an LLC this California resident is no longer considered to own real estate in Minnesota. Rather they own "personal property" located outside of Minnesota. Their estate would not need to file a Minnesota death tax return and they save $26,550 in Minnesota state death taxes on the cabin property.

In this scenario, the larger the estate and the more valuable the cabin, the greater are the potential tax savings. Though interests in trust should be considered "personal property," it is not clear whether the same tax results can be reached. Accordingly, we usually advise persons in these situations to do their cabin planning with cabin LLCs rather than cabin trusts.

What is a QPRT cabin trust?

A qualified personal residence trust, or QPRT for short, is discussed in more detail in the preceding chapter. A QPRT cabin trust meets all of those requirements; however, the difference between a QPRT cabin trust and a regular QPRT is that at the end of the initial term it turns into, for lack of a better word, a "regular" cabin trust. As such, it will contain provisions for allocating expenses, scheduling use, dealing with beneficiaries who don't want to participate, who die or won't pay. This is an outstanding way to reduce federal estate taxes (often by several hundred thousand dollars) and to protect the cabin from divorces, lawsuits, and the other challenges facing the successor owners of valuable cabins and vacation homes.

How is income tax handled after I transfer my cabin to the cabin trust or LLC?

If the cabin is transferred to a revocable "grantor" living trust, which many are, any income (if the property was rented for example) is reported on the owner's individual 1040. No separate income tax return is required for such revocable living trusts.

If the cabin is transferred to an irrevocable trust, a less common occurrence, then a separate income tax return for the trust (Form 1041) is usually required to be filed. Exceptions to this separate filing requirement might be where the trust earns almost no income and is a grantor trust. To respect the formalities of the irrevocable trust it is usually advisable to file an informational return even where no income is reportable by that trust, i.e., it is a "grantor trust" and it earns less than the amount the IRS has established for requiring the filing of a 1041.

If the cabin property is transferred into a single member LLC, then the owner reports any income (if it is rented at a profit) or any loss, on

Schedule C of their individual 1040 income tax return. No separate return is required to be filed for such single member LLCs which are treated as "disregarded entities" for income tax purposes.

A multi-member LLC will usually be taxed as a partnership and will file a separate income tax return for the LLC (Form 1065) to report any income or loss. As part of the tax preparation, K-1s are issued to each member in the LLC who then reports any income or loss on their personal 1040. This is why these are known as "pass-through" entities: the income or loss passes through to the individual owners of the LLC interests. Those familiar with "subchapter S" corporations will be familiar with this concept. Some LLCs may elect to be treated as a corporation for tax purposes including an S corporation. The utility for this in cabin planning is probably limited to situations where the cabin is being managed for rental to third parties on more or less a full-time basis, or where the cabin is being used to operate a business such as a guide service or fishing resort. Such a structure might help reduce income taxes.

If your cabin is owned more or less passively, and rental use is nominal, electing to be taxed as a corporation would probably add an unneeded layer of complexity (the LLC would have to file a corporate tax return—Form 1120). Thus, for most multi-member cabin LLCs that own a cabin passively, it is likely best to be income taxed as a partnership and file the partnership tax return (Form 1065).

How are property taxes handled after I transfer my cabin to a cabin LLC or cabin trust?

In most situations where the cabin trust is designed as a sub trust of the owner's main revocable living trust, the owner will still be considered the owner for income tax purposes. Therefore, the transfer of the cabin to the owner's revocable trust should not change its property tax classification. Some county tax assessors may raise a question about this. In our experience when shown that the property is held in a revocable living trust of which the owner is both its trustee and beneficiary, and it is thus a "Grantor trust" within the IRS rules, they will treat the property as if it were still individually owned for property tax purposes.

For similar reasons transfers of cabin properties to single member LLCs where the prior owner is the manager should also not change the tax classification. If, however, the property is transferred into an irrevocable trust or a multi-member LLC and the property was formerly homestead property, the tax classification is likely to change. Some county assessors may allow it to continue to be taxed as a homestead upon showing actual homestead use by a beneficiary or managing member of the LLC, and others may not.

If, however, the property tax classification is already "seasonal recreational" or its equivalent, which many are, then the transfer to a multi-member LLC or irrevocable trust would normally not change the property tax classification. Thus, the concern about increased property taxes mainly concerns owners where the cabin property has homestead status. You should check your state law prior to any transfer of your cabin property.

What effect does placing my cabin into a trust or LLC have on my property and casualty insurance premiums?

Insurance costs should not go up if the property held in the LLC or trust is not being run for profit and the property is not rented, but this can vary from company to company. If the trust or LLC rents the property on an ongoing basis or operates a guide or resort service or some other operating business, a commercial policy will be needed. Such policies will typically be more expensive.

In most cabin trusts and cabin LLCs where the owner and their family are the primary users of the property and any rental use is minimal or non-existent, an "endorsement" can usually be made to the existing home-owners policy. This endorsement lists the cabin LLC or cabin trust as an additional insured. Because of competition in the insurance industry, if one company is less flexible in dealing with these issues, an owner may want to shop around. They may find a new policy that will cover the entity, provide umbrella protection to them individually as well, and at a reasonable cost.

After we are gone, we want to set up a fund to help our family pay for the expenses of cabin ownership. How do we go about doing that?

An endowment fund is an incredible gift to the whole family. Where one or more new owners lack the financial resources to meet their share of expenses, the endowment allows them to continue to enjoy the family property. Creating an endowment can be as simple as directing funds to the cabin trust or cabin LLC from your main estate plan. For example, "upon my death I leave my cabin to the cabin trust I have created under Article such and such of my revocable living trust. I also leave $100,000 to my cabin trust for the payment of expenses and maintenance that my trustees, in their full and absolute discretion, deem appropriate."

Life insurance can also be used to establish an expense fund. Insurance can be owned on the lives of the cabin owners (and on the beneficiaries for that matter). At the owner's death, the insurance is paid into the cabin trust or cabin LLC. The cabin trust or LLC operating agreement may simply allow the funds to be used at the trustee's or manager's discretion, or it might specify that the funds are to be used only for major repairs such as a new roof or septic system. These choices are very specific to each family. For estate tax reasons or legal clarity, it may be advisable to direct the insurance into a separate trust from the trust holding the cabin but have both trusts managed by the same trustee(s).

Here's an example. Bob and Pat are reasonably healthy 65-year-olds. They want to have a $300,000 endowment after they are gone to help pay for expenses of the cabin for their children, at least one of which could not afford to be an owner for very long without this type of planning. If they direct those funds from their estate, the cost to them is $300,000. Instead they purchase a second-to-die life insurance policy in that amount. This type of policy pays out only at the second death, but at that time it pays $300,000. To get this coverage they were required to pay $4,400 in annual premiums. They do that for twenty years and thus have paid a total of $88,000 to the insurance company issuing the policy. Accordingly by use of this insurance, they reduced the effective cost of creating the endowment by 71%, from $300,000 to $88,000!

Can a cabin trust or cabin LLC provide creditor protection?

It can provide some creditor protection, but it is not unlimited. If the cabin is operated in a negligent manner and someone gets hurt, the entity is not likely to protect the cabin from a lawsuit arising out of the incident. The entity itself can be sued for its own negligence and unless liability insurance covers the claim, judgments could be obtained against the entity itself and through proper legal mechanisms, a creditor could force the company to pay the judgment.

What an irrevocable cabin trust or cabin LLC can do is provide a significant barrier of protection from the lawsuit reaching one of the individual members of the LLC or one of the individual beneficiaries of a cabin trust. For example, assume that the company owning the cabin has been negligent in maintaining its dock. A wealthy high profile personal injury attorney walks across the dock and it collapses. He cannot swim and drowns. His estate sues the cabin LLC for wrongful death and recovers a $5,000,000 judgment.

The cabin LLC has only $500,000 of liability insurance. The creditor seeks to collect the balance from the individual members. Provided the formalities of the entity were respected, (no commingling the LLC assets with the members' personal assets, and proper tax and other state filings were made each year), the members in the LLC would generally be liable only up to their capital contributions to the cabin LLC. So, they would likely lose the cabin, but their personal assets would remain intact. The creditor would either have to be satisfied with the insurance or would have to force the LLC into bankruptcy to try to get the cabin, and then sell it to pay the claim.

Similarly, if a successful lawsuit is brought against one member of the LLC and the plaintiff recovers a judgment against that member, the LLC interests would typically be much less attractive than the underlying cabin property would be.

For example, if the property was owned by the children as Tenants In Common and not in a LLC (or irrevocable trust) the creditor can place a lien on the underlying real estate and get paid when the property is sold. Or, having properly filed the judgment and recording the lien on the cabin, the creditor could ask a judge to sell the property and give them the amount of the judgment from the proceeds. This is known as a judgment foreclosure.

But by placing the cabin into a cabin LLC, the creditor may be limited to seeking a "charging order." See Chapter 11 on Asset Protection Planning for a broader discussion of how a charging order is an inferior remedy to a creditor, and how it can be used to reach a more favorable settlement than what might otherwise be possible.

How does a cabin trust or cabin LLC deal with buy-outs?

This aspect of cabin planning is very much like buy-sell planning for business owners. If you have been involved in a small business or are in the insurance industry, you will likely be familiar with these concepts. Buy-sell agreements are essentially contracts between business owners to buy and sell under certain conditions, namely death, disability, voluntary withdrawal, or retirement from a business. With cabin owners, especially cabin owners from different families and multiple owner situations, we do the same thing. That is, upon the death of a cabin owner or where one owner voluntarily wants to sell, the other owners may be required to buy, or at least have the right of first refusal to buy, that deceased owner's interest.

These purchase agreements can also be made between the future beneficiaries of the property as well. By properly analyzing the situation, needs and desires of the current owners and what they want to happen in the future, the right set of option agreements, and purchase rights can be established. This avoids having to negotiate the sales under less than favorable conditions.

After a person dies, his or her family may be suffering from the loss of their loved one, and possibly at a time when his or her estate lacks liquidity and needs to sell. It avoids having the family members of a deceased heir be "stuck" owning something that they do not use and can't readily sell to a third party. Such planning can create a market for the interest in the property when someone dies that might otherwise be very difficult, or as a practical matter, nearly impossible to sell. Such planning protects those who continue to own the cabin, since they know the interest of other owners cannot be sold out from under them.

How would a cabin trust or cabin LLC handle the situation where one or more beneficiaries do not pay their share of the expenses?

Most cabin plans will address this issue in some fashion. First, there is usually a penalty that applies for nonpayment, such as forfeiting the right to use the property that season. Next, after an established grace period in the cabin trust or cabin LLC has run, the non-paying trust beneficiary or LLC member can be deemed to make a legal offer to sell their interest back to the cabin trust or cabin LLC. The price and terms of this sale are usually at a discount. For example, if the non-paying beneficiary's pro-rata interest in the underlying cabin is $100,000, the trustee or manager of the LLC might be given a "put" option to buy the LLC interests at a 35% discount. A put option is the right to "put" the price at some amount in the future.

So for $65,000 the trustee or LLC manager could buy the interest. It is also common for the trust or LLC to state that the trustee or LLC manager can buy the interest over time with a promissory note. Buy-out structuring like this creates incentives for beneficiaries and members to avoid going into default, but if a serious default occurs, these provisions make it easier for the others to conduct the purchase. With clear disclosures up front, everyone knows what is expected of them.

The discount in value is justified by the way beneficial interest values are appraised. When you own real estate 100% outright, it is worth whatever you can sell it for. However, when you own that same real estate beneficially in trust with other beneficiaries, or you own an interest in an LLC with other members, the existence of trust instructions or the limited liability company's operating agreement heavily restricts its use, the right to sell, etc. Therefore, the value of that beneficial interest is definitely reduced. These are called "lack of marketability" or "minority interest" discounts.

Appraisers qualified to render opinions as to such valuation discounts for lack of marketability and minority interests would commonly value the interests at 25% to 40% or more below the fair market value of the underlying property. Thus apart from dissuading the beneficiaries or members from defaulting on their financial obligations and making it easier for others to buy the interest, valuation principles support that the property value should be discounted in some fashion in the sale.

What kinds of decisions can the managers or trustees typically make without consulting with all the trust beneficiaries or LLC members?

The trustee or manager is typically allowed to pay routine expenses like the property taxes and insurance, as well as small maintenance items. For example, it would make no sense to require a phone conference to discuss whether to fix a screen door. On the other hand, for a major repair like a new roof, then the trustees of the cabin trust or managers of the cabin LLC are often required to obtain approval of the majority of the beneficiaries of the cabin trust or a majority of the members of an LLC.

Once that vote is obtained, then the trustee or manager can allocate those larger maintenance costs along with the regular operating costs. These "assessments" become a legally binding obligation to those beneficiaries and members per the terms of the trust or the LLC operating agreement. Major decisions requiring either majority or unanimous consent are likely to be a sale or mortgage of the cabin property; larger purchases of personal property (new furniture throughout, a new dock, or a new boat) and purchases of additional real estate such as an adjacent lake lot.

What kinds of rules are found in cabin trusts and cabin LLCs?

Cabin trusts and LLCs can be regulated by a wide variety of rules. For example, trustmakers often have rules that would prohibit guests without a primary cabin trust beneficiary being present at the same time. A cabin LLC's operating agreement can similarly establish rules or empower the managers to set rules that they feel are appropriate.

Because what looks nice to one owner may be tacky to another, requiring a majority to approve of plans to decorate makes a lot of sense. Also, to avoid having the family cabin become the dumping ground for their overfilled garages back home, it is common to establish rules restricting storage on the property. Rules that set forth scheduling procedures, penalties for nonpayment of cabin expenses, (such as forfeiting the right to use the cabin until payments are brought current) and penalties for missing group work weekends are also common.

Regarding scheduling procedures, beneficiaries of cabin trusts or members of LLCs might be required to provide their preferred dates of occupancy by a certain date each year. The trustee or manager will then seek to accommodate those requests within the framework provided in the trust instructions or LLC operating agreement. That framework usually allocates the favorite time slots (July 4th, Memorial Day, Labor Day, Christmas) among the trust beneficiaries or LLC members on some kind of rotating basis.

With these rules in place, all the beneficiaries or members get their fair share of the key holiday weekends and other prime times at the cabin. It avoids the cabin hog phenomena where one TIC owner abuses their common rights.

The cabin trust or cabin LLC does not appeal to me . . . isn't there a simpler way of doing things?

One of the simplest things to do is to determine which of your heirs are going to use the property and then direct the cabin only to those heirs. This is done by having the proper instructions in your will or living trust. If there is more than one of these heirs, then, in order to avoid the problems inherent with bare TIC ownership, you would have the future cabin heirs sign a TIC agreement that would become binding upon your death. This TIC agreement will then govern the use of the property.

To equalize things for the other heirs, you would bequeath a corresponding amount of other property to them from your estate. This requires you to have other assets besides the cabin. If the cabin comprises the bulk of your estate, then it may be difficult to do this. The amount of this equalizing bequest does not have to be exactly equal to what the cabin heirs receive, just something that seems fair to you. The rest of your assets can then be left equally among the heirs.

8 | Investing

As mentioned in the front of this book, this chapter is not intended to provide you with specific investment advice. Instead, it should serve as an educational tool to help you develop an investing philosophy, and understand some of the investment options available to you. The goal is that, with the help of your advisor, you can better devise a basic investment strategy that meets your needs.

What are the three primary stages of wealth, and how does that impact my investments?

There are three major stages of family wealth. The planning and investment strategies implemented can be vastly different among the three stages. Identifying where you are on this continuum will allow for more specific recommendations to be made and to plan for the possibility of future changes.

The first stage is when individuals and families are creating their financial wealth to support their current lifestyle, and save for future objectives such as college education for their children, and their own eventual retirement.

Families who are in the first stage need to monitor their current cash flow to meet current expenses while saving and investing for future goals. Many of the investments for those longer term goals such as retirement will require a growth strategy. They also need to maintain proper insurance to guard against loss from unforeseen events while they build their wealth.

Individuals and families approach the second stage when they have built enough financial resources to support their desired lifestyle without continued employment. They have enough assets to produce an income during their lifetime to replace their own efforts in the workforce.

Many of those who have successfully achieved the second stage begin to become concerned with protecting what they have grown. Investment strategies may begin to include some income producing securities to supplement their retirement income needs. Insurance programs may also be included in the plan to protect income as well as protect assets from the large expense of long term care.

The third stage is achieved when an individual or family has accumulated more wealth than they will use during their lifetime. This wealth stage usually requires more extensive estate planning to make sure assets are passed effectively and efficiently to those chosen by the wealth holder. This stage may require reallocation of investment assets, use of legal instruments such as trusts and other entities, and insurance products to replace assets potentially lost to taxes.

What are some of the general principles of investing of which I should be aware?

It is very important to understand why and how you are allocating your investments to support various lifetime objectives. Not all investments are created to reach the same objective. Some have the objective of substantial growth over a long period of time while others have the objective of maintaining low volatility in all market climates.

The aim is to match a specific goal and time line to an investment strategy. Furthermore it is imperative to continually revisit and monitor the goals and investments to seek the maximum possibility of achieving plan success.

How do I go about building an investment portfolio?

Hundred of books have been written on investing. There are more magazines, TV shows, radio programs, and advertisements for this component of financial planning than all the other disciplines combined. It is the exotic part of financial planning, and brings out the entrepreneur and gambler in many people. However, many find that the media confuses rather than educates the public. They often leave out some basic ideas that every investor should know. Among those ideas are "The Risk Return Spectrum" and the "Time Horizon."

What is the Risk Return Spectrum?

With the creation of mutual fund portfolios and index funds (exchange traded funds that replicate the major indices), individual security selection is no longer a necessary building block of a well-diversified investment portfolio. Whole asset classes can be purchased that help to diversify the risk of owning a single security.

However, the risk of volatility remains. Volatility is the risk that the asset class may be trading below the price for which you originally purchased it when you need to sell. Asset classes have different levels of volatility. As a general rule, the higher the level of volatility, the higher the historical and expected return over a period of time. And while volatility may yield a higher return, it requires that you hold those assets for longer periods to be able to weather the ups and downs. On the next page you'll find a graphical representation of the "risk" versus the "reward" for some common asset classes.

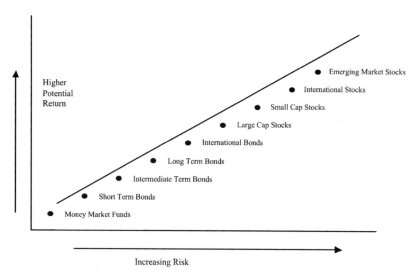

What do advisors mean when they talk about "time horizon?"

Determining when you'll need the money back is probably one of the most important decisions you should make before committing any money to an investment. As the Risk Return Spectrum illustrates, some investments are more volatile than other investments, meaning that as you move up the spectrum, each asset class increases in volatility, and therefore poses greater risk of being on a downward trend when you need to sell. The volatility of an investment decreases over time, reducing the risk of selling it at a loss, the longer you hold the investment.

As an example, if you are investing money that you would use for a home purchase expected in the next 5 years, it might be prudent for you to consider investing in money market funds or long term bonds. If you are investing your retirement assets that may not be needed for at least 10 years, you might consider investing in something like international bonds or emerging market stocks, depending on your tolerance for significant swings in the value of your investment during a shorter period, like one year.

As you consider investment allocation, you might begin by defining cash flow needs within four or five different time horizons:

- Less than 12 months
- 1–3 years
- 3–5 years
- 5–10 years
- More than 10 years

These various time horizons should be kept in mind when you and your advisor are determining your risk tolerance. Rather than determining the risk tolerance for you, as an investor, it might make more sense to determine your risk tolerance for each of the time horizons.

Many investors that are accumulating wealth are not planning on spending the value of all their investments within the next 5–10 years, if ever. Those investors are typically willing to allow more risk, defined as volatility for this discussion, for the segments of funds that fall in longer time horizons.

At the same time it is not prudent for the aggressive investor to engage in an aggressive strategy with assets that will need to be turned into cash within the next 12 months. The point is that cash flow is as important a consideration for different time horizons as is the temperament of the investor.

An investment strategy might start at the two ends of the spectrum by budgeting for the shortest term (less than 12 months) and the longest term (greater than 10 years), and then building from there.

Against popular thought, age should not be the only factor (or perhaps even the primary factor) used as the determination of risk level for an investor. For example, consider the 80-year-old college professor who is not even spending the amount he draws from his state funded pension plan and social security. If he also has a 403b plan containing $500,000, he does not necessarily need to be conservative with the 403b investment simply because he is 80 years old. There is a high probability that his 40-year-old grandchildren will end up using the money instead of the professor. In this example, asset allocation could be based on when the money will be USED, as opposed to the age of the owner of the account.

Explain the three general categories of investment needs: cash, income, and accumulation.

Another way to envision the time horizon is to classify your investment assets in three "buckets" of asset types, each with a different investment priority. Most people's investment needs can be broken down into three general categories; cash, income and accumulation.

What is a "cash bucket" and when is it used?

The "cash" bucket is a savings and investment strategy that is used to fund very short term obligations or to meet unexpected expenses. It may be used to supplement monthly income needs as well as unforeseen repairs or purchases in household items.

You might consider using bank savings accounts, money markets, and CDs. These investments, while providing fairly small yields, offer very little market risk. This gives you a higher probability that the money will be available when needed.

What is an "income bucket" and when is it used?

The "income" bucket is a portfolio of securities used to fund goals that need to be met over a mid range time line of possibly three to five years. This strategy is meant to replenish the "cash" bucket as it becomes depleted due to those unexpected emergencies or a regular monthly draw for personal income needs.

You may consider using a mix of longer term CDs, bonds, bond mutual funds, and blue chip higher dividend paying mutual funds. This mix of investments may provide higher returns than the "cash" bucket but still have fairly low volatility.

What is the "accumulation bucket" and when is it used?

The "accumulation" bucket is a portfolio of securities used to fund goals that do not need to be met for a longer time period. Typically, most investors will not expect to use these assets for five to ten years or more. This strategy is used to replenish the "income" bucket as needed.

You may consider using a wide array of investments with of an objective of growing their wealth over a longer period of time. Many of these considerations will be in a wide range of stocks and stock mutual funds. Some of the areas of investments may be in large, medium, and small companies, as well as international investing. Some consumers will continue to add some bonds into the portfolio as well. While this portfolio may have more volatility year to year, it may have superior performance over longer periods and be able to replenish the income bucket to meet more immediate concerns.

How can I sort out all the investment recommendations I receive from a variety of sources?

The first thing to remember is most of the information available to investors is produced by companies or individuals within the investment industry. Therefore, it is important to understand the possible bias of your source of information, based on the source's business model.

For example, most forecasts put out by mutual fund companies or stock brokerage firms will likely have a fairly positive short term bias toward the stock market. Firms in the business of selling investments are not typically going to recommend asset classes that are not available through them.

Is it true that "the market always goes up over time?"

First of all, remember that "the market" is simply a place and a process whereby ownership shares in a wide variety of companies are bought and sold. These companies provide goods and services that the population consumes.

The reason the market has historically gone up, over the long term, is simply because there are more people to consume the goods and services. The population is increasing, and until the population ceases to increase, we predict the market will continue to trend upwards.

Keep in mind that is the long term. However, during shorter times the value of companies can go up or down for a myriad of reasons.

How do life insurance programs play a role in the success of my financial or estate plan?

Insurance policies are an important part of your overall wealth plan. They are purchased to protect against an unexpected loss which could cause harm to the future success of your financial or estate plan for your family.

Is life insurance necessary in all financial and estate plans?

While life insurance is not compulsory in developing financial and estate plans, it does offer an opportunity to fill gaps in the plan in an efficient manner. Financial and estate plans can be developed without the use of insurance when an individual is uninsurable or wishes to use other alternatives.

How is life insurance used during each of the wealth stages?

The type and amount of insurance needed is dependent on your wealth stage as well as your financial and estate planning priorities.

Life insurance is purchased in the first stage of wealth to protect against the loss of future earnings, or loss of the income-producing wage earners. If an unexpected death or disability occurs, the current lifestyle and future savings goals are in jeopardy due to the cessation of income into the household.

Life insurance plans purchased during the second stage may be used to replace assets used during retirement to provide a desired inheritance to children. Sometimes it is purchased not only to replace, but to increase the inheritance on an income tax free basis.

When families have identified they have more assets then they will use over their lifetime, they begin to use insurance as an estate preservation tool. Life insurance may be purchased to replace assets lost to estate taxes. Insurance also may be purchased to provide larger gifts for philanthropy, or to replace those assets given to charity so that the children will still benefit.

Insurance is discussed in much greater detail in Chapter 12.

What are immediate annuities?

Immediate annuities are long term contracts issued by life insurance companies typically purchased with a single lump sum investment. An immediate annuity can provide income stream for a set period of time or for one's lifetime or for one's lifetime and their spouse's lifetime.

The amount of income you can receive from an immediate annuity will vary, generally depending upon the following factors:

1. Your current age. Typically the older you are, the larger the periodic payout over your lifetime.

2. Length of payout period selected. A shorter payout period will usually result in a larger payment schedule.

3. Amount of purchase payment, generally the larger the payment, the larger the income stream from that payment.

4. If there is an underlying investment medium. This refers to whether it is a fixed immediate annuity or a variable immediate annuity.

What is the federal income tax impact of immediate annuity income?

Because immediate annuities are purchased with after-tax dollars, each payment you receive is allocated between ordinary income, which is taxable, and a return of principal, which is not taxable.

Please remember, state and local income tax law can vary and one should counsel with their tax advisor for guidance.

What parties are involved with a deferred annuity?

There are four parties involved in a typical deferred annuity:

1. The insurance company. This is the company that issues the annuity.

2. The policy owner. This is the individual or entity that contributes the funds. The policy owner typically has the right to terminate the annuity, to gift it to someone else, to withdraw funds from it and to change the annuitant or beneficiary.

3. The annuitant. This is the individual whose life is used to determine the payout once payments begin ("the annuitization period"). An annuity will remain in force unless terminated by the owner or as the result of death of the owner or the death of the annuitant.

4. The beneficiary. This is the individual or entity that receives any proceeds payable upon the death of the annuitant or the policy owner depending on whether the annuity is annuitant-driven or owner-driven contract. Usually a single individual may be the policy owner, annuitant, and the beneficiary. In other situations different individuals or entities may be the policy owner, annuitant and beneficiary.

Can variable annuities provide protection against market downturns?

You should first understand that variable annuities are long-term, tax-deferred investment vehicles designed for retirement purposes and contain both an investment and insurance component. They are sold only by prospectus. Guarantees are based on the claims paying ability of the issuer. Withdrawals made prior to age 59½ are subject to a 10% IRS penalty tax and surrender charges may apply. Gains from tax-deferred investments are taxable as ordinary income upon withdrawal. The investment returns and principal value of the available sub-account portfolios will fluctuate so that the value of the investor's unit, when redeemed, may be worth more or less than their original value.

Various types of guarantees are available on variable annuity contracts. These may include income guarantees, principal guarantees, or death benefit guarantees. These guarantees are known as riders. While some riders are part of an existing contract, many others may carry additional fees, charges, and restrictions, and the policyholder should review their contract carefully before purchasing. These guarantees are also based on the claims paying ability of the issuing company.

Income guarantees are often available as a rider on a variable annuity contract. These may be designed to provide guaranteed income regardless of underlying market performance.

Principal guarantees may be available in several different forms. The original purchase price may be guaranteed on surrender, death, or total income payout.

Death benefit guarantees may not only include return of the original investment, but may also include a guaranteed growth factor regardless of underlying market performance.

These features vary greatly from company to company and are spelled out in detail in the corresponding prospectus. Read the prospectus and consult your advisor prior to investment to determine if one of these guarantees could be appropriate for your situation.

What is the Endowment Model strategy of investing?

Recently, "Endowment Model" investing has come into the mainstream financial media, primarily due to the investment performance of the Harvard and Yale University endowments during the past 10 years. Essentially this strategy is an expansion of Modern Portfolio Theory which says that a portfolio combination of risky investment assets which have low correlations to each other reduces the risk of the overall portfolio. Initially, endowments used the same two asset classes as many individual investors, stocks and bonds, to create their portfolios.

For several years, low correlations were available between large company and small company domestic stocks as well as between U.S. and International stocks so within the stock universe, it was possible to create a well-diversified portfolio. Beginning in the 1980's, as the world became more interdependent, and companies of all sizes began deriving more of their sales in other countries, correlations among different types of stocks began to increase so that now there is very little diversification benefit to be obtained from different types of stocks. Bonds still provide low correlations to stocks but the trade-off is lower expected returns.

Harvard and Yale found that there were other asset classes that have lower correlations to stocks, but have historically performed on par with stocks. Examples include real estate investment trusts and other alternative investments. It's been just in the past few years that access to some of these alternative asset classes has become available to most individual investors. It is now possible to invest in many of these areas through investment trusts, limited partnerships, and increasingly in mutual funds and exchange traded funds.

As with any investment, care must be taken when considering the addition of alternative investments into a portfolio. Many of these types of investments have limited or no liquidity, meaning they cannot be sold at just any time. Expenses associated with these investments are also typically more expensive than in stocks and bonds. Finally, some of these types of investments and their managers have limited track records. All of these factors make it more important to make sure the investment has been well researched by you or your advisor and determined to be appropriate for your portfolio before making a commitment.

The Endowment Model strategy of investing, as with any strategy, cannot guarantee positive investment returns every year. Even Harvard and Yale's endowments, arguably the leaders in this type of strategy, suffered significant losses during the 2008–2009 bear market. Just because asset classes have low correlations to each other doesn't mean they can't all go down at the same time. Correlations also fluctuate over time, and it remains to be seen if all the alternative asset classes will continue to keep their historical correlations or if they, like U.S. and International stocks, will become more closely related over time.

Important considerations regarding the investments and ideas discussed in this chapter:

- **Past performance is no guarantee of future results. The market for all securities is subject to fluctuation such that upon sale, an investor may lose principal.**

- **Bonds are subject to market and interest rate risk if sold prior to maturity. Bond values will decline as interest rates rise and are subject to availability and change in price.**

- **CDs are FDIC insured and offer a fixed rate of return if held to maturity.**

- **Stock investing involves risk including loss of principal.**

- **Small-cap and mid-cap stocks may be subject to a higher degree of risk than more established companies' securities.**

The illiquidity of the small-cap market may adversely affect the value of these investments.

- International and emerging market investing involves special risks such as currency fluctuation and political instability and may not be suitable for all investors.

- Investing in real estate/REITS involves special risks such as potential illiquidity and may not be suitable for all investors. There is no assurance that the investment objectives of this program will be attained.

- Alternative investments may not be suitable for all investors and should be considered as an investment for the risk capital portion of the investor's portfolio. The strategies employed in the management of alternative investments may accelerate the velocity of potential losses.

- Investing in mutual funds involves risk, including possible loss of principal. Investments in specialized industry sectors have additional risks, which are outlined in the prospectus.

- An investment in a money market fund is not insured or guaranteed by the Federal Deposit Insurance Corporation or any other government agency. Although the Fund seeks to preserve the value of your investment at $1.00 per share, it is possible to lose money by investing in the Fund.

9 | Charitable Planning

Americans are some of the most giving people in the world. Fortunately, (at least for now) the government supports our philanthropic tendencies by allowing tax benefits for charitable contributions. But for most philanthropists, the tax benefits are just icing on the cake. The real driver in most charitable planning is to provide a benefit for institutions or causes we care about; to impact our community for the better; and to lead not just a life of success, but a life of significance.

Why should I leave something to charity?

When people think about charitable giving in the context of estate and financial planning, they often think in terms of tax savings. However, history shows that the people of America are the most generous in the world. Most of them give for truly philanthropic reasons—thinking of tax savings as an extra benefit. In other words, many would still contribute even if it did not save them taxes.

During your lifetime you've no doubt supported things bigger than yourself and your family. Perhaps it's your local place of worship, a community foundation, or a national charity. Consider whether it's important to you that these charities continue their work after you're gone, and if so, what you might do to help them.

But I need to leave as much as possible to my children and loved ones. Don't I?

Leaving financial assets to other family members is what most people do. But there's no law that it has to be that way, if you decide you want to benefit charitable causes.

When most of us make gifts to our children during life, we do so with a lesson or purpose attached. Even when they get older, we continue to honor our other important charitable, education, and religious charities while also expressing our love to our children. But most people don't give their loved ones money if they know the child will mishandle, lose, or have it taken from them. At death, however, we'll be giving them more than most of our children have ever handled before.

That leads to two questions:

1. First, are they ready? If not, proper planning and advanced training will help to prepare them.

2. Second, do they need all of it?

In most situations, your children will outlive you by 20–30 years. As you consider charitable giving, you may consider if inheriting $1,000 (or $5,000 or $10,000) less will make a real difference in their lives. There probably is some amount, big or small, that will make no difference to your children. And that same amount *will* make a difference to your church or charity.

I plan to leave money to charity in my will. Is there any reason why I should do something now?

Perhaps the greatest satisfaction of giving comes from seeing the results that your donation brings, and how it can change the lives of others for the better. On a practical level, making a gift now, even in the form of a charitable remainder trust, can help the charity make plans for its future and allocate its resources wisely.

Are charitable contributions during life and/or at death an effective estate planning tool?

There are three possible heirs in any estate plan—family and loved ones, the IRS, or charity.

In many estate plans, the IRS receives 45%, the family 55%, and charity 0%. It may be possible with proper planning to reallocate the IRS portion so that it ends up closer to a split of 80% to family and 20% to charity.

During life, charitable contributions can be made outright or in trust. The contribution will generally reduce current income taxes based on a percentage of adjusted gross income and the type of property transferred. The gift to qualified charities will be removed from your estate and thereby reduce estate taxes. Also, if contributions are made to charitable trusts during your lifetime, there may be an income stream to you and your spouse with the remainder going to charity at the second death.

Also, it is possible to leave property in a charitable trust at death, whereby the income from the property goes to the named charity for a period of years, with the remainder going to the heirs; estate tax free.

All of this can be accomplished by using advanced estate planning tools and techniques discussed in more detail below. Of course, all charitable planning begins with the goals and objectives of the individual or family, not with tax considerations alone.

CHARITABLE REMAINDER AND LEAD TRUSTS

What is a charitable remainder trust?

A charitable remainder trust (CRT) is a trust where there are two separate and distinct "beneficial interests," also known as "split interests." This means that two different entities have an interest in the assets of the trust. These two interests are usually the "income interest," which means income from the trust, and the "remainder interest," which means what is left over at the termination of the trust. In a CRT, a non-charitable beneficiary receives the income interest and a charitable beneficiary receives the remainder interest.

A properly drafted CRT can allow the creator of the trust to take a Federal income tax deduction, as well as provide an income stream for life.

Is it possible that I might be able to increase my income and reduce my taxes at the same time by using a charitable remainder trust?

Yes, depending on your circumstances. If you hold property which has considerably increased in value since you purchased it, you may incur a capital gains tax if you sell the property. A properly drafted charitable remainder trust will allow you to donate the property to the trust and take an income tax deduction and establish an income stream for yourself. If the property is currently producing little or no income, the income stream from the trust may increase your present income as well.

How can a CRT increase my income?

A CRT is a tax exempt entity. If a highly appreciated asset is contributed to a CRT, that asset may be sold without paying current income tax. Conversely, if a CRT is not used, the sale will be taxable. The tax-diminished principal resulting from the taxable sale, in some cases, will generate less income than the undiminished principal resulting from the CRT sale. In addition a charitable contribution deduction is generated. The deduction is equal to the remainder value of what passes to charity at the end of the income period. An analysis must be done to determine whether the taxable sale or CRT sale best serves your interests. If you are charitably inclined, that qualitative factor must be taken into account along with the quantitative financial factors.

What is the biggest disadvantage of a CRT?

The biggest disadvantage of the CRT is that the person establishing the CRT loses access to the principal. A person who wants or needs to spend principal, generally speaking, is not a candidate for a CRT.

Does a CRT result in loss of control?

Except for the loss of access to principal, there are many levels of control that may be retained by the person establishing a CRT. If you establish a CRT, you may be trustee of the CRT and thereby retain control of the investment decisions. You can also choose the charitable beneficiary or beneficiaries. You can choose to inform the charity that it has been named as remainder beneficiary of the CRT, or you may choose not to inform. And, you can retain the power to change the charitable beneficiary or beneficiaries.

What type of property is best to contribute to a CRT?

The most common type of property contributed to a CRT is marketable securities that are highly appreciated. However, many other types of property are often contributed as well. These include raw land, commercial real estate, collectibles such as art or antiques, non-traded securities, and even cash. The consequences of contributing each of these assets differs and careful consideration must be given to the type of trust as well as the tax implications that accompany each asset.

There are some assets that are not strong candidates for contribution to a CRT. Any property that is subject to debt, such as mortgaged real estate, presents a problem. Further, property that has been pre-sold to a third party will cause the tax on the property sale to become the obligation of the seller, even though the property has been transferred to the CRT. It can also be challenging to contribute the stock of a Subchapter S Corporation. While the contribution is allowable, the S status of the Corporation will be revoked upon the completion of the transaction. This may or may not be the desired outcome.

What are some of the important rules of CRTs?

CRTs have many specific rules that apply. First, a CRT must have a minimum payout rate of 5% and cannot exceed a maximum payout rate of 50%. Furthermore, when the calculations are done to compute the desired payout rate, they must take into account that at least a 10% remainder interest is required to be left to charity.

If a CRT is established by an individual, the trust income stream can last for the lifetime of one or more individuals or for a period of years, not to exceed twenty. If a CRT is established by an entity such as a corporation, the trust may only be for a term of years, again not to exceed twenty.

There must be at least one charity designated in the CRT at the time it is created but there may be more than one; and, if desired, the grantor may reserve the right to change the charitable beneficiaries at any time.

What is taken into consideration to ensure a 10% remainder interest for the charity?

In order to qualify as a CRT, the value passing to charity must be worth at least 10% of the beginning value of the trust. Conceptually speaking, the trust has two pieces: a piece that is kept (the income retained for a period of years) and a piece that is given away (what's left in the trust that goes to charity at the end of the income period). That value will be affected by a number of factors including:

A. The trust pay-out rate. The higher the income pay-out rate, the smaller the charity's remainder value. If the pay-out rate is 8%, the charity's remainder value will be less than if the pay-out rate is 6%.

B. The length of the income period. If the income period is based on life expectancy: the younger the income beneficiary, the smaller the charity's remainder value. If the income beneficiary is 50, the charity's remainder value will be less than if the income beneficiary is 70.

C. Current interest rates. Each month the IRS publishes an interest rate (the applicable federal rate, or AFR) that is used to calculate the amount of the charity's remainder value. The lower the AFR, the higher the charity's remainder value.

Are there different types of charitable remainder trust?

There are two basic types of the charitable remainder trust—the charitable remainder annuity trust (CRAT) and the charitable remainder unitrust (CRUT).

What is the difference between a charitable remainder annuity trust (CRAT) and a charitable remainder unitrust (CRUT)?

Both the CRAT and the CRUT are irrevocable trusts which provide for an annual payment to a non-charitable beneficiary or beneficiaries (usually including the trustmaker or the trustmaker's spouse), with the remainder of the trust property distributed to the charity upon the death of the last income beneficiary.

With the CRAT, a fixed dollar amount or percentage of the initial value of the trust assets is paid to the non-charitable beneficiary annually. The payment to the income beneficiary remains level for the entire term of the CRAT. Also, a CRAT may receive only one contribution. No additional property may be added to the trust. This type of trust is most appropriate for older donors who require a steady income and are not worried about future inflation.

With the CRUT, a fixed percentage of the value of the trust assets, <u>revalued annually</u>, is paid to the non-charitable beneficiary annually. With this type of trust, the amount of the distributions to the income beneficiaries will fluctuate each year, based on the annual value of the trust. Furthermore CRUTs allow for additional contributions of property after the initial contribution.

A NIMCRUT (Net Income with Make-up Charitable Remainder Unitrust); is a variant of the standard charitable remainder unitrust (CRUT). This variant still provides for distribution of a certain percentage of the trust's assets, revalued each year, to the non-charitable beneficiary. The NIMCRUT, however, provides that if the trust's income for the year is less than the specified distribution percentage, the non-charitable beneficiary will receive only an amount equal to the actual annual income. The good news is that if the trust's income in future years exceeds the specified distribution amount, the trust will "make up" the shortfall in previous years' payments.

What things do I need to decide to set up a CRT?

There are many different options when setting up a CRT. They include:

A. **Pay-out rate:** The pay-out rate (not less than 5%, nor more than 50%, of the beginning trust value) will determine the distributions to the income beneficiary. Don't forget that the pay-out rate may be limited by the 10% charitable remainder limitation previously discussed. Unless the trust's first year is a full twelve months, the first year pay-out will be prorated; the same proration will apply during the last year.

B. **CRAT or CRUT:** If a CRAT has a 6% pay-out and is funded with $1 million, it will pay out $60,000 per year each and every year of its income term. Conversely, if a CRUT has the same 6% pay-out rate and is funded with $1 million, it will pay out $60,000 in its first year. In its second year, the pay-out will be determined by applying the 6% pay-out rate to the CRT's new balance. If the value of the CRT assets has grown to $1.1 million at the beginning of year two, then the year two pay-out will be $66,000. What if the value of the trust goes down? If the trust value is $900,000 at the beginning of the second year, the pay-out that year will be $54,000.

C. **Pay-out frequency and timing:** The income pay-outs may be monthly, quarterly, semiannually, or annually. The pay-out may be made at the beginning or end of the segment of time.

D. **Income limitations** (this applies only to CRUTs): There are three options:

> 1. Straight pay-out. A straight pay-out CRUT pays out annually without regard to trust income. If it is necessary to dip into principal in order to fund the pay-out, a straight pay-out trust is required to do so.
>
> 2. Net income pay-out (NICRUT). A net income CRUT will pay-out the lesser of:
>> a. Trust accounting income for that year
>>
>> - OR -
>>
>> b. The pay-out as determined by the trust's pay-out rate. As discussed previously, this would be calculated by applying the pay-out rate (a percentage number) to the CRT's beginning value for that particular year. This type of structure protects the trust principal, but will likely result in a lower pay-out in some years.
>
> 3. Net income with make-up payout (NIMCRUT). As explained above, this is much like the NICRUT except that the income shortfall from one year may be "made up" if there is excess income in a subsequent year.

E. **Income term:** The income term may be for the lifetime(s) of one or more people, or for a fixed term of years not to exceed 20 years.

F. **Little known investment strategy:** As the value of a NIMCRUT goes below a capital gain, the securities can be sold to lock in a loss for a given year, and repurchased the next year to establish a lower cost basis. Without this strategy, if the portfolio had losses, you would have to wait until those losses were recovered, plus a gain achieved, before getting a distribution. By using this strategy to "harvest" the losses and reset the cost basis, distributions are made available.

How are CRT income distributions taxed to the income beneficiary?

Income paid from a CRT is taxed based on a four-tier system. These four tiers (and numerous sub-tiers) must be tracked within the CRT. They are:

- Tier 1: Ordinary Income
- Tier 2: Capital Gain Income
- Tier 3: Tax Free Income
- Tier 4: Principal

When a distribution is made to an income beneficiary, the character of that income will exhaust each of the top tiers (and sub-tiers) before "proceeding" to the lower and more tax-favorable lower tiers. Hence, the worst type of taxable income (from the taxpayer's perspective) generally comes out first and the most favorable type of taxable income comes out last. That's referred to as the "worst in, first out" (WIFO) principle.

The Economic Growth and Tax Relief Reconciliation Act of 2001 created an exception to the WIFO principle, making qualified dividends (normally ordinary income) to be taxed like capital gain income at a 15% federal rate.

What are other tax consequences of CRTs?

There are several possible tax implications to be considered when utilizing a CRT. First, contributions to CRTs generally create some type of **charitable income tax deduction**. The deduction is computed using a formula that calculates the value of the gift that charity will receive in the future.

With most common contributions such as publicly traded securities, the deduction is based on the current fair market value of the assets on the date of the transfer. However, in some instances, the deduction may be based on the cost basis of the contributed property. Charitable income tax deductions can be utilized in the year of the contribution and for five succeeding years if the deduction is not fully utilized in year one. These deductions are subject to limitations depending on the property contributed and the nature of the ultimate charitable beneficiary.

The **saving of capital gains tax** is another important aspect of planning with CRTs. When an appreciated long term gain asset is contributed to a CRT and then sold, the CRT does not immediately owe any income tax. Instead, the capital gain is "stored" in the trust. As the trust pays out distributions to the income beneficiary, a portion of the income may be taxed at the capital gains rates. Thus the capital gains may be deferred over a very long period allowing the principal of the trust to be fully invested and productive.

Lastly, in most common CRTs where a husband and wife are income beneficiaries; when the last of them dies, the assets of the CRT are out of the estate for **estate tax** purposes. (Note that if the CRT is a term-of-years trust instead of a lifetime trust, and the income beneficiary dies before the expiration of the term of years, then the values of the future income stream may still be included in the estate.)

What happens to the non-charitable heirs of the person establishing the CRT?

Since the principal of the CRT passes to charity at the end of the income term, the heirs are disinherited as to the CRT assets. If this is a concern, this problem may be remedied by establishing a separate wealth replacement trust. A wealth replacement trust is another name for the irrevocable life insurance trust (ILIT) mentioned in Chapter 6. By way of reminder, an ILIT is an irrevocable trust that purchases a life insurance policy on the life or lives of the CRT's income beneficiaries. The heirs are the beneficiaries of this new trust; and the life insurance replaces the CRT principal that passes to charity at the end of the CRT's income term.

Can you give me an example of how all these different pieces fit together?

An example may make the whole process a little clearer.

Cy and Bea Pace are both 60 years old, in good health and are considering an offer to sell their business for $10 million. The business is set up as a C Corporation and has a cost basis of zero because they started the business from scratch.

For this discussion, let's assume a combined (federal and state) ordinary income tax rate of 40%, a capital gains tax rate of 20% and an estate tax rate of 45%. Cy and Bea believe their future investments can earn 7% pre-tax and net 5% after tax.

If Cy and Bea sell their business on a taxable basis, they will pay $2 million in capital gains taxes and have $8 million left to invest. This $8 million will generate $400,000 per year of after-tax income, based on their investment assumptions at 5%. When Cy and Bea have both passed away, their children will pay $3.6 million of estate taxes and end up with an inheritance $4.4 million.

Conversely, the Paces could transfer their company stock to a charitable remainder trust. Assume the same pre-tax and after-tax rates of return and assume the CRT has a 7% income pay-out to Cy and Bea for the rest of their lives.

Cy and Bea transfer their stock to their CRT. The CRT sells the stock and pays no capital gains tax. Cy and Bea receive 7% from the trust and will pay personal income tax on that distribution. We'll assume that the 7% pay-out equates to a 5% annual after-tax cash flow.

However, Cy and Bea do not wish to disinherit their children. So they establish a wealth replacement trust (ILIT) that purchases a $4.4 million survivorship life insurance policy on their lives. Each year they will make a $40,000 cash gift to the trust which will be used to pay the insurance premium. Their net annual cash flow is $360,000.

In addition, the Paces will receive a $1.6 million charitable contribution deduction. This deduction, if not fully used in the year of the contribution, may be carried forward for up to five years. Hence, during the first five years of the CRT, a significant portion of the distributions will be sheltered from income tax.

When Cy and Bea have both passed away, their children will inherit $4.4 million tax-free from the life insurance proceeds in the wealth replacement trust. Further, a charity selected by the Paces, will receive the $10 million principal value in the CRT.

This illustration does not take into account that, in the real world, investment returns vary from year to year. If you are considering the sale of a material asset, you would want to take this into account whether the sale is structured taxably or tax-free.

What is a Charitable Lead Trust?

A charitable lead trust (CLT) is an irrevocable trust which provides for distribution of annual payments to a charitable beneficiary or beneficiaries, with the remainder distributed to a non-charitable beneficiary or beneficiaries upon the death of the trustmaker, or upon expiration of a fixed period of time. It is sometimes thought of as the reverse of the charitable remainder trust.

Similarly to charitable remainder unitrusts, there are two types of lead trusts: Charitable Lead Annuity Trusts (CLATs) and Charitable Lead Unitrusts (CLUTs).

A CLAT is established so that the payment to charity needs to be calculated only when the trust is established. Generally the payment remains level over the term of the trust and is independent on the performance of the underlying assets. A CLUT recalculates its distribution annually based on a fixed percentage of the assets in the trust. Depending on investment performance, the payment to charity may go up or down.

How does a Charitable Lead Trust work?

First, the trustmaker transfers assets to the trust for a term of years. Assets could be cash, securities, fine art, or other property.

Next, annual payments are made from the trust to a designated charity or charities. Payments can be based on a fixed amount or a set percentage of the trust's value each year depending on how the trust is structured.

For tax purposes, the IRS uses a set rate to project the trust's growth. This determines the taxable gift that will pass to the heirs. If the trust grows beyond that amount, the gains or the appreciation passes to the heir's estate tax free.

To totally avoid gift tax consequences on the assets passed to the heirs, investors can "zero out" the trust by structuring the annual charitable payments so that they equal the original value of the assets donated to the trust.

One of the most common applications of CLTs is a special trust that comes into place at the death of the grantor. Called a Testamentary charitable lead annuity trust (TCLAT), this trust is used to take any assets that remain in the estate above the current remaining estate tax exemption and to create a trust that is the right combination of term and payout so as to create a "zero" remainder interest. These trusts effectively can eliminate any remaining taxable estate and therefore any estate tax. The trade-off is that the heirs will have a considerable delay in receiving these assets.

How is the charitable deduction calculated?

There are specific rules for computing the estate or charitable deduction which are based on the value of the gift to charity over the term of the trust. Generally, the longer the term of the trust, and the higher the payout rate, the larger the charitable deduction.

Are there any other special rules for CLTs?

Many advisors often refer to CLTs as the "opposite" of CRTs since they pay income to charity first and then heirs receive the benefit, which is the reverse of CRTs. However, unlike CRTs, CLTs are not tax exempt trusts. The sale of assets inside a CLT is subject to taxation either to the grantor or to the trust. Also, CLTs do not have a minimum payout percentage. Where a CRT must have a rate no lower than 5%, CLTs have no such minimum. CLTs are also governed under special rules that prohibit self-dealing and certain types of investments called "jeopardy investments."

PRIVATE FOUNDATIONS

What is a private foundation?

A private foundation is a special type of tax exempt entity that is most often established by a single family to fulfill its charitable mission. There are operating and non-operating foundations, though most private foundations are of the non-operating type.

What are the rules for private foundations?

Private foundations have very specific rules and regulations that must be strictly adhered to. Most well known is the rule that mandates a 5% distribution to charity annually. However, there are also rules against self-dealing, holding certain types of investments known as "jeopardy investments," and rules against creating excessive personal benefits from the foundation. While it is common to have family members on the Board of Directors get paid for their services, pay must be reasonable compared to other similar sized charities.

What tax rules apply to private foundations?

Contributions to private foundations generally create an income tax charitable deduction subject to the deductibility limitations. Deductions are available in the year of the gift and can be carried forward for five succeeding years if needed. Contribution may be deductible at fair market value or cost basis, depending on the type of asset contributed. Private foundations are tax exempt under most circumstances but caution must be taken if assets that create Unrelated Business Taxable Income (UBTI) are being considered.

A family with a considerable collection of art or antiques or classic cars might consider using an operating foundation, essentially establishing their own "museum." While the collection may not be housed in a single physical facility, it would allow the family to keep the collection together, exhibit it around the world by loaning to other museums, maintain it, and otherwise keep it within family control.

How much is the minimum to establish a private family foundation?

While there is no legal minimum under the law, there is a practical dollar amount needed to justify the cost. While that amount used to be $5 or $10 million, it is now common to see private family foundations established with $250,000 or less.

What is a Community Foundation?

A community foundation is an independent non-operating pubic charity working in a specific geographic area to manage a collection of charitable funds from various donors in the community. There are more than 700 community foundations nationwide; many dating back to the early 1900s. Collectively, community foundations manage more than $40 Billion in charitable assets and distribute millions of dollars to charitable organizations each year.

A community foundation is a vehicle for charitable giving, not an end user of charitable donations. Community foundations help people achieve their philanthropic dreams by accepting, managing, administering, and distributing charitable funds created by individuals and families. Gifts to the community foundation can take the form of donor-advised funds, endowments, gift annuities, charitable remainder trusts, and others.

How does a donor-advised fund at a community foundation work?

A donor makes an irrevocable gift to a special fund established within the community foundation, which usually bears the donor's or the donor's family name. The donor receives an immediate income tax charitable deduction for the gift. The gift is invested and accumulated tax free by the community foundation, similar to an endowment. The donor can request, at any time, that part or the entire fund be paid to a charity that the donor selects. The donor can select any number of charities in any proportion the donor chooses.

The community foundation makes all of the investment decisions and the donor advises the community foundation when and how much to pay out to charities selected by the donor. The community foundation is able to pool various charitable funds established by its donors for a greater market return, thus keeping overhead and expenses low, and maximizing the amounts being given to the charities selected by the donor from the donor's fund.

How does a fund established at a community foundation compare to private foundations?

There are many practical reasons why establishing a charitable fund at a community foundation might make more sense than creating a private foundation. Some of these reasons include:

- A fund at the community foundation is easy and inexpensive to establish, while a private foundation requires a donor to create a new organization, apply for tax-exempt status, pay filing fees, and incur legal and accounting expenses.

- The income tax charitable deduction limitation on a gift of cash to a community foundation is 50% of the adjusted gross income of the donor for the year of the gift, while that same gift to a private foundation is limited to 30% of the donor's adjusted gross income.

- The charitable deduction for a gift of appreciated stock to a private foundation is limited to its cost basis, up to 20% of the donor's adjusted gross income. That same gift to a community foundation may be deducted at its fair market value, up to 30% of the donor's adjusted gross income.

- A private foundation is required to pay an excise tax of 2% on its investment income and net realized capital gains, while a fund at a community foundation does not because the community foundation is a public charity.

- Gifts made to a community foundation can remain anonymous, while a private foundation is required to make available to the public the name and address of any substantial contributor.

- A private foundation must distribute at least 5% of its net investment assets to charities each year, regardless of whether the private foundation has earned any investment income that year. A charitable fund at a community foundation does not have any minimum annual distribution requirements, thus allowing the fund to grow from year to year at the discretion of the donor.

- A private foundation is subject to strict regulations on self-dealing between the foundation and those who manage, control, or contribute to it and persons or corporations closely related to them. There are fewer legal restrictions on a charitable fund at a community foundation.

- Community foundation funds have fewer investment restrictions than a private foundation. A private foundation, for example, may not hold more than 20% ownership in a particular corporation.

- There are fewer IRS reporting requirements on community foundation grants and funds than those on private foundations. Any reporting requirements are part of the community foundation's annual reporting to the IRS, and include all of the community foundation funds and grants at no additional charge to the funds the community foundation administers.

Are there advantages to private foundations?

Yes, of course. A private foundation provides the donor more direct control over operations of the private foundation than a donor can exercise over a fund at a community foundation. The private foundation often provides a more prominent connection between the donor's family and philanthropy within the community. The private foundation can also pay reasonable compensation and expenses (including subsequent generations of involved family members), relating to the foundation's activities, from donated proceeds.

What is a donor-advised fund?

An alternative to a family foundation is a donor-advised fund. Many brokerage firms and investment companies offer their own versions of donor-advised funds. These funds are established as public charities and contributions are tax deductible as charitable gifts. They can be established with a relatively small contribution (many require an initial gift of only $5000) and the expenses are often charged as an asset-based fee. This makes them substantially less expensive to establish than a family foundation.

Once contributions are made to a donor-advised fund the donor can also recommend the investment allocation for the funds. If the money is to be dispersed to another charity within a short period of time, the donor might elect to invest in a money market account for example. If the goal is to grow the account over a period of many years, the donor might choose to recommend a significantly more aggressive investment allocation. With minimum account balances, many donor-advised funds allow donors to recommend their own investment advisor.

Distributions or grants are processed on the recommendation of the donor to qualified charities. The grant can either identify the donor or they may choose to remain anonymous. Donors can also name successor donors to continue the charitable objectives of the fund beyond their lifetime.

Donor-advised funds are also established by Community Foundations or other institutions. They are accounts that are held separately for the donor that establishes the fund. Normally they allow the donor, with the consent of the Community Foundation, to distribute his or her charitable gifts to as many other charities and in any amount as the donor desires.

Some funds allow the donor to appoint his own money manager or to direct the money management independently. This type of flexibility has become very popular among the giving community since it allows a significant amount of control to remain with the donor. Further, many donor-advised funds allow the fund to remain in force for multiple generations. Contributions to donor-advised funds are deductible in the year of the contribution and for five succeeding years.

How can a donor-advised fund allow me to make charitable gifts anonymously and still receive a tax deduction? (I don't want the charity to know who I am and continue to solicit me for future gifts.)

Many donors would prefer to make gifts without their identity being disclosed. However, our tax code requires that the donor have a receipt from the charity to document gifts for income tax purposes. In order to obtain a receipt it is necessary to disclose the identity of the donor to the charity.

When a donor makes a gift to his or her own donor-advised fund the receipt comes to the donor directly from the fund. The donor can then recommend a grant to a qualified charity from their donor-advised fund. When the charity receives the gift they know it comes from the donor-advised fund, but the name of the donor behind that fund need not be disclosed. This strategy allows charitable gifts on a tax-deductible basis without the donor's identity being disclosed to the end charity.

How can a donor-advised fund help me to receive a year-end tax deduction for my charitable gift when I'm not sure which charity I want to support?

Sometimes clients would like to make charitable gifts at year-end for in-come tax planning purposes and yet are uncertain which charities they would like to support. An example of this occurred in 2004 when the tsunami struck Southeast Asia between Christmas and New Year. There was tremendous destruction and loss of lives. Many donors wanted to help the region but were unsure in the last days of the year which particular charity they might want to give to.

By using a donor-advised fund, donors were able to make a year-end tax-deductible donation and then wait until the New Year to perform their due diligence over the respective charities doing relief work in the area. They obtained the tax advantage and yet were able to select the end charity to receive the funds without the year-end rush.

MISCELLANEOUS TOPICS ON CHARITABLE PLANNING

How do I involve my children and grandchildren in family philanthropy?

One of the methods that has been implemented successfully to involve family members in philanthropy, uses current cash gifts. Here's how it works.

Gather your family members age eight or older (or any age you deem appropriate) and give each of them a specific dollar amount (i.e. $100) that he or she is responsible for giving to one or more qualified charities. In order to make his or her decision each family member is required to go with you to visit at least three charities upon which you mutually agree. During these visits you and your younger family member will learn about the charity and their mission, learn about what causes interest and excite them, and learn about what causes you care about as well.

You may choose to fund these gifts yourself or from your charitable entity. You may also elect to match gifts from your family members to encourage their cooperation and participation. After everyone has made his or her decisions we recommend a family philanthropy meeting to discuss what everyone has done.

What is a bargain sale?

A bargain sale takes place when a seller sells property for less than its fair market value. When such a sale takes place with a charity, the difference between the fair market value and the actual sales price is considered to be charitable gift. The gift portion of the transaction usually represents a charitable income tax deduction and may, therefore be useful in offsetting a portion of the taxable gain that may be realized from the same sale.

How do charitable gift annuities work?

Gift annuities are a type of bargain sale by which a donor transfers property to a charity in return for a stream of income that will be received usually over his or her lifetime. Since the donor will receive less in payments than the value of the transferred property, there is a "gift" of the difference.

Gift annuities are generally guided by the American Council on Gift Annuities (ACGA) and also fall under state regulations. Since they pay a fixed income stream, they are generally advisable only for those donors that are not worried about inflation eroding their spending power. All payments are made up of three components: there is first a return of capital; then a return of capital gains and final interest income. This can make the favorable income tax treatment of gift annuity payments a very attractive feature.

What is a charitable life estate?

The most common type of life estate entails a gift of the residence of the donor. With this gift, the donor retains the right to live in the residence for the rest of his or her life and to generally do all of the normal maintenance, pay all the bills and taxes and treat the home as if it was still their own. However, since the home will be passed to charity at death, the owner/donor will receive a current charitable income tax deduction.

The deduction is based on an IRS calculation to determine the current value of the gift to be received in the future. While this calculation may be complex, there are several computer applications that can handle this computation. As with other charitable deductions, this contribution may be deducted in the year of the contribution and for five succeeding years.

What about contributing fine art or collectibles?

One often overlooked category of assets that lends itself to charitable planning is collectibles. This may include fine art, wine, coins, stamps, classic cars, or any number of other categories. Special rules apply to these assets when they are to be considered as a charitable gift. First, unless the charity is a "purpose" charity (an Art museum to receive art), the deduction for the asset is based on the asset's cost basis instead of its fair market value. Also there are very strict appraisal rules that govern these gifts. When the value exceeds $20,000 the transaction is automatically reviewed by the IRS. When a collectible is sold it is considered tangible personal property. It is taxed at a capital gains rate of 28% (current law) not the lower 15% (current law) capital gains rate applicable to marketable securities.

I want to leave a gift to my favorite charity at my death. Is it better to leave my stock portfolio or my IRA?

At death, IRAs may be subject to both estate tax and income tax. Therefore, IRAs and qualified retirement plans can make excellent charitable gifts, especially for individuals with taxable estates. The estate tax is eliminated due to the charitable estate tax deduction. In addition, the charity does not have to pay income tax on distribution of the IRA because of its tax-exempt status. If the asset had been left to heirs, not only would the IRA have been subject to estate tax in the deceased's estate, but the heirs are still subject to income tax on withdrawals.

Gifts of appreciated securities at death can also be an excellent charitable gift, especially for individuals with taxable estates. They receive a charitable estate tax deduction for the gift and thereby reduce their taxable estate. However, if they had left that asset to their heirs the built-in capital gain would be gone due to the step-up in cost basis at death (2009 law). The heirs inherit the asset with a basis equal to the fair market value on the date of death. The heirs could then sell the asset without recognizing the built-in gain that the deceased had. Highly appreciated securities make excellent lifetime gifts to charity as the capital gains tax need not be paid by the charity on sale of the asset due to their tax-exempt status.

Consult with your advisory team when deciding which of these assets to leave to your favorite charity and which to leave to your heirs. It is not an easy question as taxable securities receive a step-up in basis, but IRA's can be deferred over the heirs' lifetime with the exception of required minimum distributions.

What are Conservation Easements?

Conservation Easements were designed by the government to provide tax incentives for land owners to preserve large spaces of land.

In addition to the preservation of land for public, recreation, open space, or historic purposes, there are significant tax benefits. First, there is an income tax deduction equal to the value of the public easement. Second, there will be a reduction in property value at death (due to easement value) for estate tax. Third, there may be an additional estate tax exclusion (up to $500,000) if certain conditions are met. Lastly, in some states there may be a state tax credit for a conservation easement.

Normally, the donor of a conservation easement may not develop the property for commercial purposes. An exception to this rule would be for farming purposes.

10 | Retirement Planning

More than ever, it's important to plan for the ultimate disposition of your IRAs and other retirement plans. The tax laws surrounding these plans are complex, and have changed several times throughout history. For some people, the retirement plan is the most significant financial asset that will be passed to children and grandchildren. Whether or not that's the case, there is no doubt that IRAs, 401Ks, pensions, and other retirement plans must be carefully integrated with the rest of the estate plan. This chapter will help you better understand how your retirement plan works, and how you can maximize the amount that is passed to your beneficiaries when you're gone.

I hear a lot about retirement planning. Is it really that important?

Historically, a personal residence was the largest asset in a person's estate. Currently, however, because of changes in tax laws and the tremendous historical growth of the equity markets, qualified retirement plans occupy a significant portion of many estates. The rise in the value of the assets held in qualified retirement plans has created new problems and opportunities. In most cases, retirement plans subject the owner, their heirs, or their estate to income tax liability, as well as potential estate tax liability.

They say that numbers don't lie. One recent study determined the following sources of income for individuals, age 65 and older (Social Security Administration, Income of the Aged Chartbook, 2006):

Retirement Plans	17.90%
Social Security	36.70%
Personal Investments & Savings	14.90%
Earned Income	27.80%
Miscellaneous	2.70%
Total	100.00%

The numbers are revealing. Retirees use part-time employment to supplement nearly 28% of their retirement income, and Social Security accounts for less than 37% of all retirement income.

Many experts suggest that your retirement income should be between 70 to 80% of your pre-retirement income. Therefore, there is one undeniable conclusion. It is up to you, and you alone, to plan for your retirement.

Now I understand that relying on Social Security alone is not wise. Should I concentrate on increasing my retirement plans or my personal investments?

The answer is both, but there is generally a reason to first utilize retirement plans. The government is concerned about you saving for retirement and gives you certain tax incentives to do so. First, you receive an income tax deduction each year when you make contributions to certain retirement plans. Second, and more importantly, the earnings each year on those retirement plans are not subject to income tax. The earnings are "tax deferred" and subject to income tax only when withdrawn by you.

Someone once said that compound interest is the most powerful force in the universe. What is even more powerful is tax-deferred compounding of interest. Look at the following example comparing a tax deductible retirement plan versus a taxable account:

EXAMPLE: You are 30 years of age and contribute $5,000 per year to a tax deductible retirement plan and $5,000 per year to a taxable account. Assuming you are in a 25% combined federal and state income tax bracket and your investment return is 6%, at age 65 the account balances would be:

Total Tax Deductible Retirement Plan	$631,341
Total Taxable Account	$337,655

The above numbers do not reflect that distributions from the Tax Deductible Retirement Plan upon retirement will be taxable. However, even considering the after-tax value of the Tax Deductible Retirement Plan, there is still more in the account:

Total Tax Deductible Retirement Plan
(assuming a 15% combined income tax rate) $536,650
Total Tax Deductible Retirement Plan
(assuming a 25% combined income tax rate) $473,505
Total Taxable Account $337,655

Therefore, it is normally prudent to first maximize your retirement plans and then concentrate on personal investments.

DIFFERENCES BETWEEN QUALIFIED RETIREMENT PLANS AND IRAs

What is the difference between an IRA and a Qualified Plan?

Generally, an IRA (also known as an Individual Retirement Account) is a type of retirement savings vehicle established by you. The government allows you this personal retirement vehicle with the hopes that the money will help supplement your government retirement plans (generally Social Security). You establish an IRA by a written agreement between you and a "qualified institution." This written agreement is known as a Custodial or Trust Agreement and the qualified institution is known as the IRA Custodian. Only certain institutions qualify under the law to be an IRA Custodian, and this includes most banks, savings and loans, credit unions, brokerage firms and insurance companies.

On the other hand, a Qualified Plan is a retirement savings vehicle established by your employer for your benefit. In order to be a Qualified Plan, your employer must comply with certain federal laws. In exchange for meeting these legal requirements, the government provides a benefit to your employer in the form of deductible contributions. In other words, when your employer contributes money to a Qualified Plan, it is entitled to an income tax deduction in the year of contribution.

TYPES OF QUALIFIED PLANS

I just graduated from college and have secured a job.
Will my employer provide me a pension plan?

Probably not, but it may offer another type of Qualified Plan. Generally Qualified Plans can be divided into two main types:

1. Account Plan (also known as a defined contribution plan); and

2. Annuity Plan (also known as a defined benefit plan).

Under an **Account Plan**, a separate account is established for you, the employee. Contributions made by you or your employer are deposited directly into your separate account. Normally you are entitled to the money in your account when you leave your employer, or you retire. If you die, you have the right to name a beneficiary who will receive any money remaining in your account at your death. Within limits, you are allowed to select how the money in your account will be invested and can periodically change the investment mix of the assets in your account. Since you control how the money is invested, all investment risk is borne solely by you.

Under an **Annuity Plan**, all money is held in one fund; a separate account is not established for you. You are normally entitled to receive benefits only when you become disabled or reach a certain retirement age. The amount of your benefits is generally tied to a formula taking into account your annual salary, number of years worked and other factors. Your benefits will generally be paid to you in the form of a monthly annuity.

An annuity is a guaranteed payment for the rest of your life. When you die, the annuity payments stop. Usually you have the option of having the annuity paid during your lifetime (single annuity) or for the joint lifetimes of you and another individual, usually your spouse (joint annuity). If you elect a joint annuity, your monthly benefit will be less than a single annuity. Furthermore, you generally have the option of electing a term certain. A term certain guarantees payment for a specific period of time, regardless of whether you are alive. Thus if you elect a five year term certain, and die after two years, the annuity payments will continue to your beneficiary for another three years. Unless you have elected a term certain, the annuity payments stop when you die (for a single annuity) or when both of you die (for a joint annuity). For that reason, there are no remaining benefits to leave to your family. The guarantees are based on the claims paying ability of the issuer.

Under an Annuity Plan, you have no ability to choose how the assets are invested. Your employer is in essence "guaranteeing" your future annuity payments. Since you have no control over how the money is invested, all investment risk is borne by your employer.

Historically, most, if not all Qualified Plans were Annuity Plans. The most common was the pension plan. Unfortunately, pension plans are not easy to establish and maintain. There are many complex rules that employers must follow each year and the administrative costs can be very high. For these reasons and others, most employers have switched to Account Plans.

Today, most Qualified Plans are Account Plans. They are also known as defined contribution plans. The most common Qualified Account Plans are:

1. Money Purchase Pension Plan;

2. Profit Sharing Plan;

3. Regular 401(k) Plan;

4. Roth 401(k) Plan;

5. Savings Incentive Match Plan for Employees (SIMPLE) 401(k) Plan;

6. Savings Incentive Match Plan for Employees (SIMPLE) IRA;

7. Simplified Employee Pension Plan (SEP);

8. Stock Bonus Plans; and

9. Employee Stock Ownership Plans (ESOP).

TYPES OF IRAs

Are there different types of IRAs?

Yes. The law provides for three different types of IRAs:

1. Deductible IRAs;

2. Non-Deductible IRAs; and

3. Roth IRAs.

Historically, IRAs fell within the two categories of Deductible and Non-Deductible. The main difference between the two types involved your ability to deduct contributions and the taxation of distributions.

With a **Deductible IRA**, you receive an income tax deduction for each contribution. Normally this will provide you with an immediate income tax savings, which in turn helps "finance" the cost of your contribution. Each year, the earnings inside your IRA accumulate tax deferred . . . you do not pay current income tax on those earnings. This tax-deferred growth allows you IRA account to grow much faster than a normal investment subject to income tax each year. Once you begin withdrawing money from your Deductible IRA, both your original contributions and all accumulated earnings are subject to ordinary income tax.

With a **Non-Deductible IRA**, you do not receive an income tax deduction for your contributions, but the earnings are tax-deferred just like a Deductible IRA. Upon withdrawal, your contributions are not subject to income tax (since you did not get a deduction when you made the contribution) but all earnings are subject to ordinary income tax.

A **Roth IRA** is a hybrid between a Deductible IRA and a Non-Deductible IRA. You receive no income tax deduction when you contribute to a Roth IRA, but the earnings are tax deferred, and maybe even tax free. You may withdraw your contributions at any time, tax free. In fact all distributions are first deemed to be your original contributions, and only thereafter your earnings. But here is the best part. If you do not make a distribution of earnings until the later of 59½ or five years from the establishment of your first Roth IRA, then all of your earnings are **income tax-free**!

Can I invest in an IRA?

As a general rule, you are allowed to decide which type of IRA you want: Deductible, Non-Deductible and Roth. In fact you may be able to establish more than one type in a given year. However, the government is always concerned that these moneys be set aside and used for retirement, not as a wealth accumulation and transfer vehicle for your family when you die. Therefore, the law provides limits on your overall contributions and further reduces your ability to make contributions based upon your income and your participation in an employer provided Qualified Plan. Therefore, in order to be eligible to make contributions to an IRA you must meet a series of tests.

a. Earned Income

In the year of your contribution, you must have "earned income" equal to or greater than the amount of your contributions to an IRA. Earned income includes wages, salary, tips, commissions, and earnings from self–employment, but does not include interest, dividends, capital gains or rental income. If you are married and file a joint income tax return, you can consider the earned income of both you and your spouse.

b. Contribution Limit

If you have sufficient earned income, you are limited to a maximum contribution amount each year. The maximum contribution limit is shown in Table 1 below and applies to all IRAs in a given year (Deductible, Non-Deductible and Roth).

For example, if you are 40 years of age and contribute $4,000 to a Deductible IRA in 2010, then the most you could contribute to a Roth IRA for 2010 is $1,000 (assuming you could meet the other tests provided below).

If you are married, the contribution limit applies to each of you.

TABLE 1 Total Annual IRA Contribution Limits		
Year	Overall Contribution Limit Deductible, Non-Deductible and Roth IRA (under age 50)	Overall Additional Catch-up Contributions Deductible, Non-Deductible and Roth IRA (age 50+)
2010	$5,000	$1,000
2011 and thereafter	$5,000★	$1,000★
★Indexed for inflation		

If you are 50 or older, you are allowed to make additional contributions each year. Known as "catch-up" contributions, these additional contributions allow you to set aside more for retirement since your retirement years are quickly approaching. Again, the amount of the catch-up contribution provided above is the total cumulative amount for all IRAs for a given year.

c. Participant in Employer Provided Plan

Your contribution limit to a Deductible IRA could be reduced and even eliminated if you or your spouse participates in an Employer Provided Retirement Plan at work. See Table 2 below.

TABLE 2 Reduction or Elimination of Deductible IRA Contribution for Those with Employer Provided Retirement Plan		
Year	Deductible IRA Contribution Limit Begins Reduction When AGI Reaches	Deductible IRA Contribution Limit Eliminated if AGI Reaches
Single or Head of Household		
2010	$56,000	$66,000
2011 and later★	$56,000★	$66,000★
Married Filing Joint Return		
2010	$89,000	$109,000
2011 and later★	$89,000★	$109,000★
★Indexed for Inflation		

If you are married, and both you and your spouse are participants, then the above table reflects the reduction or elimination of each of your contributions. If one spouse is not a participant then the nonparticipant spouse's contributions begin to be phased out when your combined AGI reaches $167,000 and is totally eliminated at $177,000.

d. Reduction or Elimination of Roth IRA

Your contribution limit to a Roth IRA is first reduced to the extent you have made contributions to a Deductible IRA for the same year. Furthermore, your contribution limit to a Roth IRA could be reduced or eliminated if your modified AGI exceeds certain limits. See Table 3 below.

TABLE 3	Reduction or Elimination of Roth IRA Contribution	
Year	Roth IRA Contribution Limit Begins Reduction When Modified AGI Reaches	Roth IRA Contribution Limit Eliminated if Modified AGI Reaches
Single or Head of Household		
2010	$105,000	$120,000
2011 and later	$105,000★	$120,000★
Married Filing Joint Return		
2010	$167,000	$177,000
2011 and later	$167,000★	$177,000★
Married Filing Separately		
2010 and later	$0.00	$10,000
★Indexed for inflation		

e. Reduction of Non-Deductible IRA

Your contribution limit to a Non-Deductible IRA is reduced by any amounts that you have contributed to a Deductible or Roth IRA in the same year. There are no income limits on contributions to a Non-Deductible IRA.

f. Contribution Deadline

A contribution to any IRA must be made no later than April 15th following the year for which the contribution is made.

g. Age Limit

Finally, you are not allowed to make contributions to a Deductible or Non-Deductible IRA beginning in the year you reach 70½. However, you may continue to make contributions to a Roth IRA (assuming the other tests are met) regardless of your age.

Which type of IRA is best for me?

That's a personal decision that should be based upon many factors, including:

- Your age
- Your need (or desire) for a current income tax deduction
- Your current income tax bracket
- Your anticipated income tax bracket at retirement
- Your expected need to use the IRA prior to retirement
- Your expected need to use the IRA after retirement

There has been much talk between the advantages and disadvantages of a Deductible IRA and a Roth IRA. In a perfect world, if everything remained constant, there would be no difference between the two. Let me give you an example.

EXAMPLE: You are 30 years of age and want to contribute $3,000 to either a Deductible IRA or a Roth IRA. Assume you are currently in a 25% combined income tax bracket and will be in the same income tax bracket at retirement. Also assume a 6% investment return. At a combined 25% income tax rate, you would have to make $4,000 in order to make a $3,000 nondeductible contribution to a Roth IRA ($4,000 × 25% is $1,000 tax). Therefore, for a true apple to apple comparison, $4,000 would be invested in the Deductible IRA and $3,000 in the Roth IRA. At age 65 and assuming the immediate liquidation of the account, each account would net the following:

Deductible IRA	$442,953
Roth IRA	$442,953

Unfortunately, we don't live in a perfect world. However, the following observations can be made:

Reasons to invest in a Roth IRA:

- You anticipate your income tax bracket will be higher at retirement

- You don't want your retirement funds to subject your social security payments to possible income taxation

- You want access to your contributions (without penalty) prior to 59½

- You want the flexibility of not taking distributions from your account during your lifetime

- You do not anticipate using the money during your lifetime

- You can live without the income tax deduction each year

Reasons to invest in a Deductible IRA:

- You need (or desire) the current income tax deduction

- Your income tax bracket will be lower at retirement

- You are concerned that the government might, in the future, tax Roth IRAs.

LIFETIME DISTRIBUTIONS FROM RETIREMENT PLANS

Can I withdraw my retirement plan dollars at any time?

That depends upon the type of retirement plan.

Generally, with regard to an **IRA**, you are allowed to withdraw any amount any time. However, if you are under 59½, then the 10% penalty tax will apply unless you meet one of the exceptions. By law, you may not borrow from your IRA, sell your IRA, or give your IRA away. Any of these transactions would be deemed to be a distribution of the IRA to you and subject to income taxation.

For **Qualified Plans**, normally you cannot withdraw monies from the plan while you are still employed (known as "in-service withdrawals"). Some types of Qualified Plans (like a 401(k)) might allow you to borrow money from your account. However under federal law, the maximum amount you can borrow is the lesser of 50% of your vested account balance or $50,000. Also you must still pay interest on the amounts borrowed. You should check with your employer to see if your Qualified Plan allows for loans to you. Additionally, some Qualified Plans allow for withdrawals for certain hardships such as unreimbursed medical expenses, college education expenses, funeral expenses, and the purchase, repair, or foreclosure prevention of your principal residence. There are strict rules determining "hardship" including the requirement that you have no other fund in which to meet the need. Finally, hardship withdrawals are still subject the 10% penalty tax for early withdrawals. Again, you should check with the Human Resources department of your employer to see if hardship withdrawals are allowed.

I need to withdraw funds from my retirement account now. How can I avoid the 10% penalty tax?

It is the government's intent that your IRAs and Qualified Plans be used for your retirement, not on an "as needed" basis. Therefore the law imposes a penalty for early withdraws. If you withdraw money from your IRA or Qualified Retirement Plan prior to 59½ you will generally be subject to a 10% "excise" tax. In addition all amounts withdrawn will normally be subject to ordinary income tax.

However, there are certain exceptions provided under the law. If you meet one of these exceptions, then you will not be subject to the 10% excise tax. Most of the exceptions are provided below, but you should always consult with your tax advisor prior to taking an early distribution from your IRA or Qualified Plan.

a. **Your Separation from Service.** If you have separated from service (left your employer) and in the year of your termination you are age 55 or older then distributions from the Qualified Plan maintained with that employer will be exempt from the penalty tax. This exception does not apply to IRAs or Qualified Plans of other employers.

b. **Distributions Not Included in Your Gross Income.** If any distribution is not included in your gross income, then it will not be subject to the 10% penalty. Normally this would include withdraws of non-deductible contributions (including all contributions, but not earning, on a Roth IRA) or rollovers.

c. **Your Death.**   If you die, all distributions to your beneficiaries are exempt from the 10% penalty tax.

d. **Your Disability.**   If you become disabled, then you are not subject to the penalty tax. You meet the definition of disability if you are "unable to engage in any substantial gainful activity by reason of any medically determinable physical or mental impairment which can be expected to result in death or to be of long-continued and indefinite duration."

e. **Substantially Equal Payments.**   If you begin to take distributions that are part of a series of substantially equal payments based upon your life or life expectancy, then the 10% penalty tax does not apply. Generally the law provides three methods to determine the payments: the life expectancy method, the amortization method or the annuity method. Be aware that the payments must continue until the later of you reaching 59½ or 5 years. If payments are increased, decreased or stopped prior to that time, then the 10% penalty will apply. Also, in order for the penalty not to apply to your Qualified Plan, you must have also left your employment.

f. **Your Divorce.**   Distributions from your Qualified Plan to your ex-spouse pursuant to a divorce will not be subject to the 10% penalty tax. However, caution must be utilized since only distributions pursuant to a Qualified Domestic Relations Order (QDRO) issued by the divorce court will escape the penalty. The law also provides for the transfer of your IRA to your former spouse if it is pursuant to a divorce decree.

g. **Your Unreimbursed Medical Expenses.**   Distributions that do not exceed the amount of your unreimbursed medical expenses for a given year (after subtracting 7.5% of your adjusted gross income) are not subject to the penalty.

h. **Your Health Insurance if You Are Unemployed.**   Distributions from your IRA that do not exceed the cost of medical insurance premiums for you, your spouse and your dependents during a period of your unemployment may be exempt from the penalty tax.

i. **Qualified Higher Education Expenses.**   Distributions from your IRA for certain Qualified Higher Education Expenses for you, your spouse, children or grandchildren are not subject to the penalty tax. These expenses generally include tuition, fees, books, supplies, equipment and room and board for post-secondary institutions.

j. First-Time Home Purchasers. Distributions from your IRA for the first-time purchase of a home for you, your spouse, or your descendants or ancestors is exempt from the penalty tax provided the funds are used within 120 days of your receipt. Furthermore, your lifetime limit is $10,000. First-time is defined as not owning a home within 2 years from the date of the purchase of the new home.

I am retired and currently don't need to access my retirement plan to live on. I've decided not to take any distributions. Is that ok?

It probably is NOT ok. Congress intended that your retirement plan funds be used for your retirement and not as a wealth accumulation and transfer devise. Therefore, most retirement plans require that you begin taking minimum distributions once you reach a certain age. Failure to take these minimum distributions will result in a 50% penalty tax. These rules are known as the Minimum Distribution Rules and are somewhat complex.

Ok. So when do I have to start taking funds out of my Retirement Plan?

The first date that you must begin taking distributions from your Retirement Plans is known as your Required Beginning Date.

For your **Deductible and Non-Deductible IRAs**, your Required Beginning Date is **always** April 1st of the year following the year in which you turn 70½.

For **Roth IRAs**, there are no requirements that you withdraw funds during your lifetime. This is one important distinction and advantage of a Roth IRA.

For Qualified Plans, the **general rule** is that your Required Beginning Date is April 1st of the year following the year in which you turn 70½. However, there is an **exception** if you are still working. With regard to plans maintained by your employer, you can postpone distributions until April 1st of the year following the year in which you separate from service (provided that the plan allows this exception). This exception applies only if you are an employee and you own 5% or less of the employer. If you are an employee and in addition you also own more than a 5% interest in the employer, the IRS is concerned that you could manipulate your retirement date and thus indefinitely postpone your Required Beginning Date.

In addition, the ability to postpone your Required Beginning Date applies only to Qualified Plans maintained by **your current employer**. The Required Beginning Date for Qualified Plans from your *former* employer is the same as that for IRAs—April 1st of the year following the year in which you turn 70½.

Now I am really confused. How much and how often do I need to take distributions once I reach my Required Beginning Date? Let's start with how often.

Once you reach your Required Beginning Date, you must withdraw a minimum amount from your IRA or Qualified Plan at least annually, known as a Required Minimum Distribution (or RMD). Each calendar year in which a RMD is required to be withdrawn is known as a **Distribution Year**. The **first Distribution Year** is actually the year in which you turn 70½ (or the year in which you separate from service, if the exception for Qualified Plans described in the preceding answer applies).

The normal rule is that a RMD must be withdrawn no later than December 31st of the Distribution Year. However there is an exception for the **first** RMD. The first RMD can be postponed until no later than your Required Beginning Date (April 1st of the following year). However for the second and all subsequent Distribution Years, the RMD must be made by December 31st of that Distribution Year.

If you postpone your **first** RMD until the calendar year of your Required Beginning Date, you will have to take two RMDs in one taxable year (the first RMD by April 1st and the second RMD by December 31st). This could be bad or good depending upon your other taxable income. In many circumstances this "bunching" of income in one taxable year could force you into a higher income tax bracket resulting in higher marginal rates and possibly the loss of itemized deductions.

If, however, you anticipate a significant drop in taxable income in the next calendar year (for example you retire) postponing your **first** RMD could result in an overall reduction of income taxes.

Obviously there is no "one" answer as to whether you should postpone your **first** RMD until the calendar year of your Required Beginning Date. This decision should be made only after you have consulted with your income tax advisor.

Now let's talk about how much.

The RMD will depend upon the type of retirement plan and the options available under the plan. There are two general options that satisfy the Minimum Distribution Rules: the annuity method and the life expectancy method.

The Annuity Method

As discussed previously, an annuity is a guaranteed stream of income for the rest of your life. Under the Annuity Method, as long as the periodic payments are made in intervals no longer than one year and any term certain period is not longer than 20 years, the Minimum Distribution Rules will be satisfied if the first periodic payment begins by your Required Beginning Date. Normally this method is available only for defined benefit Qualified Plans, and certain IRAs that are designed as an annuity.

The Life Expectancy Method

The second method is by far the most popular method and generally must be used for all defined contribution Qualified Plans and most IRAs. Under the Life Expectancy Method, the Required Minimum Distribution is determined by dividing your account balance as of December 31st of the prior year by the life expectancy number obtained from a table published by the IRS. The life expectancy number is also known as the "Divisor." With one exception, you must use the Divisor from the following table found on the next page (known as the Uniform Table).

The Uniform Table (as of 2010)	
Age	Divisor Number
70	27.4
71	26.5

(Continued)

| The Uniform Table (as of 2010) (Continued) ||
Age	Divisor Number
72	25.6
73	24.7
74	23.8
75	22.9
76	22.0
77	21.2
78	20.3
79	19.5
80	18.7
81	17.9
82	17.1
83	16.3
84	15.5
85	14.8
86	14.1
87	13.4
88	12.7
89	12.0
90	11.4
91	10.8
92	10.2
93	9.6
94	9.1
95	8.6
96	8.1
97	7.6
98	7.1
99	6.7
100	6.3
101	5.9
102	5.5
103	5.2
104	4.9

(Continued)

The Uniform Table (as of 2010) (*Continued*)	
Age	Divisor Number
105	4.5
106	4.2
107	3.9
108	3.7
109	3.4
110	3.1
111	2.9
112	2.6
113	2.4
114	2.1

There is one exception to using the Uniform Table for calculating your **lifetime** Required Minimum Distributions. If the only beneficiary of your retirement plan during the entire calendar year is your spouse, and if your spouse is more than 10 years younger than you, then you must use your actual joint life expectancy (obtained from another table published by the IRS) to determine the Required Minimum Distribution **for that year**.

Note that the ability to use the actual joint life expectancy of you and your "more than 10-year younger spouse" is determined on a year-to-year basis. If your spouse dies or you divorce your spouse during a Distribution Year, the law allows you to continue to use the actual joint life expectancy table for that Distribution Year. However, for each subsequent year you must revert back to the Uniform Table (unless you again marry a more than 10-year younger spouse!). The advantage of using the divisor from this second table is that the divisor will be larger than that of the Uniform Table and will therefore result in a smaller RMD.

What if I own more than one IRA or Qualified Plan?

You must compute the Required Minimum Distribution for each IRA, and then add all Required Minimum Distributions together. You then have the option to withdraw the total of all the Required Minimum Distributions, in equal or unequal installments, from any one or more of your IRAs to the complete exclusion of others.

The previous rule does not apply to Qualified Plans. You must compute your Required Minimum Distribution for each Qualified Plan, and you must withdraw the RMD from that plan.

NAMING BENEFICIARIES OF RETIREMENT PLANS

Are there any restrictions on who I can name as the beneficiary of my retirement plans?

With regard to your IRAs, normally you have the freedom to choose who will receive any remaining funds at the date of your death. This is done through a beneficiary designation form that must be completed, signed by you, and delivered to your IRA Custodian prior to the date of your death. You have the right to choose one or more "primary" beneficiaries and one or more "contingent" beneficiaries. Contingent beneficiaries are those who are entitled to your Account balance in the event that all primary beneficiaries die before you. Normally, you are not restricted as to whom you can name as a beneficiary. You can name your spouse, your children, or other individuals. In addition, you can name entities, such as a corporation, a charity, a trust, or even your estate.

The same is usually true with regard to your Qualified Plans. As a general rule, you have the freedom to decide who will receive any remaining funds at the date of you death. A beneficiary designation form can be obtained from your employer. If your employer has a Human Resources (HR) department, they normally can provide you with the form.

However, sometimes there are legal restrictions on who you can name as a beneficiary of your IRA or Qualified Plan. Most restrictions on IRAs are based upon state law. If you are married and live in a community property state, state law may provide that you must name your spouse as your beneficiary or obtain your spouse's consent if you name someone other than your spouse.

Most restrictions on Qualified Plans are based upon federal law. The Employee Retirement Income Security Act of 1974 (ERISA) and the Retirement Equity Act of 1984 (REA) are two federal laws that govern most Qualified Plans. These laws were enacted to protect both employees and their spouses. If you are an employee, the main protection is found in the "anti-alienation" rules. These rules prevent you from transferring your interest in your Plan during your lifetime and also prevent others (such as creditors) from gaining access to your benefits.

In addition, these rules protect your spouse by providing default provisions in the event of your death.

In general, if you die before distributions have begun, then your spouse must receive some or all of your remaining benefits either outright or in the form of a qualified preretirement survivor annuity. Once you start taking distributions, then your remaining benefits must be paid to you in the form of a qualified joint and survivor annuity. Upon your death, the continuing annuity amount paid to your spouse must be at least 50% and not more than 100% of the annuity amount paid to you during your lifetime.

However, you can waive the right to receive benefits in the form of a qualified preretirement survivor annuity or qualified joint and survivor annuity provided that your spouse consents. In other words, if you want to name a beneficiary other than your spouse, he or she must consent. Your spouse's consent must be in writing and must be notarized or signed in the presence of a Plan Representative. You employer (again generally the Human Resources department) can assist you with regard to obtaining these spousal consent forms.

What happens to my Retirement Plans when I die?

As discussed in a previous answer, your beneficiary has the legal right to the remaining proceeds in your retirement plan at your death. Federal retirement plan laws require that, after your death, your beneficiary must continue withdrawing the proceeds from your retirement plan over a certain period of time. The period of time depends upon three factors:

- The written provisions contained in the retirement plan;
- When you die; and
- Who you name as a beneficiary.

Based upon the above factors, the period of time can range anywhere from 1 year to over 80 years!

Why wouldn't my beneficiary just withdraw all of the remaining proceeds after my death?

There are several good reasons for your beneficiary **not to** immediately withdraw the plan proceeds after your death.

First, upon withdrawal, the proceeds will generally be taxed to the beneficiary at ordinary income tax rates. The only exceptions would be for non-deductible contributions and qualified earnings on a Roth 401(k) or Roth IRA.

Second, as long as the proceeds remain in the retirement plan, all monies (including earnings) continue to be tax-deferred until withdrawn. Thus the same tax deferral that you obtained during your lifetime will continue for your beneficiary. This continued tax deferral will generally result in the proceeds growing at a faster rate than if withdrawn and immediately taxed.

Third, under federal or state law, your beneficiary might have better protections (such as creditor or divorce) if the money is left in your retirement plan.

So, what are the distribution options available to my beneficiary upon my death?

First, the options available to a beneficiary will depend upon the written terms of the IRA or Qualified Plan, so the plan document must be reviewed.

As a general rule, a beneficiary normally has the right to immediately withdraw all of the plan proceeds.

Assuming the beneficiary does not want to immediately withdraw all of the proceeds, then federal law provides a "maximum" period of time over which the beneficiary must deplete the account.

This maximum period of time depends upon which of three categories your beneficiary falls under: Designated Beneficiary, Non-Designated Beneficiary, or Surviving Spouse.

What is a Designated Beneficiary?

A "Designated Beneficiary" is a term of art under the Internal Revenue Code. It does not mean the individual or entity that you have named as the beneficiary to receive your IRA or Qualified Plan proceeds at your death. Rather, the beneficiary you have named either falls or does not fall within the category of "Designated Beneficiary" under the Internal Revenue Code. If the beneficiary you have named falls within the "Designated Beneficiary" category, then as a general rule, that beneficiary is allowed a longer period to time to withdraw your remaining plan proceeds after your death.

There is a simple way to remember if your named beneficiary falls within the category of "Designated Beneficiary": Does the beneficiary have a heartbeat? In other words, is the named beneficiary an individual? If, so, then he or she falls within the Designated Beneficiary category.

What is a Non-Designated Beneficiary?

As previously discussed, if your named beneficiary is not your surviving spouse and is not an individual falling within the Designated Beneficiary category, then by default, the beneficiary is classified, for IRS purposes, as a Non-Designated Beneficiary.

Again, there is a simple way to remember if your named beneficiary falls within the category of "Non-Designated Beneficiary": If the named beneficiary does not have a heartbeat, it is usually classified as a Non-Designated Beneficiary.

Therefore, if your named beneficiary is an entity, a charity, or your estate, it is a Non-Designated Beneficiary.

If your named beneficiary is a trust, then it too generally falls within the Non-Designated Beneficiary category. However, there is an exception if the trust meets certain requirements.

So, bottom line, what difference is it to my beneficiary if he, she or it is classified as a Designated Beneficiary, a Non-Designated Beneficiary or my spouse?

The major difference is the length of continued income tax deferral available to the beneficiary after your death.

As discussed in the previous answers, there is a maximum period of time after your death over which your beneficiary must withdraw all remaining funds. The longer the period of time, the more potential there is for continued income tax deferral and faster growth.

What is maximum period of time my beneficiary has to withdraw my plan proceeds after my death?

As a general rule if your named beneficiary is an individual (a "Designated Beneficiary"), that beneficiary can withdraw your plan proceeds over a period of time (a fixed number of years) that equals his or her life expectancy. A table published by the IRS (See the Single Life Expectancy on page 184) provides the life expectancy of a beneficiary based upon his or her age.

For example, if your beneficiary is 55, then based upon the table, his or her life expectancy 29.6 years.

For each year after the year of your death, your beneficiary must withdraw at least a minimum amount, known as the annual Required Minimum Distribution. Your beneficiary must withdraw his or her first annual Required Minimum Distribution by December 31st of the year following your death and then by each December 31st thereafter.

The amount of the first annual Required Minimum Distribution is determined by dividing the value of your retirement account as of December 31 of the year of your death by the life expectancy of your beneficiary in the year following your death (also known as the "Initial Divisor").

For example, assume that you die in June 2010 and your beneficiary is your son who is 54 at the date of your death. The value of your account on December 31, 2010 is $200,000. Your son must take his first annual Required Minimum Distribution by December 31, 2011. The amount of this first distribution (for 2011) will be determined by dividing $200,000 into his life expectancy in 2011. Since he will be 55 in 2011, his life expectancy is 29.6 years (the "Initial Divisor"). This results in a Required Minimum Distribution of $6,757 for 2011 ($200,000/29.6 = $6,757).

For each subsequent year, when determining the annual Required Minimum Distribution, the Initial Divisor will be reduced by one. So the Divisor will be 28.6 in the second year, 27.6 in the third year, 26.6 in the fourth year, and so on until all of the proceeds have been withdrawn.

What is the distribution period if my beneficiary is a Non-Designated Beneficiary?

Since a Non-Designated Beneficiary does not have a life expectancy, the IRS provides a maximum number of years depending upon when you die.

Single Life Expectancy Table (as of 2010)							
Age	Life Expectancy	Age	Life Expectancy	Age	Life Expectancy	Age	Life Expectancy
0	82.4	29	54.3	58	27.0	87	6.7
1	81.6	30	53.3	59	26.1	88	6.3
2	80.6	31	52.4	60	25.2	89	5.9
3	79.7	32	51.4	61	24.4	90	5.5
4	78.7	33	50.4	62	23.5	91	5.2
5	77.7	34	49.4	63	22.7	92	4.9
6	76.7	35	48.5	64	21.8	93	4.6
7	75.8	36	47.5	65	21.0	94	4.3
8	74.8	37	46.5	66	20.2	95	4.1
9	73.8	38	45.6	67	19.4	96	3.8
10	72.8	39	44.6	68	18.6	97	3.6
11	71.8	40	43.6	69	17.8	98	3.4
12	70.8	41	42.7	70	17.0	99	3.1
13	69.9	42	41.7	71	16.3	100	2.9
14	68.9	43	40.7	72	15.5	101	2.7
15	67.9	44	39.8	73	14.8	102	2.5
16	66.9	45	38.8	74	14.1	103	2.3
17	66.0	46	37.9	75	13.4	104	2.1
18	65.0	47	37.0	76	12.7	105	1.9
19	64.0	48	36.0	77	12.1	106	1.7
20	63.0	49	35.1	78	11.4	107	1.5
21	62.1	50	34.2	79	10.8	108	1.4
22	61.1	51	33.3	80	10.2	109	1.2
23	60.1	52	32.3	81	9.7	110	1.1
24	59.1	53	31.4	82	9.1	111+	1.0
25	58.2	54	30.5	83	8.6		
26	57.2	55	29.6	84	8.1		
27	56.2	56	28.7	85	7.6		
28	55.3	57	27.9	86	7.1		

If you die before your Required Beginning Date, your beneficiary must withdraw all plan proceeds by December 31st of the fifth year following your death. There is no minimum amount required each year, provided the whole account is liquidated prior to the fifth year deadline.

If you die after Required Beginning Date, your beneficiary can take withdrawals over your remaining "assumed" life expectancy obtained from the Single Life Expectancy Table. For example, if you are 73 years of age at your death in 2010, then under the IRS table, your assumed life expectancy (for a 73 year old) is 14.8 years. Your Non-Designated Beneficiary will have to take annual Required Minimum Distributions in the same manner as a Designated Beneficiary described in the previous answer, except the Initial Divisor for the first Required Minimum Distribution will be your life expectancy in the year of your death reduced by one (in our example $14.8 - 1 = 13.8$) and then further reduced by one for each subsequent year.

I have named my spouse as the beneficiary of my retirement plans. I have been told that when I die my spouse should immediately roll over my retirement plan to her own IRA. Isn't that correct?

It depends. Generally, your spouse has three options upon your death:

- Taking a lump sum withdrawal;
- Rolling it over to her own IRA; or
- Leaving it in your plan.

Taking a lump sum withdrawal is usually not recommended since federal and state income tax would be due on the whole amount (except for nondeductible contributions and qualified earnings on a Roth IRA or Roth 401(k)).

Rolling it over is usually advised in order to defer income taxes. Once your spouse rolls the plan proceeds to her own IRA she is now treated for all purposes under federal retirement plan laws as the owner. Therefore she immediately benefits from the continued income tax deferral and she does not have to begin taking distributions until she reaches her required beginning date. Since she is now the owner, she can name new beneficiaries who will receive any remaining plan proceeds upon her death. However, if your spouse is under 59½, then any distributions she takes prior to reaching 59½ will be subject to the 10% penalty tax unless an exception applies.

Unknown to many, your spouse has a third option. She can elect to keep the proceeds in your plan. Under this option, she does not have to take distributions from your plan until you would have reached 70½. But more importantly, if she is under 59½ and needs to access the money, any withdrawals <u>are not</u> subject to the 10% penalty tax. Furthermore, if she is younger than you, once you would have reached 70½, she can then rollover any remaining proceeds and therefore continue to postpone distributions until her required beginning date.

Consider the following example:

EXAMPLE: You are 60 when you die and your spouse is 55. Your spouse is the beneficiary of your IRA. If your spouse elects to leave the proceeds in your IRA, she does not have to take any distributions until you would have reached 70½ (over 10 years later). If prior to 59½ she needs to take withdrawals to live on, she can do so without incurring the 10% penalty tax. Once you would have reached your required beginning date, she can then elect to roll over any remaining proceeds to her own IRA and can continue to defer any withdrawals until her required beginning date (five years later).

Three other observations need to be made with regard to this third option:

1. First, the account must remain titled in your name after your death. Normally the account will be titled something like: "John Smith, deceased, IRA, for the benefit of Mary Smith." If the account is titled directly in your spouse's name, then it will be deemed to be a rollover account.

2. Second, your spouse has the option of naming new beneficiaries if she should die prior to her withdrawal of all the IRA proceeds. If she does not name new beneficiaries, then upon her death, the remaining proceeds will be distributed to any contingent beneficiaries that you originally named, and if none, then the default beneficiaries contained in the plan document. Those original contingent

or default beneficiaries might not be the same beneficiaries that she desires.

3. Finally, depending upon her age when she dies, the beneficiaries might have to take distributions over your spouse's remaining life expectancy, rather than their own life expectancy. Therefore, it is normally recommended that she roll over the IRA proceeds at some point prior to her death.

Ideally, after your death, your spouse should have a meeting with her professional advisors (including her estate planning attorney, financial advisor, and accountant) to discuss her goals, objectives, and financial needs in order to make the appropriate decision.

What is a "Rollover" IRA?

In the context of a surviving spouse, a rollover IRA is an IRA that your surviving spouse has inherited from you and rolled over into his or her own IRA or a new IRA in your surviving spouse's name. Once the IRA has been rolled over, your spouse owns the assets of the IRA, has complete control of the assets, and is free to dispose of those assets as he or she sees fit. The surviving spouse is the only person that has that option.

What is an inherited IRA?

An inherited IRA is an IRA that remains in your name after your death for the benefit of your beneficiary. It is the way to allow your beneficiary to take distributions over his or her life expectancy (if a Designated Beneficiary).

The law does not allow a beneficiary (other than your spouse) to roll over your IRA into his or her own IRA. To do so, would be taxable event to the beneficiary. Instead, the beneficiary must keep the IRA title in your name. For example, your name is John Smith and your beneficiary's name is Jane Wilson. After your death, your IRA account should be titled something like: John Smith IRA, deceased, for the benefit of Jane Wilson.

This ability to leave the IRA in a tax deferred environment helps to create the opportunity for a significant amount of wealth to be generated without being subject to income taxation on an annual basis.

Can my revocable living trust be named as a beneficiary of my IRA?

A trust can be named as a beneficiary of your IRA. If the trust does not qualify as a "Designated Beneficiary", then the trust will be required to withdraw the IRA assets over a shorter period of time than if you had named an individual. If you die before your Required Beginning Date, then the withdrawal period is five years. If you die after your Required Beginning Date, then the withdrawal period is based upon your "assumed life expectancy" found in a table published by the IRS.

As a general rule, a living trust is not a natural person (does not have a heartbeat) and therefore does not have a life expectancy. This would normally argue against naming the trust.

However, structured properly, a trust can qualify as a "designated beneficiary," thus making it possible to "look through" the trust and use the life expectancies of the trust beneficiaries for distribution purposes if the following conditions are satisfied:

A. The trust must be valid under applicable state law.

B. The trust must be irrevocable or become irrevocable at the time of your death.

C. All trust beneficiaries must be individuals and must be identifiable from the trust document.

D. Documentation regarding trust beneficiaries, or a copy of the trust document, must be provided to the plan administrator or IRA custodian no later than October 31 of the year following your death.

If your trust has multiple beneficiaries and some are not individuals, then this can disqualify your trust from "Designated Beneficiary" status. Furthermore, if your trust has multiple beneficiaries and all are individuals, then generally all trust beneficiaries must take distributions over the life expectancy of the oldest trust beneficiary.

It may be advantageous to name the living trust as beneficiary of the retirement plan. For example, let's say you want your spouse to be the primary beneficiary of your IRA, and your children from a prior marriage as contingent beneficiaries. At death, your surviving spouse could roll the IRA proceeds to his or her own IRA and meet your objective for the primary beneficiary. However, then he or she could make his or her own beneficiary designation, effectively disinheriting your children. A solution would be to name a trust as the primary beneficiary. Properly designed, it would protect your children from being disinherited by their step-parent.

Naming the trust as a beneficiary gives the estate planner greater flexibility for post-death planning. It can also afford your beneficiaries some protections that they may not be able to provide for themselves. Moreover, it may give you the opportunity to use your federal estate tax exemption when you may not have enough other assets to do so otherwise and thus limit or eliminate potential estate taxes.

Should I change the ownership of my retirement plan to my living trust?

Successful implementation of a living trust requires funding the trust or, in other words, titling one's assets in the name of the living trust. Otherwise, assets not "in" the living trust at the time of death may be subject to probate, in spite of the existence of the living trust.

Retirement plan assets are an important **exception** to this guideline. For example, putting IRA assets in the name of a living trust will trigger income taxes and, if under age 59½, penalties.

Therefore, ownership should not be transferred, but your trust could be named as the beneficiary. You should consult with your professional advisors prior to naming your trust as a beneficiary to discuss the advantages and disadvantages.

What is a "Stretch Out" IRA?

Assuming that your beneficiary is younger than you, the term "stretch out" describes the ability for your beneficiary to withdraw the IRA assets over his or her life expectancy, rather than your remaining hypothetical life expectancy. The beneficiary will still have a Required Minimum Distribution to withdraw each year, but if he or she uses his or her life expectancy rather than your life expectancy, that Required Minimum Distribution will be less each year, allowing the assets in the IRA to continue to grow tax deferred.

COORDINATING MY RETIREMENT PLANS AND MY ESTATE PLAN

What does it mean to coordinate my retirement plans with my estate plan?

Your retirement plan is a financial asset; therefore you need to plan for it just like all of your other assets. Ideally, your estate plan (including your will, living trust, and financial powers of attorney) is designed to deal with all of your financial assets. However, your retirement plan has some unique features that present challenges.

1. Beneficiary Designations. Your retirement plan is a contract. Upon your death, the IRA trustee or qualified plan custodian is contractually obligated to transfer any remaining funds to your named beneficiary, regardless of any contrary desire you state in your will or living trust. For example if the named beneficiary of your IRA is your son, but in your will you leave all your property equally to your son and daughter, your son will receive all of your IRA. Under law, the beneficiary designation trumps your will! To complicate matters, many wills and living trusts state that all death taxes are paid out of the balance of the remaining will or trust property and are not paid by the beneficiary actually receiving the retirement proceeds. Thus in our above example, if federal estate tax was due, both children would equally share in the payment of the death tax on the IRA even though your son received all of the proceeds. Again, probably not what you wanted. Therefore, you must match (coordinate) your beneficiary designations with your will and any living trust.

2. Income Tax Deferral. As discussed earlier in this chapter your beneficiary might be able to have years of continued income tax deferral after your death. It is important that your beneficiary designations be designed to ensure that this can happen.

3. Estate Tax Reduction. If you are married, and you die before your spouse, your will or living trust might create two trusts upon your death. The first trust, known as a Family Trust, will hold an amount of property equal to your federal estate tax exemption amount ($3,500,000 in 2009). The balance of your property (if any) will go

to a Marital Trust. The Family Trust is designed to provide for the needs of your spouse during her lifetime, but exclude the assets of the Family Trust from her taxable estate when she dies. If you need to use your retirement plans to "fill-up" the Family Trust, your beneficiary designations needs to be coordinated to ensure that this can happen.

4. Protective Trusts. Your goal might be protecting your beneficiaries from "outsiders" upon your death. Outsiders could include a beneficiary's spouse or ex-spouse, creditor, or the government if the beneficiary has or incurs a significant health problem. In order to ensure the best protections, your property should be left in trust for your beneficiary. If you name your beneficiary directly as the beneficiary of your retirement plan, then he or she will likely lose those protections. Again, coordination is essential.

Should I name my spouse or my living trust as the beneficiary of my retirement plans?

The quick answer is both, the longer answer is how?

Let's assume that your living trust will be divided into a Family Trust and Marital Trust upon your death as described in the above answer.

If you knew the year of your death, your federal estate tax exemption allowed at your death, and the amount and value of your property when you die, then planning would be easy. Unfortunately it is not, and therefore usually the best estate plan will provide flexibility to deal with these unknowns.

In order to have flexibility after your death, it is usually recommended that you name both primary and contingent beneficiaries on all retirement plans.

Flexibility is provided by the use of a disclaimer. A disclaimer is a legal "no thank you." Under the law, you are never required to accept property that someone leaves you upon his or her death. State law will provide a period of time for you to refuse to accept the property. Normally your refusal has to be in writing, cannot be changed and has to be delivered to the person or entity holding the property. Once you sign a disclaimer, the property then passes as if you had died before the person leaving you the property. For federal gift tax purposes, if you sign the disclaimer within 9 months of the death of the person leaving you the property and you do not accept any benefits of the property within that 9 month period, then you are not deemed to have made a gift.

With a retirement plan, if the primary beneficiary disclaims the right to receive the proceeds, then the contingent beneficiary becomes entitled to the proceeds.

So, the question becomes who do I name as the primary beneficiary and who do I name as the contingent beneficiary. In its most simplistic form you could do either of the following:

Primary Beneficiary: your spouse

Contingent Beneficiary: your living trust

or

Primary Beneficiary: your living trust

Contingent Beneficiary: your spouse

Either way will provide flexibility after your death.

The main tax benefit of your spouse being the recipient of your retirement plans is that she can roll over the proceeds into her own IRA and continue the income tax deferral until she reaches her required beginning date. Upon her death, structured properly, any remaining funds can be stretched out over the life expectancy of her named beneficiaries.

The main tax benefit of your living trust being the recipient of your retirement plans is the ability to allocate the funds to fully maximize the value of the Family Trust for federal estate tax purposes. In addition, if you are concerned that the remaining funds remain in your bloodline or your spouse needs protection from outsiders, then, then your living trust should be the recipient.

Some advantages of naming your spouse as the primary beneficiary are:

- Your spouse is in total control of the decision making process. He or she alone decides ultimately where the proceeds go: spousal rollover, or the living trust, if the spouse disclaims.

- The spousal rollover option is always available.

Some advantages of naming your living trust as the primary beneficiary are:

- Your Trustees are in control of the decision making process. The
  Trustees will decide whether to keep the proceeds (usually to
  fully fund the Family Trust) or disclaim the proceeds in order for
  your spouse to roll over the proceeds. If your spouse is not the
  sole Trustee after your death, then any Cotrustee is able to assist
  and provide guidance to your spouse. Sometimes it is very hard for
  a surviving spouse to make sound financial decisions during the
  grieving process.

- It tends to slow down the decision-making process after your death,
  with a greater likelihood that input can be obtained from all of your
  professional advisors. Once your surviving spouse rolls over the proceeds, the ability to later disclaim the proceeds is lost. Often times,
  the rollover is completed before all the options can be evaluated.

- The ability to fully fund the Family Trust is always available.

- If the Trustee disclaims the proceeds, then your spouse can still retain any limited power of appointment that you have granted her in
  the Family Trust.

You should consult with your professional advisors prior to naming the
primary and contingent beneficiaries of your retirement plans.

RETIREMENT PLANS AND TAXES

I have heard that there are a lot of taxes associated with my retirement plans. Could you please explain?

During your lifetime, distributions from your retirement plans are subject
to ordinary income tax when withdrawn. The only exceptions are your
non-deductible contributions and qualified earnings from Roth IRAs
and Roth 401(k)s. After your death, your beneficiaries will pay ordinary
income tax (except as provided above) when they receive the proceeds.

Upon your death, the remaining value of each retirement plan is
included in your taxable estate for federal death tax purposes. Also most
states that have a state death tax include the value of retirement plans in
your taxable estate.

Finally, if you decide to leave your retirement plan assets directly to one generation of your family (such as your living grandchildren) and bypass an older generation of your family (such as your living children) a federal generation skipping tax could be due. Congress wants to tax property at every generational level. In order to discourage wealthy clients from "skipping" one generation in order to avoid death tax at that generation, the generation skipping tax was created. The generation skipping tax is in addition to the federal estate tax and the tax rate is the same as the highest federal estate tax rate.

How do I coordinate investing and taxes within my individual retirement accounts?

With few exceptions, IRAs can invest in the same types of investments in which your taxable accounts can invest, including stocks, bonds, mutual funds, etc. However, your choice of what you invest in with your IRA may be different than what you invest in with your taxable account because IRA's differ from taxable accounts in their time horizon and their tax treatment.

Time Horizon

Time horizon means when you need your money back from an investment. Investments that are actively traded have a level of volatility risk associated with them. Of course cash, certificates of deposit and non-traded money market funds do not have volatility risk from trading. However, bonds, stocks, mutual funds, etc all trade daily and fluctuate in price from the date of purchase to the date of sale. The longer you can hold an investment the better the chances that you can maximize that investment's return potential and minimize selling the investment at a loss.

Retirement accounts have restrictions on withdrawal. Generally, no withdrawals are allowed without penalty until the owner reaches age 59½. Also, distributions will be required starting after age 70½. Depending on your age, these restrictions may mean that funds held in your IRA have a longer time horizon than the funds held in your taxable accounts. These longer time horizons may suggest that they could be invested in more aggressive or volatile investments.

Tax Considerations

Retirement accounts can grow tax deferred until withdrawal. Consequently, this is a good place for frequently traded securities, or to rebalance your assets without tax consequences. This also means that you should defer withdrawing these funds until required allowing you to earn as much from the deferral of taxes as possible. The price that you pay for this benefit is that all preferentially taxed items lose their preferential tax characteristics in a retirement plan.

For example, long term capital gains and Qualified Dividends are both taxed at maximum rates of 15% (currently through 2010). When these gains occur in an IRA, they are not taxed in the year that they occur or are received like taxable accounts. However, years later when they are withdrawn they are treated as ordinary income and maybe taxed at a maximum federal rate of 35%. The other price that you pay for the benefit of tax deferral of holding investments in your IRA is that your losses are not deductible in the year of the loss and cannot be used to offset gains that you have in your taxable accounts. Instead they just reduce the amount available for withdrawal and hence the amount taxed.

Although it is difficult for even the most seasoned financial planner to determine the proper allocation between a client's taxable accounts and IRA accounts, one approach might look like the chart on the next page.

Taxable Accounts

Investment	Reason
Municipal Bonds[1]	Double tax free and greater liquidity for immediate needs
Growth Stock Portfolio[2]	Higher appreciation potential, lower dividends (ordinary income), capital gains tax treatment on appreciation

IRA

Real Estate Investment Trusts[3]	Generates high amounts of income taxed at ordinary income tax rates

Hedge Fund of Funds[4]	May generate mostly ordinary income
	Many funds may result in late receipt of K-1's adding to complexity of personal income tax return not an issue in an IRA account
Tactical Money Manager	Frequent trading may result in high short term capital gains taxed at ordinary income tax rates

Important considerations concerning the investments above:

1. Municipal bonds are subject to availability and change in price, and are subject to market and interest rate risk if sold prior to maturity. Bond values will decline as interest rates rise. Income may be subject to the alternative minimum tax. While federally tax free, other state and local taxes may apply.

2. Stock investing involves risk including loss of principal.

3. Investing in real estate/REITS involves special risks such as potential illiquidity and may not be suitable for all investors. There is no assurance that the investment objectives of this program will be attained.

4. Fund of hedge funds involves special considerations and risks not associated with investment in traditional mutual funds. Each fund's investment program is speculative and includes risks inherent in an investment in securities as well as specific risks associated with the use of leverage, short sales, options, futures, derivative instruments, investments in "junk bonds," non-U.S. securities, illiquid investments, and limited regulatory oversight. Each fund is a non-diversified fund and invests in Hedge Funds that, from time to time, may invest a substantial portion of the assets managed in an industry sector. Higher fees, potential investor income qualifications, and strategy limitations must be considered in any suitability determination.

RETIREMENT PLANS AND ASSET PROTECTION

Are my retirement plans protected from my creditors?

Yes, but the extent of protection depends upon the type of Retirement Plan, and state and federal laws.

If you file bankruptcy, federal law protects your Qualified Plans, regardless of their size. Federal bankruptcy laws also protect up to $1,000,000 of your IRAs, plus an unlimited amount of your Qualified Plans that have been rolled over to IRAs.

For this reason, it is always recommended that you roll over your Qualified Plan to a new IRA that contains only the rollover amounts. By doing this, you can always keep track of the rollover amounts and their subsequent earnings. Also please keep in mind that *under the federal bankruptcy laws, each state can adopt their own rules with regard to the amount and protection of IRAs.*

In a non-bankruptcy setting, federal retirement plan laws (ERISA) generally protect your Qualified Plans from your creditors. With regard to your IRAs, the laws of the state of your residency will determine the amount of protection.

Therefore, it is always recommended that you first check your state law protection of IRAs before you roll over a Qualified Plan into and IRA.

Does this same protection apply to my beneficiaries?

Generally no. The federal retirement plan laws (ERISA) does not give protection for the beneficiaries of Qualified Plans. Also, to date only one state court has extended the state law protection for the owners of IRAs to their beneficiaries.

Therefore, if you are concerned about protecting your retirement plans from the creditors of your beneficiaries after your death, you should consult your estate planning attorney. Through the uses of trusts, you should be able to provide better protection.

ROTH CONVERSIONS

What is a Roth Conversion?

A Roth conversion is the ability to transform (convert) your existing traditional IRA or qualified plan into a Roth IRA.

Prior to 2010, you could convert only in a given year if your modified adjusted gross income (for federal income tax purposes) was under $100,000. Beginning in 2010, there is no income limit.

There are two ways to convert to a Roth IRA. The first, and usually the preferred method, is the direct method (trustee to trustee transfer). Under this method, you direct the trustee of your plan to directly transfer the funds to the Trustee of your new or existing Roth IRA. You never receive the money. The second method is the rollover method. Under this method, you receive a distribution (check) from your existing plan and roll it over (contribute it) to a new or existing Roth IRA within 60 days.

Do I owe taxes if I convert to a Roth IRA?

Absolutely! In general, the full value of the amount converted will be included in your gross income in the year of conversion. There is an exception for any amounts converted that were originally nondeductible contributions.

What about the 10% penalty if I am under 59½?

If you convert the entire amount withdrawn from your existing plan, then you are not subject to the 10% penalty for withdrawals prior to 59½. If you do not convert the entire amount, then you will be subject to the 10% penalty tax for all amounts withdrawn but not converted.

Can I change my mind?

Yes, within limits. For example, assume that you convert your deductible IRA on March 3, 2010 when the value is $200,000. By December 31, 2010, the Roth IRA is now worth $120,000. If you do nothing, you will report and pay tax on $200,000 of taxable income, even though the Roth IRA is now worth only $120,000!

In order to rectify this situation, the law allows you to undo (un-wind) your Roth conversion. This is called a re-characterization. In essence, the money in the Roth IRA is transferred back to the deductible IRA. The re-characterization must be completed by the due date of your federal income tax return, including extensions. Therefore, you would have until April 15, 2011, or October 15, 2011 (if you file a timely extension).

Once you re-characterize your Roth IRA back to your deductible IRA, you are further prohibited from again converting your deductible IRA (reconversion) until the later of:

The beginning of the year following the year in which the amount was originally converted to the Roth IRA, or

30 days after the day on which you re-characterized (transferred the amount from the Roth IRA back to the deductible IRA).

Thus, if you converted on 3/3/2010 and re-characterized on 11/6/2010, you could not again convert to a Roth IRA (reconversion) until 1/1/2011.

Is there any advantage of converting in 2010?

Possibly. If you convert in 2010, you have the choice, for federal purposes, of reporting the taxable income:

1. all on your 2010 income tax return and paying the tax by 4/15/2011; or

2. ½ on your 2011 income tax return and paying the corresponding tax by 4/15/2012 and ½ on your 2012 income tax return and paying the corresponding tax by 4/15/2013.

The major advantages of reporting the tax in 2011 and 2012 are the deferral of paying the tax and the ability to spread the tax into two tax years. This could result in a lower tax rate than if all of the income was reported in one year. However, some feel that the present administration will raise income taxes over the next few years, especially on the wealthy. If that does happen, it might be better to pay the entire tax in 2010. You should consult with your tax professional prior to making any decision.

You should also consider any state income tax consequences.

Should I convert my deductible IRA or qualified plan?

To answer that question, you must first decide if legally you can convert. Generally you can convert a traditional IRA at any time. However, for a qualified plan, you generally must be retired or have terminated your employment with the company. If you are still employed, then you can convert only if your plan allows for an "in service" withdrawal. You should check with the human resources department of your company.

Once you have determined that you can legally convert, the harder question is should you.

There is no right or wrong answer but will depend upon your individual financial circumstances and goals. Having said that, factors that would lean towards conversion include:

- You have significant losses or loss carryovers that can offset the taxable income from the conversion. This would lower your overall effective income tax rate.

- You will not need to use the funds for your retirement. Once converted, you are not subject to any Required Minimum Distributions during your lifetime. This allows the value of the Roth IRA to increase more rapidly for your beneficiaries.

- You anticipate that your income tax rates will increase in the future and there is a significant time horizon between your conversion and your withdrawal of the funds. The longer the time horizon the more conversion makes sense.

- You have a short life expectancy and your estate will be subject to death taxes. Paying income taxes today will result in a reduction in your taxable estate at your death and can result in overall lower income and death taxes.

- Your retirement plans will be needed to fund your Family Trust (a trust designed to hold an amount of property equal to your federal estate tax exemption amount—see Chapter 4). After your death, Required Minimum Distributions will not result in taxable income and therefore will not be taxed at higher compressed trust income tax rates.

- You have funds outside your retirement plan to pay the income tax. In essence this allows more money to be invested in a tax-free environment.

- Your beneficiaries are in a high income tax bracket. If you do not need to access the retirement funds during your lifetime, then after your death, the proceeds will be income tax free for your beneficiaries.

- Your spouse will be in a higher income tax bracket after your death. After your death, your spouse will likely file as a single individual. The tax rates for married filing jointly are more favorable than single.

You should consult with your tax, financial and legal professionals prior to making any conversion decision. Over the last several years, many software programs have been created that will analyze the financial impact of a conversion based upon certain assumptions. Your planning professionals should have access to those programs. Also, please keep in mind that it is not an all or nothing decision. You can always convert some today and some later.

11 | Asset Protection Planning

Asset protection comes in all shapes and sizes. Once the concern of the very rich, or those with potentially great liabilities; asset protection is now for everyone. Whether it's structuring protection for a nest egg in the event of a financial disaster, or preserving what's left of a small estate for children and grandchildren, asset protection is worthy of consideration.

ASSET PROTECTION IN GENERAL

What is the basic premise of asset protection planning?

The basic premise of asset protection planning is that you are able to choose which jurisdiction controls your property rights. This is often difficult for people to understand, because most people never have the opportunity to choose which set of laws affect any part of their life. For example, we have no choice of who controls the traffic laws that we all must adhere to—that is decided by the municipality that you are driving in, and there is no way to change that.

Similarly, none of us in the U.S. can decide which set of tax rules apply to us—the Internal Revenue Service takes care of that, and there is no way around it. However, wealth usually takes the form of personal property. Securities, for example, whether publicly traded or privately held, are personal property; and personal property is usually governed by the laws of wherever the property is located. That's why the location, or domicile, of the owner of that property is so important. As we will see, some countries allow you to be much more protective of your property than other countries.

What is the goal of Asset Protection Planning?

The goal of Asset Protection Planning is to develop a wealth preservation plan that is effective and that will leave you with peace of mind if disaster strikes. Asset protection strategies are generally not designed to take control of all of your assets, such as your daily living expenses, mortgage payments, or other loan payments. Rather, they are designed to take a certain portion of your wealth and allocate it to structures that would likely frustrate the efforts of future creditors. The goal here is to reassure the client that they have wealth that is beyond the reach of creditors that they can rely on to rebuild in the unlikely event that disaster strikes. It is not designed to shield assets that are needed for short-term or mid-term financial needs.

Other goals of asset protection planning include:

- To take the decision out of the hands of the local judges and juries
- To allow lawsuits to be tried and heard by the jury
- To allow the negotiation of the favorable settlements
- To allow long-term planning
- To avoid having one lawsuit ruin your life and the life of the your family
- To allow discovery of assets but have the assets protected
- To allow the professional to continue to practice.

Why would someone want to shield their assets from creditors?

In today's litigious society, there is virtually no way to anticipate how your assets are exposed to potential creditors. If you own a business or practice a profession (medical, legal, accounting, engineering, or architecture), it is truly impossible to foresee the financial pitfalls that exist. Even though many businesses are operated as corporations or limited liability companies (which traditionally offer protection from business debts), there is a growing trend toward attaching certain business liabilities to the business owner. For example, certain tax obligations can attach to the business owner, as well as liability for sexual harassment lawsuits (even if the unlawful acts were committed by a non-owner employee), and a wide variety of environmental regulations routinely impute liability to the business owner.

Although most business owners are careful and diligent about how they run their company, we simply cannot ignore the wide variety of risks that the owner is exposed to. For that reason alone, it makes sense to learn more about asset protection planning, and decide if any of these strategies are appropriate for you.

Why are professional liabilities so troubling?

A professional (Doctor, Lawyer) is personally liable for professional liabilities. The usual state laws that shield an owner of a company from the liabilities of the company are typically not available.

These liabilities are especially severe as the professional may have conducted himself or herself beyond reproach and if sued in the wrong county with the wrong judge or jury, the professional may be unable to win. Many times the professional will be forced into an unfair settlement due to the danger of submission to a jury.

Why should I be worried about local judges and juries?

The movement of judges and juries toward large awards is a disturbing trend. As the voters elect judges, it is safe to say that the judges are representative of the voters, who elect them. For defendants out of state or out of county, there is a natural leaning toward the local and known party. The legal community has recognized that this exists and this is referred to as "home cooking."

Juries may focus on the injury and wish to compensate the injured party, without strict regard as to the person actually causing the harm. Sometimes bad things happen without fault. Sometimes persons are held liable for being in the wrong place at the wrong time.

It has become increasingly difficult for the juries to be filled with persons with business backgrounds. If a person has the ability to take off three weeks for a trial, that person either does not have a business commitment or that person is independently wealthy. Either way juries have been awarding larger and larger sums.

When is the best time to do this type of planning?

The best time to do this type of planning is when you need it the least. You can't typically buy insurance on your boat while the boat is sinking. By the same token, you can't typically protect your assets after you've been sued or after you've committed an act that is likely to end in a lawsuit. Stated in legal terms, you cannot protect your assets from *current* or from *reasonably anticipated* creditors. There are state laws (Fraudulent Transfer Rules) that address "fraudulent conveyances." A fraudulent conveyance is any convey-ance of an asset designed to hinder, delay, or defraud a creditor. You need to do this type of planning when there are no threats to your wealth—otherwise, the planning is very much at risk, and likely ineffective.

Are there any exceptions to the Fraudulent Transfer Rules?

Generally exceptions to the Fraudulent Transfer Rules under state law are transfers completed in the normal course of business, transfers for full value, transfers which do not create insolvency, and a transfer occur-ring before a known creditor exists.

What is the penalty for violation of the Fraudulent Transfer Rules?

The penalty for a violation of the Fraudulent Transfer Rules is to undo the transfer, and the remedy is against the recipient of the property. This is a situation where legal counsel is a must. As an example, if a doctor has a known claim and transfers a Certificate of Deposit to his wife, and if the creditor is successful in its claim, the creditor can bring suit against the wife and recover the funds.

If I have a known creditor, can I still do asset protection planning?

The existence of a known creditor should not stop asset protection planning. Planning may still occur concerning other unknown future creditors. Generally the planning should except known creditors but planning could continue.

OFFSHORE ASSET PROTECTION

If I Move Assets to an Offshore Trust, am I Hiding Those Assets?

Offshore entities have the reputation of hiding assets. However if a person has a serious creditor, it is reasonably certain that the creditor will have the ability to ask the right questions and discover the existence of an Offshore Trust and the assets in that trust. Therefore, the goal is to create a private trust with assets held by the trust, so that if and when the creditor finds out about the trust, the creditor cannot reach the assets.

Where do the assets actually reside if they are in an asset protected structure?

There is a lot of misunderstanding about where assets in an asset protection planning strategy are actually kept. Some people have misgivings about having to go overseas to find their assets, which are hopefully intact. This is not the case at all, and a reputable advisor would not suggest that you put your assets in a stranger's hands. Maintaining control of your assets is a cornerstone of any of this planning. The assets can still he held in a U.S. financial institution, probably with the same financial advisor you are currently working with. The key is that *ownership* of those assets resides in a foreign country, one with more favorable asset protection laws.

What is the basic structure of an offshore asset protection plan?

Typically, a trust is established for the benefit of the client, along with a limited liability company ("LLC"). The trust's situs (similar to domicile) is in a country with favorable asset protection laws, so that the assets in the trust are governed by that country's laws. A trust needs a trustee, so the trustee must be located in that country. However, the trustee does not have actual possession of the underlying financial assets.

The underlying financial assets are owned by an LLC. The LLC is owned by the trust. The LLC is managed by its Manager, who has control over the LLC assets. Generally, the manager is the client, so the client retains control over the assets. In this manner, we can separate *control* over the assets in the hands of the manager, (the client), from *ownership* in the trustee who is domiciled in a country with favorable asset protection laws. Therefore, the client can continue to manage and invest the assets, but actual ownership of the LLC belongs to the offshore trustee.

What are the key issues involved in asset protection planning?

We believe the most important issues involved are:

1. How much of your assets to protect;

2. Where to protect these assets;

3. How to protect these assets;

4. Steps involved in the process; and

5. Costs for implementing the plan, and any maintenance costs.

These issues and others are discussed in the questions and answers that follow.

How much of my assets should I put into an asset protected structure?

This answer varies, depending on several criteria:

- your net worth,
- your tolerance for working with these planning strategies, and
- the level of risk to which you are likely to be exposed.

Even knowing these things, there is no definitive answer to this question, but there are several guidelines to follow. You need to keep sufficient assets outside of these planning structures to pay your anticipated living expenses for the foreseeable future, at least five (5) years.

For clients with a net worth of approximately $10 million, a 20%–30% allocation is probably reasonable. For higher net worth clients, that percentage may climb to 60% or 70%. It really depends on your particular situation, your goals, and the risks you and your assets face.

Also, keep in mind that this is "nest egg" planning, and is not meant to contain the vast majority of your assets. In other words, if you are wiped out by a malpractice lawsuit (as an example) it would be beneficial to have one or two million dollars protected with which to start over.

What are the advantages of "Nest Egg" planning, where the client protects enough assets to start over in the event of a drastic financial loss?

If you keep a majority of your assets out of the asset-protected vehicle, and by transferring the protected assets before you have financial difficulties, the transfer is unlikely to be characterized as a fraudulent conveyance. If, on the other hand, you transfer all of your assets to a protected vehicle, thereby leaving yourself insolvent, the courts are more likely to find a fraudulent conveyance occurred.

Are there asset protection planning techniques available that do not involve the use of an offshore trust?

There are now some U.S. states that passed laws allowing the establishment of an asset protection trust. Alaska was among the first of those states, quickly followed by Delaware and Nevada. There are at least ten states that allow this kind of domestic asset protection planning. This trend is in response to voter demand for this type of legislation, with the hope that people can protect a portion of their assets without moving ownership of these assets offshore. As often happens, there is some competition among the states for the most aggressive legislation, because, with the trusts attracted to those states, there almost certainly follows more tax revenue.

What are the main differences between domestic and offshore planning?

The primary difference between a trust established in any of the U.S. states versus a trust established in a foreign country is that a federal judge can exercise authority (jurisdiction) over the U.S. trust, but may not be able to exercise authority over a foreign trust. The U.S. has treaties in place with several countries that allow a U.S. judge to make rulings about property located in that country. However, there are also several countries that expressly legislate that judicial systems in other countries will not be recognized. In short, notwithstanding state laws regarding asset protection planning, a federal judge could always overrule that legislature or court order, and the assets which the client thought were protected are no longer protected. These situations are very fact specific, so it is very difficult to predict if or when this would happen, but it remains a huge concern for advisors and clients. Many advisors don't believe the domestic asset protection system has yet been thoroughly tested, and for this reason will not recommend or use a domestic asset protection trust.

Which statutory elements are important to consider in foreign asset protection planning?

Each foreign (offshore) jurisdiction has its own statutes that regulate how it will handle assets under its jurisdiction. There are several elements in asset protection statutes, and each of them impacts how effective planning will be in that specific jurisdiction. Here are some key considerations:

1. Statutory Certainty Regarding Non-Recognition of Foreign Judgments. This would include specific language that judgments from other countries will not be recognized.

2. Statute of Limitations for Challenging Asset Protection Trust. Statute of limitations is the time in which a claim must be brought in order for the court to rule on the claim. The shorter this period is, the more advantageous that country's legislation is from a protection standpoint.

3. Burden of Proving Fraudulent Intent is Always on Creditor. Certain bodies of law require the creditor to prove that assets were moved improperly. This is a very difficult burden to meet, and therefore very effective for planning purposes.

4. "Beyond a Reasonable Doubt" Standard of Proof Required in Establishing Fraudulent Intent. This is the highest standard of proof in the judicial system, and very difficult to meet.

5. Statutory Certainty That the Asset Protection Trust Remains Valid if Fraudulent Transfers Took Place. Even if certain transfers to the trust are later found to be improper, the assets which were transferred properly remain protected.

6. Statutory Presumption Against Fraudulent Intent. Some countries include this presumption in their law, which helps from a protection standpoint.

7. Statutory Certainty That a Settlor Can Be a Beneficiary. This allows the settlor to benefit from the assets in the trust without affecting the asset-protection qualities of the trust.

8. Statutory Certainty That a Settlor Can Retain Some Degree of Control. This allows the settlor to continue to make investment and management choices for the assets in the trust.

9. Statutory Posting of Bond Before Litigation. Some legislation includes a requirement that a litigant must post a bond with the court system before filing a lawsuit. This is very helpful from a protection standpoint.

What are some other qualities that are important in choosing an offshore jurisdiction?

Other qualities to look for in an offshore jurisdiction include:

1. Economic and Political Stability of the Jurisdiction;

2. Costs associated with the Asset Protection Trust;

3. Ease of travel and communication;

4. Availability of banks and investment advisors;

5. Crime rates in the jurisdiction; and

6. Influence of other countries.

What protection is afforded by different jurisdictions?

Offshore Asset Protection Trusts - Comparison of Jurisdictions

Country	1	2	3	4	5	6	7	8	9
	Statutory certainty regarding non-recognition of foreign judgments	SOL for challenging an APT	Burden of proving fraudulent intent is always on creditor	"Beyond reasonable doubt" standard of proof required in establishing fraudulent intent	Statutory certainty that trust remains valid if fraudulent transfers determined to have taken place	Presumption against fraudulent intent if transferor remains solvent following transfers	Statutory certainty that settlor can be a beneficiary	Statutory certainty that settlor can retain some degree of control	Posting of bond required before litigation can commence
Bahamas		X	X		X		X	X	
Belize	X						X	X	
Bermuda		X	X		X				
Cayman		X	X		X				
Cook Islands	X	X	X	X	X	X	X	X	
Cyprus		X	X				X		
Gibraltar		X			X	X			
Labuan	X	X	X	X	X	X	X	X	
Mauritius		X	X	X			X		
Nevis	X	X	X	X	X	X	X	X	X
St. Vincent and the Grenadines	X	X	X	X	X	X	X	X	
Seychelles		X	X	X			X		
Turks & Caicos		X	X			X			

At this time, which country has the most advantageous asset protection legislation?

At this time, many believe the country of Nevis has the best asset protection planning legislation. Nevis is a small island in the eastern Caribbean that has been very aggressive in attracting these types of trusts. Keep in mind that certain countries are always in the process of strengthening their legislation, in an attempt to attract more trust business. Right now, Nevis has the most attractive legislation, but that title is constantly being challenged. Here are some things that make Nevis attractive:

- Nevis is the only jurisdiction with all nine statutory elements listed above.
- It is the only jurisdiction in the Caribbean with a bond requirement.
- Nevis enjoys great political and economic stability and is consistently rated among the world's most stable countries.
- The cost structure for trusts established in Nevis compares favorably with other jurisdictions.

There is no Nevis income tax levied on trust earnings. Keep in mind that for U.S. citizens, income generated in a Nevis trust remains subject to income tax in the U.S.

What other elements make Nevis an attractive choice for asset protection planning?

Nevis enjoys ease of travel and communications. It is 225 miles southeast of Puerto Rico. Thus, it is much closer for U.S. residents than the Cook Islands, another jurisdiction that traditionally favors asset protection trusts, but which is located in the South Pacific. Nevis is on the same time zone as the eastern United States, and trust companies and banks are the major industry in Nevis. At one time, sugar cane was the major industry in Nevis, but today the major businesses there are in the financial services business, and, of course, tourism.

What is the social and political environment in Nevis?

Nevis enjoys a 90%+ literacy rate, has virtually no crime, and has no outside influence of other countries. Nevis belongs to the Federation of St. Kitts and Nevis. However, Nevis enacts its own legislation pertaining to Asset Protection Trusts. The Federation of St. Kitts and Nevis is primarily for civil defense and commerce, but Nevis remains fiercely independent, and has retained control over its own legal and political system.

Is the income earned on an offshore trust subject to U.S. taxation?

Yes, absolutely. Generally, U.S. residents are subject to taxation on their worldwide income. The fact that assets are in a foreign trust that is protected from creditors does not change this. Asset protection trusts are not designed to reduce taxes, and income they earn is taxable, just as it would have been if it were earned in the U.S.

Are there any special tax reporting requirements for assets held in an offshore trust?

Yes, there are additional IRS reporting requirements for assets in an off-shore trust. These additional requirements mandate that the amount of assets in the trust is disclosed, information about the trustee is disclosed, the country where the trustee is domiciled is listed, and a reporting of the income earned on these assets. These additional reporting requirements have increased since the passage of The Patriot Act, and other laws designed to reduce money laundering and other financial crimes.

How effective is offshore asset protection planning?

In short, offshore asset protection is very effective. Done properly, an offshore asset protection trust can frustrate and defeat collection efforts of the most powerful creditors in the U.S., including the Internal Revenue Service. Again, the planning must be done at a time when the client is not under financial duress. Also, this type of planning has been effective in divorce proceedings, as a state court divorce judge has no jurisdiction over a foreign trustee.

Can real estate assets be protected with an offshore asset protection trust?

Generally, the answer is no. Keep in mind that the underlying premise of this type of planning involves moving ownership of property to an offshore trustee that is not bound by U.S. court decisions. While real estate can be owned in an offshore entity, the real property itself is still in the U.S., and real property has long been within the domain of the state court where the property is located. Therefore, we can't completely remove real estate from the jurisdiction of U.S. courts.

What if a Judge demands that I move my assets back to the United States?

When judges want to transfer known assets to a creditor and the judge is told that will not happen, the court may resort to its contempt power. Generally, if a court orders a person to do something, and if the person has the ability to do that something, but does not do what the judge has ordered, the court may cite the person for contempt and place that person in prison, until that something has been done or until that person agrees to follow the judge's instructions.

One defense to this action is the "impossibility of performance" defense. The impossibility of performance defense is that a court cannot order a person to do something the person is unable to do and then punish the nonperformance. If assets are in an offshore trust and the trustee of the trust refuses to obey the order of the person to transfer the funds, the court cannot impose sanctions on the person.

Will I still have to carry professional liability insurance once an asset protection trust is in place?

Generally, yes. It used to be unspeakable for lawyers, doctors, and other professionals to go without professional liability insurance. Things change, however. "Going naked" as the practice is sometimes called, is being discussed and being done by some professionals. This raises an interesting question. If a Professional is judgment proof and carries no medical malpractice insurance, would anyone go to the time and expense to file a lawsuit against this Professional?

Benefits of Professional Liability Insurance   Professional liability insurance should not be dropped without due consideration. With some medical malpractice insurance companies, about 50% of the premium goes to fund defense costs; this will of course vary company by company. The funding of the costs of defense can be extremely valuable for the professional who avoids paying for attorney representation. Also, the insurance company is probably in a better position to know which attorneys are best suited to defend the case. Of course, there is also the benefit of the insurance actually paying the liability.

Defense Strategy   Having professional liability insurance, coupled with offshore asset protection planning, often offers the best defense strategy. A creditor may be satisfied with receiving the insurance policy limits in settlement, especially when it realizes that other assets are protected and out of reach. If there is no insurance policy in place, however, a creditor is much more likely to attempt to reach the protected assets.

OTHER ASSET PROTECTION TECHNIQUES

What other asset protection planning techniques are there?

There are several other techniques available; mostly for the ownership of business assets. As discussed in Chapter 14, corporations, limited liability companies, limited partnerships, and business trusts are effective ways to shield the business owner from personal liability. As a practical matter, business owners are often called upon to personally guarantee certain business obligations, which would negate the benefit of the business entity. Also, as part of a comprehensive estate plan, the use of irrevocable trusts and qualified personal residence trusts can protect certain assets. All of these planning techniques must be coordinated to have maximum effect.

How does borrowing out equity help to protect my assets?

Generally, borrowing the equity out of an asset at risk and placing the funds somewhere inaccessible by a creditor is one of the best asset protection techniques available. A creditor will have little use for an asset with no net value.

For an asset to have no net value, the fair market value of the assets should be less than the liabilities against the asset. This may be accomplished by securing borrowed funds against the asset. For example if a person has a building worth $1 million and secures a note of 1.5 million against that property, the property has no net value for the creditor.

Borrowing out equity is especially useful for real estate. This troublesome asset has a difficult characteristic: real estate cannot be moved. Therefore, it will always be subject to the jurisdiction of the local judges and juries.

A few years back, an arm of the government had received word of continuous drug activity in apartment complexes. Based on a telephone call, this arm of the federal government conducted raids and found illegal drugs in the apartment complexes and commenced to seize the apartment complexes, under valid drug forfeiture laws. The apartment complexes with heavy indebtedness were not seized, as there was no equity. The real travesty of the story is that most of the calls reporting drug activity were from the apartment managers and owners to the police seeking help to rid the apartment complexes of drugs. The lesson of the story is that third party indebtedness will be respected.

So if I want to protect my assets, what is a possible plan of action?

Asset Protection Technique Table The table below lists various types of assets, and possible methods of protection:

Asset to Protect	Possible Method of Protection
Qualified Retirement Plan Funds	Federal Law Protection: No action needed (but no spousal protection)
Individual Retirement Account	Roll to Qualified Plan or Retain and Rely on State Exemption if any
Personal Checking Account	Maintain a Modest Balance
Cash Assets, Marketable Securities	Offshore Partnership and Offshore Trust
Real Estate	Partnership and Off Shore Trust and Indebtedness
Personal Residence	Non-liability spouse ownership, Indebtedness, Tenancy by Entirety
Future Earnings	Deferred Compensation Program
Professional Firms	Owner Agreements

Determine Asset Protection Goals   Identify the most feared creditors and the assets most needing protection. For some, it will be clients, for others the spouse. The plan should address the anticipated risks and use the correct tools, the most common of which are discussed below. The level of asset protection planning should be weighed with the value of the asset to protect and administration tasks being created.

Retirement Funds and IRAs   Fund these assets and rely on Federal and state exemptions. Note that these may not be protected from spousal claims.

Cash and Marketable Securities   If there is cash or marketable securities that would generate income tax on sale, these can be placed in a Partnership held by an Off-Shore Asset Protection Trust without recognition of gain. Preference is given to placing assets in the Partnership to be held by Offshore Trust so that management can be retained with asset protection.

Entity Level Liabilities   Real estate should be conveyed into an entity to protect against liabilities generated from the property. Insurance should be purchased. This is basic entity level asset protection. However this does not address personal liabilities.

Real Estate   Real estate is an asset protection problem. It cannot be removed from the local jurisdiction, and carries many potential liabilities. Possible solutions include: conveying the property into a Partnership which is then owned by an Off Shore Asset Protection Trust; mortgaging the property and the proceeds transferred as cash to the partnership owned by the offshore trust; or pledging the real estate to secure other liabilities.

Personal Residence   The personal residence may be conveyed to the spouse that has fewer potential liabilities. For example, a surgeon may have more potential liabilities than does his wife who does not work outside the home. Alternatively, the personal residence could be encumbered with liabilities so that the net equity fits within any state law exemption. In addition, title may be held as tenancy by the entirety so that the creditor of just one spouse cannot access the property.

Professional Firms   These are usually required by state law to be owned individually. Owner agreements provide protections. The buildings and equipment may be owned outside of the business by an asset protected entity, and leased to the business. Also keep the cash and investments low by distributing to the principals, and placing in asset protection vehicles.

Results of the Plan   Generally the results of the plan are to make the person judgment-proof. Even if a lawsuit produces a judgment of massive proportions, the collection of the judgment is still another matter. If the creditor cannot get to the asset, it does the creditor no good.

12 | Life Insurance

Life insurance can be a critical part of successful planning. Though sometimes overlooked by clients and planners alike, life insurance can play a key role in the success of any estate and financial plan. In this chapter, the authors explore a wide variety of uses for life insurance—some of which you may have never before considered!

COMMON USES FOR LIFE INSURANCE

What are the general purposes for life insurance?

Life insurance is a unique asset used to accomplish any of the following:

1. The creation of an estate where circumstances have kept the estate owner from accumulating sufficient assets to care for his loved ones in the event of a premature death.

2. To protect a business value due to the loss of key employees.

3. For debt reduction. Personal and business loans can be paid off with life insurance proceeds.

4. To equalize inheritance. Most estates are made up of various illiquid assets and the liquidity nature of death benefit proceeds allows for equalization among children.

5. Accelerated death benefit. Terminally ill individuals can receive a portion of their death benefit prior to death on an income tax free basis to pay for medical bills, and other expenses and/or to prevent dying destitute.

6. To pay for death taxes and/or estate settlement costs. These costs can exceed 50% of the fair market value of an estate.

7. Pay off a home mortgage.

8. Fund a business transfer. Many businesses have multiple stockholders. Life insurance proceeds upon the death of one stockholder provide ready cash to finance the transaction.

9. To replace charitable gifts. If large assets are gifted to charity there are fewer dollars that can pass as an inheritance. Life insurance can replace that lost inheritance.

10. To supplement retirement funding. Certain life insurance products can supplement retirement funding by accumulating additional funds for retirement years.

We'll explore several of these uses in more detail in the pages that follow.

Note that all life insurance policies are subject to substantial fees and charges. Death benefit guarantees are subject to the claims paying ability of the issuing life insurance company.

I am in business with a partner. How can we use life insurance to preserve our business in the event that one of us dies?

Business owners with partners can use life insurance to fund buyout obligations. In many cases, businesses made up of multiple owners will want to know that if one of the partners dies, the surviving partners will take over the business.

The cash liquidity of life insurance proceeds provides benefits for the surviving partners in that they do not have to take on their deceased partner's family as joint owners. It also provides benefits for the surviving family in that they have a cash inheritance and don't have to worry about learning the intricacies of a business they may have no interest in running.

The amount of cash needed will vary from business to business and may not be the only vehicle used to fund a buyout. Cash from business reserves can also be used, as can cash contributed by surviving partners. Other strategies include promissory notes or the issuance of preferred, non-voting stock. But in many cases, life insurance is an important part of the solution.

I am in business for myself and am worried that a lawsuit against me or my business could put all of my assets in jeopardy. Is there any asset protection benefit that comes with life insurance ownership?

One little known benefit of life insurance (and annuities in some cases) is that the cash value may be protected from creditors under the laws of many of the states in the U.S. In the event of a bad business decision or lawsuit outcome, some of your cash could be protected. It is beyond the scope of this book to detail the specific states and circumstances where cash value may be protected. But a quick Google search on "life insurance protected in bankruptcy" will yield numerous articles on this issue. For more information on how this might apply in your situation, you should consult with your professional advisor.

What role does life insurance play in an estate plan for a taxable estate?

Many taxable estates do not have sufficient liquidity (cash) to pay estate taxes within nine months after death. Clearly, estate assets could be sold to the detriment of the beneficiaries, and if the market for those assets is strong, this might be a satisfactory solution. On the other hand, if the market is down or if the people charged with selling the assets do not appreciate their true value, a sale could result in devastation of the estate value.

Therefore, life insurance (if structured properly) can provide the estate with immediate liquidity to buy time and flexibility for the executor and heirs to determine the best course of action. Life insurance proceeds guarantee that the assets can be sold in an orderly manner, including holding the assets to a later date if the market is in a slump.

As a side note, the most important part of providing life insurance (estate liquidity) in a plan is to ensure that the insurance proceeds are not themselves subject to estate taxes at your death. This is discussed in more detail on page 222 and in Chapter 6, regarding Irrevocable Life Insurance Trusts.

Can I use life insurance to pay for my final expenses such as burial, funeral, etc.?

Life insurance is often used to pay final expenses. These can include funeral and burial costs, costs of estate administration, legal fees, or outstanding medical bills.

Can I use life insurance to meet my charitable goals?

Another use for life insurance is in charitable giving. This is a little more complex, but might be especially helpful for clients who want to leave something to charity but do not want to substantially impact the inheritance they leave their children.

One plan is to purchase life insurance and leave the death benefit to charity with the rest of the estate going to family members. This has the advantage of allowing you to change your mind over time regarding your choice of charities, and has the most flexibility in terms of future choices. Since you own the policy you can elect to continue it, or you could elect to borrow or withdraw some amount or all of the cash value of the policy to deal with emergencies or other life changes.

If you are willing to give up some flexibility, another common approach is to buy a life insurance policy and give it to charity today, continuing the premium payments by making annual gifts to the charity. This has the advantage of making your current gifts to charity tax deductible, subject to certain adjusted gross income limitations.

However, the disadvantage to giving the policy to charity is the loss of the ability to change beneficiaries if you lose confidence in the charity, or decide you'd rather give it to another. You also lose access to the cash value.

It is also possible to reverse the order of things, especially with larger taxable estates, so that the taxable assets go to charity (with no tax) and the life insurance proceeds go to the children as their inheritance (also with no tax if properly structured.)

Can I use life insurance in combination with a testamentary charitable lead trust?

Another approach to charitable planning, usually involving a larger estate subject to estate tax, combines the use of a charitable lead trust (CLAT) with life insurance held in a life insurance trust (ILIT). In this strategy, you plan to leave the taxable portion of your estate to charity in trust at your death.

The CLAT pays out income every year to the charity for a period of years. At the end of the period of years, whatever is left in the CLAT goes to your heirs, tax free. At the same time, you purchase life insurance in an ILIT to keep the death benefit out of your estate.

When you die, the charitable planning strategy reduces your estate tax to zero, and life insurance replaces the amount of money going to charity that otherwise would have gone to your heirs. For more details on this approach, see Chapter 9 on charitable planning techniques.

How would I use life insurance in combination with a charitable remainder trust?

Life insurance can also be used in combination with a charitable remainder trust (CRT).

In this strategy, you give an asset to the CRT today and you receive payments from the CRT over time. At the end of the trust, the assets remaining in the CRT go to charity.

Life insurance purchased by you during life in an ILIT is used to replace the assets passing to charity through the charitable remainder trust. Again, greater detail can be found in Chapter 9.

I have a family business. Some of my children are involved in the business and others are not. How do I balance the inheritance and compensate the children who work in the business for their sweat equity contribution?

This is common scenario in family businesses, but one that is not always easy to solve. Most business owners want to take care of all their children, and provide for them as equally as possible. But most owners do not want to do so at the expense of the business itself, and often want to recognize those children working in the business for the effort they put forth to continue to increase the value of the business.

If cash flow is a problem (and it often is for business owners), there may have to be a plan that makes all of the heirs partners in the business. While seeming to be a fair and reasonable approach, this strategy usually ends up making *everyone* unhappy.

The heirs who are not in the business would like to see it sold and cash proceeds distributed. The heirs working within the business don't want input from their new partners who know nothing about it. There is also often internal conflict around the issues of executive compensation. The non-business heirs may believe those heirs in the business are paying themselves too much for the work they are doing.

A better alternative is to purchase life insurance on the founder. The beneficiaries of the life insurance death benefit are typically those children or grandchildren who are not in the business, or a trust for their benefit.

This approach frees up the children in the business to do what they think is best for the business without having to worry about having their every decision scrutinized by those heirs not in the business. It tends to satisfy the children not in the business because they have cash in hand and are free to invest or consume it in any way they see fit without having to constantly go "hat in hand" to the business for a payout.

The key to success with this strategy is to carefully think through what is fair (and not just what is equal) and to purchase insurance that will meet the goals of the founder, including the goal of keeping the business running as a healthy and profitable entity well into the future.

Can life insurance be used for wealth creation?

Many clients are in the process of building wealth but it may be years before they realize the fruits of their investments or labors. If such a client dies prematurely, life insurance can be used to create wealth immediately for heirs and loved ones.

Of course the amount of the inheritance can be tailored to the needs and want of a particular person. Where one person might feel comfortable leaving a sum of $100,000, another might want to leave an inheritance in the millions. Generally speaking, either goal can be achieved.

Can life insurance be used to help fund education?

Life insurance can help pay for education in several ways. First, like living expenses, educational expenses could be met from life insurance proceeds in the event of a breadwinner's death prior to fully funding a child's education. As with living expenses, each family will compute the amount of money they need based on their own idea of what constitutes an adequate education. For one family, public schools and universities may make sense. To another, private schools and an Ivy League graduate education may be deemed a necessity. Regardless of the choice, life insurance can help to complete an educational funding plan.

A second way life insurance can help is by allowing families to build up the cash value of a life insurance policy with the idea that the cash will be used to pay for living expenses or educational expenses in the future. The advantage of life insurance over any other investment is the fact that life insurance also provides death benefit protection in the event of an untimely death of the breadwinner prior to full educational funding. Historically, the fixed cash value would grow only 2%–4% per year. From 2000 to 2009, a steady return at that level looked very good due to the market collapse during those years.

How can life insurance help my family in financial emergencies?

At some point, nearly every individual and family runs into a situation where cash is needed. Many of these families will not have saved enough in the early years of employment or family life to be able to meet these emergencies. Cash value built up in a life insurance policy is one way to meet these needs. Loans or withdrawals can be made from the policy to help a family in a time of need.

Loans will reduce the policy's death benefit and cash surrender value and have tax consequences if the policy lapses.

How can life insurance help me when I have twin goals: leaving a good inheritance for my children while also ensuring I have enough to take care of me while I am alive?

This is a difficult situation which presents real life conflicts for many. In spite of the bumper stickers proclaiming that "I am spending my children's inheritance," it is our experience that many clients feel like they should be good stewards of their wealth and should pass an inheritance on to their children and grandchildren.

At the same time, they feel like they have worked hard to build an estate and now want to enjoy what they have built and know that they have enough money to last them for the rest of their lives.

One possible solution to this dilemma can be found with life insurance. Simply purchase a life insurance policy with a death benefit sufficient to meet your inheritance goals. This takes care of the inheritance component thus freeing up the balance of your assets to be used in whatever way you desire, without ever having to worry about whether you are spending your children's inheritance.

How much life insurance do I need?

The amount of life insurance needed will depend on a variety of factors including:

- How the insurance is to be used;
- Whether or not you own a business and your plans for its succession;
- Whether or not you have a taxable estate;
- The liquidity of your assets;
- Your age and current earning capacity;
- And many more.

Your advisory team, using detailed financial modeling and reasonable assumptions, can help you quantify the amounts needed for these various coverage needs. Your life insurance agent or financial planner may have software that helps with these calculations.

TYPES OF INSURANCE

What are the various types of insurance and where should each be used?

Generally speaking there are two types of insurance: term insurance and permanent insurance.

When should I use term insurance?

Term insurance provides a death benefit for a period of time in exchange for a premium payment. The minimum term available is usually one year. It is generally the case that this type of term insurance, often know as annually renewable term, is inexpensive at younger ages and becomes more expensive as the insured gets older.

Annual renewable term was historically used to cover a risk that is limited in duration, and where low cost in the early years is a driving factor in the choice of insurance. Candidates for this type of coverage could include: young people just starting out; entrepreneurs obligated to provide coverage as additional security on a short term bank loan; or business owners with limited current cash flow.

Most term insurance issued is "level premium term" insurance. This product calls for a level, predictable premium payment for a given term of years. Because the premium amount is predictable, this type of term insurance is probably the most popular type issued today. Business owners and households can use the predictability to plan their budgets around the fixed premium.

The disadvantage to using term insurance is that sooner or later the term ends. If insurance is desired after the term, new insurance must be applied for. If health has become an issue in the intervening years, replacement insurance may be either very expensive or in some situations, not available at all. For this reason, many companies created a term insurance product that provided a contractual right to convert to a permanent insurance product, sometimes without any additional medical underwriting or exams.

When looking at term insurance, it is important to talk with your agent about conversion rights, and understand when and under what circumstances it is possible to convert. Most policies have limits in terms of when you can convert without evidence of good health.

So what is permanent insurance and how is it different?

The second major category of insurance is often called "permanent insurance," although not all permanent insurance is permanent in the way most people think of that word.

Historically, permanent insurance meant whole life insurance. This type of insurance really was designed to be permanent. The insurance company calculated the amount of premium you would need to keep the policy in force until age 100.

Basically, the insurance company combined a term insurance product with a savings account. Each year as you built up more and more money in the savings account, the amount of term insurance in the contract decreased until age 100, when the amount in the savings account was designed to be equal to the death benefit. Premiums for whole life insurance tend to be the highest of all types of permanent insurance.

Whole life insurance is used by many as a way to have a death benefit and as a guaranteed cash value that grows tax-free under current law.

Who should buy whole life insurance?

Whole life insurance is great for anyone who needs insurance over his or her lifetime while accumulating cash value over the long term. This can include young families and business owners as well.

In fact, this type of policy is often used in business situations to address a buyout of a co-owner in the event of disability or retirement, because the cash value in the policy over time functions as a sinking fund. The longer the business operates, the greater the value and buyout obligation. This increase can be matched by the increasing cash value in the policy. Of course the death benefit function can also be used in a buyout situation where one of the partners dies.

The disadvantage to whole life is usually the cost relative to the death benefit. Often, young families and young businesses need a large death benefit to cover a calamity. Such a large death benefit in a whole life policy would be more expensive than most young families or business owners could afford. For this reason, a combination of term and whole life is often recommended so that both the need to provide protection for a period of time (term insurance) and the need to have cash savings (whole life) can be met. Because this is a compromise, neither goal can be fully met, but oftentimes you will achieve a satisfactory result.

What other types of permanent insurance are available?

In the 1980s, insurance companies began to use computers to calculate premium and run illustrations for whole life policies. During this process, they began to realize that computers would allow them to do all sorts of complicated mathematical equations that would allow them to design a new type of permanent insurance product. This product is broadly known as universal life insurance.

The new technology effectively allowed insurance company actuaries to break a policy down into its component parts, (death benefit protection, expenses, premium amounts, and investment returns), and then manipulate the various components to arrive at infinite combinations of death benefit and premium.

This ability to manipulate the parts gave the company and the insurance agents the ability to design insurance policies that better fit the unique needs of the insured. Whether the insured was looking for more cash value, a lower premium, or a guaranteed death benefit, all became possible with the new flexibility. This explains why universal life has become one of the main products of choice in today's estate planning market.

I have heard that you can now invest in the stock market inside an insurance policy?

For those with a need for insurance, coupled with a desire for higher investment returns than usually seen in life insurance policies, there exists the variable universal life policy. This type of policy functions like a universal life contract and has lots of flexibility.

One key difference is that the owner of a variable life insurance policy can invest cash value in a vast array of sub-account portfolios, thereby having the possibility of benefiting from increases in the stock market. These gains can outpace the returns normally seen in a life insurance policy, resulting in higher cash value or lower premiums or both.

On the other hand, stock markets do not always go up, as we have seen in these turbulent times. This means that returns could be much lower than those found in a traditional insurance policy. The lower returns could cause the owner to have to pay significantly higher premiums or let the policy lapse, meaning the loss of the death benefit. As in any investment question, the issue comes down to how much investment risk you are willing to take.

230 The Complete Guide to Estate & Financial Planning

Variable insurance guarantees are based on the claims paying ability of the issuer. Withdrawals made may be subject to fees when distributed, and treated as ordinary income. Outstanding policy loans at death, and withdrawals, will reduce the policy death benefits and cash values. The investment returns and principal value of the available sub-account portfolios will fluctuate, so that the value of an investor's unit, when redeemed, may be worth more or less than the ongoing value.

Are there any other insurance product designs which can result in lower premiums today?

Another design to consider is the so called Term/Perm Blend. In this approach, the company combines a permanent policy which pays dividends, with a low-cost term policy.

Each year, as dividends are paid, they are used to buy paid up permanent coverage. At the same time, a little of the term death benefit is surrendered. Assuming a good and constant stream of dividends, the term death benefit should be completely replaced by whole life sometime in the future. This can be a good way to purchase a whole life contract at a price that might be seen as more affordable in the early years.

Of course there is no magic. If dividends are not as high or as consistent as originally thought, the term will become more and more expensive to replace, and the dividends will not be able to purchase as much permanent insurance, leaving the insured with less death benefit or much higher premiums. This of course is the lesson with all insurance. The less premium you pay, the less death benefit you are likely to get.

One other product design which offers lower premium payments for a guaranteed death benefit is called Guaranteed Universal Life (GUL), commonly known as Term to Age 100, 110, or 120. For this or any other insurance product decisions, it's important to seek the counsel of a qualified insurance professional.

CHOOSING AN INSURANCE COMPANY

How do I choose an insurance company?

There are a number of factors that go into picking the right insurance company or companies for your insurance needs. The final decision will depend on what you are trying to accomplish.

Some factors that are commonly used by advisors when consulting with clients about their insurance needs include the following:

1. Ratings

Ratings help in a general way to determine which companies are the strongest financially. Most ratings systems work on an easy-to-understand alphabetical structure similar to the credit markets. So a company that has a triple-A (AAA) rating is likely to be more financially sound than a company with a B rating. These ratings involve the opinions and judgments made by the ratings services.

There are five key ratings services in the market today, including Standard and Poor's, Dun and Bradstreet, Weiss Research, Moody's Investor Services, and A.M. Best. The problem is that these various agencies have different scales with different letter ratings that do not necessarily correspond from one agency to another. In addition, not all insurance companies have ratings from each of the agencies.

In addition, a company called Vital Signs has created a product called Comdex. This places the company on a percentile ranking from 1 to 100. An insurance company with a Comdex score of 90 would place it in the top 10% of all companies in financial strength. This percentile ranking has greatly simplified the understanding of all of the various ratings for the consumer. A Comdex score of at least 75 is desirable.

2. Underwriting

In addition to ratings, another key factor in your decision will be to look at how each insurance company rates you as the insured person. This is important because the better the rating you are assigned, the lower the insurance cost.

Some companies, often those with higher credit ratings, are very selective about who they select to insure. This results in lower claims and higher profit for the company. Other companies specialize in insuring people with health problems; sometimes even with significant health problems. These are companies that are generally charging higher premiums to compensate for the increased risk.

If you are in poor health, your choice of carriers may be limited.

3. Years in Business

How long a company has been in business in some ways speaks to an ability to stay in business. On the other hand, a number of larger companies who had been in business for many years have been struggling with changing markets and the economy in general; and some of that group have merged out of existence or been purchased by other more successful insurance companies.

4. Insurance Pricing

The actual pricing offer you receive for your insurance is also a factor in choosing a company. In larger cases, you will want to make sure that your underwriting file is seen by more than one company so that you will receive competitive bids.

Insurance companies have business cycles and find that at certain points in these cycles they either want or do not want certain types of insurance risks. When they want to take in certain types of risks, they have been known to be more favorable in their underwriting. This results in lower premium pricing than you might see from other companies at a given point in time. As long as the company with the lower premium meets the minimum rating screen that you and your advisor have established, it will make sense to go with the lowest premium possible.

5.   Costs and Internal Rate of Return

A calculation of internal rate of return (available from most companies as part of their illustration) will help you to compare one policy illustration or design with another. Because insurance costs, crediting rates, expenses, and other moving parts in an insurance contract vary from company to company, a way to compare the whole picture is to look at the death benefit at a given point in time relative to the premiums paid to that point in time. A good place to start is to look at the period of time around your life expectancy. If one policy shows that the internal rate of return (IRR) of 8.5% at life expectancy and another is showing an IRR of 6.8%, you will want to explore the policy features that are creating the difference.

6.   History of Paying Dividends or Consistent Crediting Rates

Another important feature to examine is the financial performance of each company under consideration as reflected in the actual performance of their insurance products. This is important because part of what you are evaluating is the ability of the insurance company to earn a return on your money for the cash value component of your life insurance product.

In the end, your choice of company is likely to be driven by a combination of all of these factors, resulting in your choosing a company that has good ratings, offers a product that fits your needs at a price you can afford, from a company that has a good financial track record.

What is "insurable interest?"

This is a question which must be addressed in every insurance application but is not an issue for most people. The question is whether the person applying for and buying the insurance has a legitimate reason to buy insurance.

For those applying for very large insurance policies in an estate planning setting, this is an issue that will often be raised. All states require that there be an insurable interest to prevent people from "gambling" on another's life.

You and your advisors can usually address this issue at the beginning by being very clear with the insurance company about the need and purpose for the insurance as well as the parties who will be involved as owner, beneficiary, and premium payer of the policy.

KEEPING LIFE INSURANCE OUTSIDE THE ESTATE FOR TAX PURPOSES

Is there a way to keep life insurance proceeds out of my estate for estate tax purposes?

For most assets, estate inclusion is based on ownership. If you own the asset at the time of death, it is subject to estate taxes. If you do not own the asset at the time of death, it is not taxable.

By the same token, if life insurance is owned by you at the time of death, the face amount of the death benefit will be included in your taxable estate and subject to estate taxes. There are two other ways life insurance may be included in your taxable estate:

A. **Three year rule:** If you own a policy on your life and gift the policy to another person within three years of your death, the face amount will be included in your taxable estate and subject to estate taxes.

B. Incidents of ownership: If you possess any incidents of ownership at the time of your death (or transfer those incidents of ownership within three years of your death), the face amount will be included in your taxable estate and subject to estate taxes (see Treasury Reg. § 20.2042-1(c)). This refers to the right of the insured or the insured's estate to the economic benefits of the policy.

It includes the power to change the beneficiary, to surrender or cancel the policy, to assign the policy, to revoke an assignment, to pledge the policy for a loan, or to obtain a loan against the policy cash surrender value. Certain reversionary interests in a trust may constitute an incident of ownership.

Hence, to successfully exclude life insurance from your taxable estate, you cannot own the policy nor possess any incidents of ownership in the policy. The best way to accomplish this is to have the policy purchased from inception by someone other than you. The best owner is an Irrevocable Life Insurance Trust (ILIT) discussed in greater detail in Chapter 6.

I already own an insurance policy on my life. Can it be successfully removed from my taxable estate?

Yes. This can be done by gifting the policy to the desired person or to an irrevocable trust. If you die within three years of this transfer, however, the proceeds will still be included in your taxable estate. The three year rule may be avoided if the policy is sold at its fair market value to the desired person or to an irrevocable trust.

Are there any special problems involving community property?

Yes, if you and your spouse are subject to community property law, and an irrevocable trust owns insurance on your life. If, under the terms of the trust, your spouse is a beneficiary, there is a potential trap. The insurance premiums are generally funded by way of gifts from you to the trust. If the gift is made from community property, under state law, your spouse is deemed to have made half the gift, and will have made a transfer with a retained interest.

To successfully remove something from a person's taxable estate, there cannot be any retained benefits. If your spouse makes a gift of cash to the trust, and is also a beneficiary of the trust, some (perhaps as much as one-half) of the trust assets will be includible in her estate at the time of her death. Hence any gifts to the irrevocable trust should be given from the insured's *separate* property.

Can an employer-provided policy be successfully removed from the taxable estate?

Yes. Typically an employee does not own the policy, but does have an "incident of ownership" since he or she has the right to name the beneficiary (see previous discussion of "incidents of ownership"). If the insured employee irrevocably assigns all incidents of ownership in an employer-provided policy to the desired person or to an irrevocable trust, the death benefit will be excluded from the insured's taxable estate. If the insured dies within three years of the assignment, however, the policy proceeds will still be included in the taxable estate.

MISCELLANEOUS QUESTIONS ABOUT LIFE INSURANCE

What is second to die or survivorship life insurance?

"Second to die" life insurance, also known as survivorship life insurance is not really a type of life insurance. Rather it is a standard life insurance policy in all respects except one. It insures two people instead of one and pays only after the second of the two dies.

This type of policy design is typically used in estate planning and most often involves insuring a husband and a wife. The insurance works nicely in that most estate plans contemplate no estate tax until the death of both spouses, and most spouses don't plan to benefit other family members until they are both gone.

The real reason most people look at survivorship insurance is cost. All else being equal, it is more cost effective to insure two lives rather than one. This is because there is a great likelihood that premiums will be paid for a much longer time in a survivorship case than with a single life policy. Actuaries tell us that the joint life expectancy of two individuals currently age 65 is almost 22.8 years while the life expectancy of one 65 year old is only 17.7 years. The insurance companies are able to spread out payments over a longer period of time thereby lowering premiums.

Second to die life insurance can also be useful in cases where one spouse is healthy but the other is not. In such cases, the insurance company will focus on the healthy spouse in making its underwriting and pricing decisions. It can also be used in cases involving insured people who are not husband and wife. For example, such plans have been used to insure siblings or business partners.

Second to die insurance coverage is available in whole life, guaranteed universal life, universal life, variable universal life, and blended products.

I don't have a lot of cash for life insurance, is there a way for me to finance the purchase?

Over the last five or six years, insurance agents and their clients have tried to find various ways to borrow money to buy life insurance. In the early years, the focus was on clients who needed insurance for liquidity and estate tax payment, but did not currently have the cash for the premium payment. Enter premium financing.

Under this structure, a client would borrow money (either individually or in a trust) and use the borrowed funds to buy life insurance. The idea was that when the client became more liquid, usually through the sale of an asset like a business or real estate, the loan would be paid off, and the client would take over the premium payments from their own cash flow.

In its simpler, earlier form, premium finance has significant merits. It deals with a real insurance need and allows a client to bridge a period of time when they are simply not able to pay premiums due to illiquidity constraints.

As happens to many good ideas, this one was ultimately perverted resulting in a concept described as stranger-owned life insurance (STOLI). In this scenario, a client would essentially pledge their life expectancy to others in exchange for a cash payment today. All of the life insurance was purchased with borrowed funds and the loan was to be repaid by selling the insurance in a life settlement, and using the proceeds to pay off the loan. Most insurance companies now consider this to be a violation of the "insurable interest" rule mentioned earlier.

At its heart, premium finance is still alive and well, though much harder to execute because of the restrictions and policies set in place by the insurance companies.

I have been told that I need an exit strategy with my premium finance.

In this context, an exit strategy simply means a plan to repay the loan. And such a plan is critical to the successful use of premium finance.

In many cases, the exit strategy will be that assets will be sold at some point in the future and the cash from the sale will be used to repay the loan.

Another common exit strategy involves use of a grantor retained annuity trust (GRAT), which could have the benefit of removing significant assets from your taxable estate while allowing you to accomplish your exit strategy from the premium finance.

As in many estate planning strategies, the goal in this one is to remove rapidly appreciating assets with the GRAT to make sure that there will be enough left over at the end of the day to pay off the premium loan amount.

Over the past number of years, the stock market's ever-rising performance meant that the use of a GRAT as an exit strategy was successful. The recent economic crisis and its aftermath, however, have caused many to rethink entering a premium finance plan and others to have difficulty exiting as planned.

On the other hand, current loan interest rates are very attractive. If investment returns tick up in the near future, premium finance will likely be more attractive than ever.

I am more worried about long term care than I am about savings or death benefit. Is life insurance at all useful to me in the long term care arena?

One of the key issues facing clients today involves funding for long term care. Of course, long term care insurance is a possible way to deal with this as is paying for care out of your own assets. Another lesser known way to pay for long term care can be found in riders to certain life insurance contracts that provide benefits for long term care.

In such policy riders, the company agrees to pay some of the death benefit in advance if an insured needs long term care. The specifics of each policy vary from company to company and the benefits change as insurance companies discover what works and what does not. But for families who need life insurance and want to protect their nest eggs against long term care expenses, this might be a good option.

Of course long term care expenses are just another form of living expense and the cash value build up in some permanent life insurance contracts could also be used to pay long term care costs, even without the long term care rider.

Because in each case, benefits (or cash) are being paid out in advance of the death of the insured, the advancement for long term care costs will have an impact on the death benefit ultimately received by your heirs. In some cases, the death benefit may be entirely gone. In others the death benefit may be greatly reduced.

It is important to think through the possible outcomes with a skilled life insurance professional prior to making decisions that could cause the loss or reduction of the policy's death benefit.

Riders are additional guarantee options that are available to a life insurance contract holder. While some riders are part of an existing contract, many others may carry additional fees, charges, and restrictions, and the policy holder should review their contract carefully before purchasing. Guarantees are based on the claims paying ability of the issuing insurance company.

I thought my life insurance policy was paid up. Why are my premiums reappearing?

Many consumers misunderstand or misuse the terminology "paid up" as it applies to a life insurance policy. A policy is paid up only if no more premiums are required on a contractually guaranteed basis. That is not the same as a vanishing premium or premium offset. In both of these circumstances, the absence of ongoing out-of-pocket premiums is dependent on future interest rates and/or dividend scales being maintained at the current level on an ongoing basis.

The generally declining interest rate environment we have been in over the past two decades has caused life insurance to fail to perform as initially illustrated. The "vanishing premiums" were dependent on ongoing interest rates being sustained at the initial level. Interest rates declined, resulting in either longer premium payment periods or the reappearance of premiums that had previously been able to be stopped.

Can my life insurance policy "crash?"

If you purchased a policy other than Term or Fully Guaranteed Whole Life within the last 25 years, your policy has the potential to lapse, even if you have made all your premium payments. Most universal life, variable universal life, and other whole life variants were created with premiums based upon performance projections that have not been achieved. This means at some point these policies will require large amounts of additional funding to keep them in force. Warning signs include declining cash values and current policy illustrations at the guaranteed rate showing cash values going to $0 within the next several years.

If you haven't had your policy reviewed by your advisor recently, have them do so. Make sure they obtain a current set of in-force projections that includes one at the guaranteed rate. You may also consider having an objective third party advisor who specializes in life insurance analysis, perform the review.

What is a modified endowment contract?

Life insurance policies issued on or after June 21, 1988, can be tainted or defined as a "modified endowment contract" (MEC), if the cumulative premiums paid during the first seven years (the "seven pay test"), at anytime exceed the total of the net level premiums for the same period.

If a life insurance contract is tainted or defined as a modified endowment contract, any withdrawals taken from the contract will be taxed at current income tax rates until all of the policy earnings have been taxed. There is also a 10% penalty tax if the owner is under the age of 59½. The exception to this taxation is in the case of disability or any annuity installment payment.

In most cases, you will want a premium structure that avoids MEC status. On the other hand, there are times when MEC status will have no practical impact, such as when access to cash value is not a critical factor. An example would be when the policy is being purchased for the sole purpose of providing a death benefit, as is the case in many estate planning situations.

The key is to work with qualified professionals to design a premium payment schedule that fits your needs and goals while avoiding MEC status if possible.

13 | Medicaid and Long Term Care Planning

As the Baby Boomer generation continues to age, senior citizens are facing unique challenges in preserving their estates. Two specific concerns are avoiding a complete "spend down" of the estate for the expenses of a prolonged final illness or long term confinement in a nursing home. These concerns are magnified for smaller estates that can least afford the financial depletion. If you're concerned that you won't have anything left to leave to your loved ones, this chapter may be of interest.

What are some considerations when purchasing a long term care policy?

There are many advantages to purchasing a long term care policy, especially before age 50. These policies are used to cover the costs of your eventual disability and long term care. Some important features to consider include:

- This type of policy, properly designed, shifts the risk from you to the insurance company.
- It should be valid for your lifetime if you qualify health-wise.
- It should pay 100% of the benefits for care at home as well as care in an institution.
- It should include an inflation rider if you are under age 75.
- If a lifetime policy is not going to be used, the value of the other riders becomes questionable.
- One "rule of thumb" that has been used by some advisors is that if the annual premium for a policy with these features is less than

15% of the projected income from retirement assets, it is probably worthwhile.

- This is an estate planning matter, more than a pure insurance decision.

Some of these features will add to the cost of the policy, so that has to be weighed when choosing your specific features. Your advisor can provide counsel in this regard. By having a long term care policy, you can protect the estate for your heirs.

I hear a lot about "Medicaid planning." — What is that all about?

Medicaid planning is a concept that encompasses a number of different techniques that are designed to help preserve your assets in the event you or your spouse require long-term care as a result of a serious medical condition. Many people who have significant health problems require round-the-clock assistance. *Medicare* provides only *limited* coverage for those persons who primarily require "custodial" assistance for "activities of daily living" such as bathing, toileting, cooking, and transferring in and out of bed. The costs for such custodial care—which in a nursing home setting can be up to $15,000 per month in some parts of the United States—are generally your responsibility.

Some people will have the foresight to purchase *long-term care insurance* as mentioned in the previous question, to cover most if not all these costs. But the vast majority of Americans do not purchase long-term care insurance, leaving only two primary sources to cover the long-term care expenses: personal assets or the Medicaid program.

Medicaid is designed as a "safety net" to provide health care coverage for the poor. It is technically a type of "welfare" benefit. Under current law, a person can qualify for Medicaid coverage for long-term care costs only after their assets (excluding a primary residence) have been reduced to a very low amount—in some states as little as $2,000, up to a maximum in other states of $13,800. Most people who have significant long-term care requirements end up "spending down" virtually all of their assets until they achieve Medicaid eligibility.

We have worked and sacrificed our whole lives to preserve our assets. Is there any way to qualify for Medicaid without having to spend down most of our assets?

Yes. Under current law, there are a number of planning techniques available to help you protect at least a portion of your assets and to qualify for Medicaid for long-term care coverage. There are really two types of planning: *proactive* planning that is designed and implemented well in advance of any long-term health care needs; and *crisis* planning that is put in place at the time you require long-term care. In almost every circumstance, engaging in proactive planning will preserve more of your assets.

How can proactive Medicaid planning protect my assets?

In general terms, you must be mostly impoverished to be eligible for Medicaid benefits. One way to become impoverished is to spend all of your assets for that long term medical care. All "countable" assets will have to be "spent down."

Another way to become impoverished is to give all your assets away to the people who would eventually inherit them, before they are all spent on those medical costs.

The only problem is that if you give away those assets within five years of entering the long term care facility, you will still have to pay the equivalent value of those assets for your care, before you can take advantage of the Medicaid program.

Proactive Medicaid planning techniques are based on a fundamental concept: effectively transferring your assets in a manner that will "trigger" the start of the current five-year "look back" period so that when and if you need long term care, the transferred assets will no longer be part of your "countable" assets subject to a Medicaid "spend down." The good news is that available planning techniques will allow you to transfer assets in a manner that will still provide you with significant access and control.

To help protect your assets in the event of a potential long-term health care crisis, you might consider including as part of your overall estate plan, an irrevocable trust that, for the sake of this discussion, we'll call a "Medicaid asset protection trust" (MAPT). A MAPT is a particular type of *irrevocable* trust, used because *revocable* trusts are not effective asset protection vehicles. As discussed in earlier chapters, since the Trustmaker of a revocable trust has access to the assets, under Medicaid rules the assets are deemed "available" to the Trustmaker and must be "spent down" before the Trustmaker becomes eligible for Medicaid coverage.

However, assets that are transferred to a properly structured MAPT will be deemed transferred as of the date the assets are titled in the name of the MAPT. This transfer will "start the clock running" on the five-year Medicaid "look back" period.

How does a "Medicaid asset protection trust" (MAPT) work?

Typically, the Trustmaker will reserve rights to all income earned by the trust-owned assets during the Trustmaker's lifetime, and the lifetime of his or her spouse, if applicable. The Trustmaker and his or her spouse will also retain the right to reside in any residence transferred to the MAPT. The MAPT must explicitly prohibit the Trustmaker and spouse from having any distributions of trust *principal*.

It is because of this prohibition that the principal is deemed irrevocably transferred at the time of funding. However, your children, grandchildren, or other family or friends can be beneficiaries of the trust principal, and they can always make gifts to you or for your benefit should you ever have a need that cannot be met by your income alone, or assets retained by you outside the MAPT.

A significant advantage of the MAPT over outright gifts to children is that the Trustmaker retains the right to all the income from the trust. Not only do most people establishing MAPTs want to keep the income for their lifestyle needs, an additional benefit is that the Trustmakers often will be in a lower income tax bracket than their children. For clients who have no intention to use the principal but need the income, this feature has great appeal.

Also, the trust structure allows the client to make what is in effect a gift "with strings attached." The Trustmaker can retain the power to replace the Trustees (who may be the Trustmaker but are often one or more children), and can even retain the power to change the ultimate beneficiaries of the trust (i.e., the parent can disinherit a child and give their share to a grandchild, another child, etc.).

You can also transfer a primary residence to a "grantor" MAPT. This ensures that as long as you have lived in the residence at least two out of the five years prior to a sale, and if the residence is sold during your lifetime, you will be entitled to the capital gains tax exemption for homeowners (up to $250,000 of gain for individuals, and $500,000 of gain for married couples under current law).

In addition, in many states you will retain the right to all property tax exemptions usually available only to individual owners, even though the residence has been transferred to the MAPT.

What if I don't create a MAPT and someday need long-term care?

When a person applies for nursing home Medicaid coverage, under current law all "uncompensated transfers" (i.e., gifts) made by a Medicaid applicant to a person other than a spouse during the five-year "look back" period prior to the Medicaid application date will create a period of Medicaid ineligibility known as the "Medicaid Penalty Period."

The length of the Medicaid Penalty Period will be based upon (1) the total amount of the uncompensated transfers during the look back period, and (2) a figure known as the "Regional Rate." The Regional Rate is the amount deemed to be the average monthly cost of a stay in a nursing home in your particular region. Some states have a single Regional Rate, while others have multiple regions throughout that state with different Regional Rates.

Here's an example of how a Medicaid Penalty Period would be calculated:

Assume that in recent years your health begins to decline. As of June 2009 you have total assets of $220,000. You live in an area with a Regional Rate of $5,000 per month. Based on the advice of your friend Marge from the coffee shop, in June 2009 you made a gift of $200,000 to your daughter. Assume that in June 2010 you can no longer live at home and you enter a local nursing home. By that time you have $10,000 of total assets remaining in your name, thereby falling below your state's permitted Medicaid asset threshold of $13,800. You apply for Medicaid to cover the monthly nursing home costs.

Will you then be Medicaid eligible? Yes, but not until after expiration of the Medicaid Penalty Period, which will be **40 months**. This Penalty Period is determined by dividing the total amount of gifts you made during the 5-year look-back period ($200,000) by your Regional Rate ($5,000), which equals a 40-month Penalty Period.

But, you say, I wouldn't have the $200,000 needed to cover the private cost of nursing home care during the Penalty Period. How will my care be paid for? In theory, the funds to cover the nursing home cost during the Medicaid Penalty Period would come from the children or other persons who received the gifts. In imposing a Medicaid Penalty Period, the government hopes to discourage family gifts during a "crisis" period, thereby requiring your own funds, rather than Medicaid money, be used to pay for your long-term care.

Prominent among the various planning techniques devised by elder law and estate planning attorneys to help preserve assets in a "crisis planning" situation is the "promissory note" strategy. With this planning technique, the prospective Medicaid applicant will make gifts of some of their assets to children or other family members, with the remaining assets being loaned to the same persons. The repayment obligation for the loaned proceeds is memorialized in a promissory note. The "promissory note" technique is attractive because the federal law governing Medicaid transfers—the Deficit Reduction Act (or "DRA")—sets forth specific "safe harbor" guidelines.

Here's how the promissory note technique might be used: a widow needing nursing home care has total assets (all liquid) of $220,000. $13,800 of her assets are "exempt," leaving her with $206,200 in non-exempt assets. Her elder law attorney recommends that she purchase a pre-need funeral trust for $6,200, leaving $200,000 of excess resources.

The attorney will advise the Medicaid applicant to make a gift of approximately one-half of her assets, or $100,000, to children or other designated recipients. The amount of the gift will determine the length of the Medicaid "penalty period" for which the client will remain on a private pay basis. If the Regional Rate is $5,000 per month, a $100,000 total gift will create a 20-month private pay period. The applicant will be advised to immediately lend the remaining half of her assets to the beneficiaries, leaving the applicant with only her $13,800 of exempt assets.

The loan is memorialized by a promissory note that must be irrevocable, non-assignable, cannot be canceled upon death, and must be paid out in equal installments over a period no longer than the lender's actuarial life expectancy. A reasonable rate of interest must be charged; many attorneys will typically use a rate of interest roughly equivalent to the "applicable federal rate," or "AFR."

Upon completion of these transactions, the client will be "otherwise eligible" for Medicaid, and will submit a Medicaid application. Submission of a valid application will trigger the commencement of the Medicaid Penalty Period. The promissory note payments, combined with the client's other income, are used to cover the cost of the nursing home care during the Medicaid Penalty Period. After the promissory note is fully paid at the end of the 20-months private pay period, the client would be eligible to receive Medicaid benefits.

In some states promissory notes are not readily accepted by the state Medicaid agencies, notwithstanding the guidelines provided under the DRA. As an alternative to a promissory note, an immediate annuity can be purchased that will pay to the Medicaid applicant a stream of income sufficient to cover the nursing home obligation during the Medicaid Penalty Period.

Why is the well spouse at risk without long term care insurance?

If a person has long term care needs and is uninsured they will typically still get the care they need. They will either be able to pay for that care or will spend down their assets and be able to qualify for Medicaid. What often goes overlooked is the dilemma of the well spouse. Not only does the well spouse often have the difficult task of caring for the disabled spouse, but also they are often left with very little at the end of their spouse's lifetime. You should take into consideration when you are looking at insuring this risk the potential plight of the well spouse. They can spend their life and all their assets caring for their ill spouse. When that spouse passes away the well spouse may still be left with many years of health and no assets with which to enjoy them.

14 | Business Planning

The wealthiest people in America are not primarily those who have inherited great wealth or those that head the country's largest corporations—although many of these are quite wealthy. Rather, the wealthiest (including prominent names like Warren Buffett and Bill Gates) gained their wealth through building their own businesses. For most business owners, the business is their primary asset. If you own a business, it's critical that you and your advisors design a comprehensive plan; from the starting point of choosing the type of business entity, to the eventual exit strategy and plan for business succession.

TYPES OF BUSINESS ENTITIES

What are the most common forms of business?

The most common forms of businesses include: sole proprietorship, general partnership, limited partnership, corporations (which may be either Subchapter S or Subchapter C corporations), and limited liability companies.

What is a sole proprietorship?

When someone starts a business, they are a sole proprietor. For example, if Mary works as a nurse for a hospital, she is an employee; however if she comes home after work and helps her elderly neighbor with his medications, and that elderly neighbor pays her for her help, she now has her own business. If she does not incorporate, or form some other formal business entity, she has a sole proprietorship.

What is a corporation?

A corporation is an artificial person or legal entity created in compliance with state law. It may be owned by one or more shareholders who themselves may be natural persons or a legal entity. The law regards a corporation as having a personality and existence distinct from that of its owners or shareholders. A corporation can acquire, hold, and convey property; sue and be sued in its own name; and generally do all things in a legal sense that a natural person may do.

The shareholders' rights are determined by the corporation's charter and the applicable state laws. While the shareholders are the owners of the corporation, that fact by itself does not make them agents for the corporation. Unless shareholders are officers, directors, or controlling shareholders in certain situations involving a duty of loyalty to the corporation, they do not owe a fiduciary duty to the corporation.

As a creature of state law, a corporation cannot do business in states other than the one that created it without first qualifying to do business in that state by complying with that state's laws.

A corporation is subject to greater governmental regulation, and the statutory formalities respecting the formation and operation of corporations must be strictly observed. For a small business these may be nuisance factors that must be considered in determining the appropriate form of business organization.

I have heard about an "S corporation," what does that mean and what is the difference?

An S corporation is an entity formed as a corporation under applicable state law for which an election is filed with the Internal Revenue Service to be taxed as an "S" corporation. The "S" refers to a sub-chapter in the voluminous tax code, but is often thought of as the "small business" corporation.

This election with the IRS results in the corporation being treated as a pass-through entity for federal income tax purposes. That allows the taxable income, gains, losses and expenses of your company to "pass through" to your individual tax return. You, and not the corporation, are personally liable for the taxes due, if any. You may also claim losses as deductions personally, rather than at the corporate level.

In general, the drawback of S corporations is the maze of complexity that shareholders and their advisors must consider in formation and operation. There are many restrictions for an S corporation that do not apply to other pass-through entities. These restrictions include the following:

- Only a domestic corporation may file an S corporation election.
- An S corporation cannot have more than 100 shareholders.
- Generally, only natural persons can be shareholders. Certain other organizations can also be shareholders, such as the following: the deceased shareholder's estate; a bankrupt shareholder's estate; specified trusts, including qualified subchapter S trusts, and electing small-business trusts; and specified tax-exempt organizations.
- An S corporation cannot have a nonresident alien as a shareholder.
- An S corporation cannot have more than one class of stock.
- Certain businesses are prohibited from operating as S corporations.
- S corporation status can be terminated inadvertently.

There are also restrictions on the capital structure of an S corporation. Although it can have a subsidiary, it must be a "qualified subchapter S subsidiary," generally defined as a 100% owned corporation that is not otherwise ineligible to be an S corporation. Where the applicable election is made effective, the subsidiary is not treated as a separate corporation.

Certain trusts may own stock in S corporations, such as testamentary trusts, which can hold the stock for up to two years, grantor trusts, if treated as 100% owned by one individual who is a U.S. citizen, and qualified subchapter S trusts. Further, electing small-business trusts may hold stock in S corporations.

What is a C Corporation?

Unlike an S Corporation, the net income of a Subchapter C Corporation ("C Corporation") is taxed at the corporate level first before being taxed at the individual level. Many large companies are Subchapter C corporations. You may have unlimited shareholders; and a variety of types of people and entities may own stock in a C Corp.

What is a Limited Liability Company?

A Limited Liability Company (LLC) is a non-corporate business entity created per state statute. Structured properly, it provides personal asset protection for the business owner while still allowing the pass-through advantages of an S Corporation. Unlike an S Corporation, it does not generally have limits on numbers or types of members. (In a LLC, the owners are called members, whereas in corporations, they are called shareholders.) The LLC may have less cumbersome filing and reporting requirements, but that varies from state to state.

What is a Partnership?

A partnership is when two or more people conduct a business venture that is not established as a corporation or LLC.

What is the difference between a General Partnership and a Limited Partnership?

A General Partnership exists anytime one or more person runs a business. No formal filings are required with the state and all partners are joint and severally liable for any business activities. In addition, the income and expenses of the partnership pass through to the individual partners.

A Limited Partnership is a creature of state statute, meaning you must file formal papers with the state in order to have this type of partnership. It does require more than one person, but unlike the general partnership, you can limit your liability as a partner to your contribution to the partnership. It is also a pass through entity.

Limited Partnerships consist of two types of partners: limited partners and general partners. The limited partners have limited control and say in the partnership operations, but also have liability that is limited to their contribution. The general partners have control over the management of the company, but they also have unlimited liability.

TAX TREATMENT OF BUSINESS ENTITIES

How do you file a tax return if you are a sole proprietor?

A sole proprietor generally files his company taxes on Schedule C of his regular 1040 tax return.

How will my newly formed LLC be treated for tax purposes by the IRS?

A domestic LLC with only one member is disregarded as an entity separate from its owner and must include all of its income and expenses on the owner's tax return. Also by default, a domestic LLC with two or more members is treated as a partnership. A domestic LLC may file Form 8832 to avoid either default classification.

How is a corporation taxed?

S Corporation income and losses pass through to the shareholders and are recorded as part of their individual 1040 tax return.

A C corporation, however, is subject to separate tax procedures and rates by the federal and state taxing authorities. A corporation is taxed separately on its own income. This causes some advantages and some disadvantages, all of which must be considered carefully.

Corporate taxation may result in "double taxation." Income received by the corporation is taxed at the corporate level according to the corporate tax rates then in effect. The profit remaining after taxes is then available to be distributed to the owners or shareholders as dividends, which are taxed again as personal income to the shareholder. This double taxation is recognized as a distinct disadvantage of the corporate form, as compared with other forms of business enterprise.

Larger corporations with many shareholders simply accept the disadvantage, but in smaller, closely held corporations, double taxation can be minimized. One way to minimize the effect of double taxation is to pay the shareholders a reasonable salary. Whenever shareholders are officers or employees of the corporation, and this is frequently the case in smaller organizations, they may be paid reasonable salaries that are deductible as a corporate expense, and thereby reducing or eliminating the amount distributed as a dividend.

BUSINESS ENTITIES AND ASSET PROTECTION

What types of entities provide the best asset protection?

If you think of asset protection as a continuum flowing from left to right, with the left end of the continuum providing no asset protection and the right side providing the greatest asset protection, then sole proprietorship and general partnership would be on the far left.

The owner, in a sole proprietorship, and the partners, in a general partnership are all personally liable for acts of their businesses. In a general partnership, you are not only liable for your own acts, but are also responsible for the acts of your other partners, even if you were not aware they were doing something wrong.

In the middle of our asset protection line, we would place corporations. Corporations do provide limited liability protection, meaning you will not lose your personal assets to a corporate liability and you are generally not personally responsible for corporate debts. Following the proper procedures however is the key. Corporations typically require formal filing requirements; proper notice of meetings to all shareholders; annual meetings; annual minutes; election of officers, etc.

If you fail to meet these requirements, a creditor may be able to invalidate your corporation by "piercing the corporate veil." This means if they can prove you did not act like a corporation by meeting formal requirements, they can go after your personal assets. In addition, if you are sued for a personal liability, such as you causing an accident outside of company business, you can lose both your personal assets and your corporate assets.

Furthermore, the judge in a lawsuit can award your stock to a creditor. If you own all or a majority of the stock, this would allow the creditor to liquidate your company, as well as all of your personal assets. Corporations do provide good asset protection, but they are not the best entities.

On the right side of our asset protection line would be properly structured LLCs and Limited Partnerships. Established in the right jurisdictions, these entities can be structured in a way where they provide the best asset protection for families and/or individuals domestically. This strong asset protection is created by state statutes that allow a creditor to collect personally from a partner or member only through a charging order.

What is a charging order?

A charging order is a legal remedy available under certain state statutes for creditors of limited partnerships and LLCs. If a member or partner has an outside liability, which simply means he causes liability with a non-business asset (such as a car accident while not working or a slip and fall at his home), the court has no ability to force the LLC or LP to liquidate its interests and pay the creditor.

In traditional lawsuits against an S or C corporation or general partnerships and sole proprietors, a court can have the creditor "step into the shoes" of the owner and force a liquidation of company assets. With a charging order, all the creditor can do is wait for a partner or member to take a distribution from the entity, at which time they can collect against that member or partner. The problem for creditors is they do not typically want this remedy. It can create a "phantom income" problem for them.

What is phantom income and why is it a problem for creditors?

For income tax purposes, many LPs and LLCs are considered a "pass through" entity. This means that the company is not taxed on its income, but all taxable income (or loss) "passes through" and is taxed to the underlying owners. Each owner must include his, her or its share of the company's taxable income and losses on the owner's income tax return, regardless of whether or not the owner actually received any distributions from the company. For example, assume that you own 25% of an LLC. The LLC has total taxable income of $100,000 for the year. You must report on your individual income tax return your share of the taxable income ($100,000 × 25% = $25,000). You must report the income even if the company made no distribution of cash or other property to you during the taxable year. This is known as phantom income.

When a creditor has a charging order, it "steps into the shoes" of the owner. Depending upon state law and the nature of the charging order, a creditor may be considered the owner for income tax purposes. Not all tax accountants and attorneys agree that this is a problem, but it is a grey area most creditors want to avoid.

Are certain jurisdictions better for asset protection, and if so, which ones?

Yes, certain states have intentionally written their laws to be a safe haven for business owners and for people wishing to protect their personal assets. Other states have written their laws to create the least amount of tax to the business owner. Some of these states include Wyoming, South

Dakota, Nevada, Delaware, Texas, Florida, and Oklahoma. Other states may also be favorable. It is best to discuss the various jurisdictions with a qualified attorney prior to creating your entity.

If I do not live in these jurisdictions, can I still form my business in these states?

Yes, you can form businesses in states in which you do not reside and operate these businesses normally. You will likely need to hire a local company or attorney to act as your registered agent to satisfy state law, but that is generally a minimal expense. Discuss the process with a qualified business planning attorney.

Are there reasons for using business entities for estate planning?

Yes, business entities can be used for estate planning for a variety of reasons. Some of these reasons include:

- Keeping the business in the family;
- Efficient gifting to the other family members;
- Protecting family interests from a possible divorce;
- Consolidation of family assets;
- Restrictions on transfer of business interests to non-family members;
- Privacy of family matters;
- Reduction in value of the family assets for estate tax purposes;
- Protection of family assets from creditors, etc.

BUSINESS SUCCESSION AND BUY/SELL AGREEMENTS

What is a buy/sell agreement?

A buy/sell agreement is an agreement among owners of a company regarding issues such as the sale of the business in the event of the death, disability or divorce of an owner, and the proper value of the business if one owner wishes to sell their interest in the company to another.

My business partner and I each own 50% of the stock in our small business. My attorney and CPA tell us that we need a buy/sell agreement. Why is that so important?

Quite simply, a "buy/sell" agreement is essential to the long-term viability of a business that will eventually see its owners go through a critical life event such as disability or death.

Imagine this common scenario: in 1962 high school friends Herman and Calvin started their plumbing supply business, "H & C Plumbing Supply, Inc.," with the modest goal of providing a nice life for their growing families. Through hard work and good business sense, in 2010 H & C Plumbing Supply—which now employs 40 people, including one of Herman's sons, Alan, and one of Calvin's daughters, Susan—has a fair market value of $10 million.

But Herman and Calvin's success comes with strings attached. Like owners of most successful closely-held businesses, the value of their business interests is by far their largest asset. Since the asset is illiquid, a premature death for either Herman or Calvin might prove disastrous.

For example, the deceased owner's estate will need to pay what might be a substantial federal and state estate tax—in cash—within **nine months** of the owner's death. If there is insufficient cash to pay the tax, either the estate will need to sell the deceased owner's interest in the business at a "fire sale" price, or pay the tax late with substantial penalties and interest.

Tax issues aside, without planning, an owner's unexpected death may create a situation where the remaining owner is now a business partner with the deceased owner's surviving spouse, who typically has had little to no involvement in the business.

To ensure the preservation of the equity of their business as well as their legacy, business owners must plan ahead for the inevitable day when they will "leave" the business—whether the departure is made vertically (during lifetime) or horizontally (after death)!

All closely-held businesses should have a formal plan to ensure the preservation of the business upon an owner's death. The buy/sell agreement is a planning tool used to provide a "road map" that will address various contingencies such as the death, disability, or retirement of an owner, and those circumstances (if any) when an owner can sell their interests in the business to a third party.

Herman and Calvin need to take time from their busy schedules and sit down with their attorney, accountant, financial advisor, and insurance professional to devise a strategy to address the various life events that are part of any successful buy/sell agreement.

A fundamental component of any buy/sell agreement is a mechanism to provide for the disposition of an owner's business interest upon death. A common scenario would be for Herman and Calvin to purchase life insurance on each other's life in a **cross-purchase** arrangement, with a death benefit equal to at least the value of each owner's interest in the business. Since closely held businesses are often difficult to value, Herman and Calvin are well-advised to use a business valuation specialist to determine H & C Plumbing Supply's actual value so that the appropriate amount of insurance can be purchased.

In a cross-purchase agreement, each owner is contractually obligated to purchase from the deceased owner's estate (or trust, if applicable) the deceased owner's interest in the business. Assume in our example that Herman dies first. Upon Herman's death, the business would need to be valued to determine the value of Herman's interest in the business at the time of his death. Calvin would use the life insurance proceeds from the policy he owns on Herman's life to purchase Herman's interest in the company from Herman's widow, Wilma. If the life insurance is insufficient to pay the full amount of Herman's interest in the company, the agreement should provide a mechanism—typically in the form of installment payments for a set term of years at a set rate of interest memorialized by a promissory note and secured by Herman's stock—to pay to Wilma the balance of the purchase price.

To help prevent a scenario where too much of the purchase price must be paid for via installment payments, it is critical that the owners' determine their company's value periodically and, if feasible, increase the amount of life insurance on each other's lives.

In businesses with three or more owners, it may be unwieldy to use a cross-purchase arrangement, as each owner would need to own a policy insuring the life of each other owner. An alternative to the cross-purchase arrangement is a **redemption agreement** in which the business entity (i.e., the corporation, LLC, etc.) is the owner of the insurance policies insuring the lives of each owner.

Upon the death of an owner, the entity uses the life insurance on the deceased owner's life to purchase from his or her estate the deceased owner's business interest. For example, assume H & C Plumbing Supply has a third shareholder, Rocky, with each shareholder owning one-third of the company stock. Upon Herman's death, H & C Plumbing Supply would purchase Herman's stock from his estate. Calvin and Rocky will now each own 50% of the remaining issued and outstanding stock in H & C Plumbing Supply.

A third alternative is the **hybrid**, or **"wait and see"** arrangement. In a hybrid buy/sell agreement, the corporation has the first "option" to purchase a deceased shareholder's stock. If the corporation does not exercise the option, then the remaining owners will have the option to purchase the deceased owner's stock. If the individual shareholders do not exercise the option, then the corporation will typically be required to purchase the stock.

The hybrid agreement has gained greater usage over the past few years, as it affords greater flexibility to address the different tax impact of a corporation's purchase of an owner's stock as opposed to a purchase by the individual shareholders. Regardless of the structure used for the agreement, competent tax assistance is a must to ensure the best results.

Is a buy/sell agreement needed for any reason other than the death of an owner?

While it is critical that a buy/sell agreement provide for the successful transfer of a business owner's interest in the business after his or her death, it is equally important that the agreement take into account other critical life events such as disability, retirement, and sales of business interests to third parties.

An unexpected disability can be as serious a problem as death for a business owner. Most business owners work long hours, and if a closely held business were to lose the services of one of its key players for any significant period of time, the business's operations could be severely hampered.

The owners of a closely-held company should ensure that disability coverage is in place covering each of the owners. Such insurance might provide, at a minimum that income "lost" because of the absence of an owner due to disability is available to the business to cover overhead.

The company's buy/sell agreement can provide that the non-disabled owners would have the option to purchase the interest of a permanently disabled owner, and disability insurance can be obtained to help fund the purchase of those interests. Even if disability insurance has not been obtained, the cash value of any life insurance on the life of the disabled owner may be used to fund the buy-out. None of these options are possible, however, unless the buy/sell agreement has been drafted to include specific disability buy-out provisions.

It is also critical that in drafting the agreement the business owners address the common situation where an owner retires or otherwise leaves the business. Many "boilerplate" agreements incorporate a loosely based definition of "retirement" that essentially allows a business owner to walk away at any time, and requires the remaining owner or owners to immediately purchase the departed owner's interest. Not only might the remaining owners have to come out of pocket with significant amounts of cash—or be burdened with large promissory note payments if the agreement provides for installment payments—but they must do so at a time when the business has lost the services of a key person. Properly counseled, very few business owners would opt for such a result.

One solution might be to permit a "retirement" only if an owner reaches certain milestones (for example, attaining the age of 62 with a minimum of 20 years service). The buy/sell agreement might specify that an owner who departs the business prior to the stated retirement milestones might have no ability to sell his interests to the other owners or to any third parties. Or, the agreement could specify that the remaining owners have the option to buy out the departing owner, but are not obligated to do so if the economics do not make sense.

Language can be included that provides that an owner who leaves prior to the "permitted" retirement date would not share in the appreciation of the business if it is sold to a third party at some future date, and might in fact be required to take less than the fair market value of their interest (valued as of the date of their departure) if the business's value subsequently declines. This mechanism is designed to protect the remaining owners if the value of the business suffers as a result of the lost services and good will attributable to the departed owner.

Another important consideration in buy/sell planning is determining when, if at all, that an owner can sell his interest to someone other than another current owner. Owners in most closely-held businesses wish to restrict any sales to third parties except if the remaining owners unanimously agree to such a sale. While such restrictions impair the liquidity of an owner's interest, they also ensure that all owners will be "partners" only with those persons with whom they are comfortable working.

The buy/sell agreement might also include provisions for "tag along" and "drag along" rights. "Tag along" rights protect minority owners in circumstances were the majority owners contract to sell the majority interests to any third party. A tag along provision might provide that the majority owners can sell their interests only to third parties if minority owners are afforded the same sale rights and at the same sale price per share. Under a "drag along" provision, if the requisite percentage of ownership interests required under the buy/sell agreement vote to sell the entire company or its stock to a third party, then owners of the minority interests would be obligated to participate in the sale.

Buy/sell planning presents many unique challenges and opportunities. Successful planning requires that business owners commit the requisite time and resources necessary to engage in thorough discussions with their professional advisors. A well-designed buy/sell agreement can ensure that the business will survive beyond the current ownership group. But if a business has a poorly designed agreement—or like too many businesses, no agreement at all—then that business's long-term survival will be questionable at best.

How often should a buy/sell agreement be updated?

These agreements should be discussed annually in the company's annual meetings and updated as circumstances dictate. Some buy/sell agreements have a valuation clause which will automatically set a new business value each year based on net income, etc.

How do you establish a purchase price for a business under a Buy/Sell Agreement?

The simplest way to establish a price is to have all parties agree upon a value in writing that is equal to its true fair market value (an arm's length transaction). In the past, some agreements have used book value based on the company's financial statements. This is typically the "bare bones value" and most likely will not be accepted by the IRS for Federal Estate Tax purposes.

Another method is a formula approach which factors in net profits, goodwill (in some cases), and capitalization rates. In recent court cases, independent qualified business appraisers have used the formula approach. The IRS has the right to challenge any business value used for buyout purposes. However, the more "arm's length" the transaction appears with the formula approach, the greater the chance of successfully defending the value.

KEEPING THE BUSINESS IN THE FAMILY

How do I ensure my business stays in the family?

A buy/sell agreement is the best way to ensure the business goes to your family, along with a source to fund the transfer of the business to them. Normally, the company carries enough insurance to allow the company to either buy out non-family members or provide the company money to allow the kids to buy in.

My business is my most significant asset. Since only one of my children works in the family business, how do I protect his interests while providing an equal inheritance to my other children?

"Fairly" dealing with family business assets can be difficult for owners of closely-held businesses. When only one child or less than all the children works in the family business, careful planning is required.

In most cases the business owner wants to ensure that the business interests—typically corporate stock or membership interests in a limited liability company—will pass via a will or a trust to the child or children actively involved in the business. Some transfers may be accomplished during the parents' lifetimes, while in other cases the parents will prefer to pass the interests only upon their deaths.

There are many questions when planning a disposition of a closely-held business to family members. First, are the members of the family currently employed in the business capable or interested in continuing the business at the owner's death? Is the surviving spouse working in the business? If not, how will she draw income from the business if not employed? If there is no family heir capable or interested in the business, will the non-family employees decide to move elsewhere? If the business had to be liquidated, what value would it bring? Without the owner behind the business, will customers transfer their business to a competitor? What value might the IRS put on the business for estate tax purposes? And, as in this example, if some family members work in the business and others do not, how do you treat all family members fairly at the owner's death?

If you intend that the inheritances are in fact equal, it is imperative to obtain a qualified valuation to determine what your business is in fact really worth. Only then can you determine whether you have enough "other" assets that will permit you to leave the business assets to the "active" children, with some or all of the remaining assets to the "non-active" children.

In cases where the value of the business is significantly greater than the non-business assets, life insurance may be the great equalizer. If you are insurable, you can obtain sufficient life insurance (preferably owned in an *Irrevocable Life Insurance Trust*) that will leave the death benefit to the non-active children, with the business assets of equivalent value to pass to the active children.

But what if you're uninsurable or you cannot afford enough insurance to equalize the value of the business and non-business assets? In such cases, you might consider including in your business operating documents (e.g., a corporate shareholders' agreement or LLC operating agreement) a provision that affords the active children the right to buy out the interests of the non-active children in the business for that portion of the business value that exceeds the value of any life insurance or non-business assets.

For example, assume that you have two children, one who is active in the business and one who is not. Assume your business is worth $2 million, and you have $1 million in other assets. You might leave your non-active child the $1 million in non-business assets, and the active child $1.5 million worth of the company stock. Your estate planning documents can provide that the active child would have the right to buy out his sister's share in the company for $500,000. If there's life insurance available, those proceeds would be used to fund the buyout. If insurance is unavailable or insufficient, then you might stipulate that the buyout would be made in installment payments memorialized by a promissory note, typically secured by business assets, or by the stock or membership interests being purchased.

Keep in mind that any lifetime gifts of business interests will be subject to the annual gift exemption ($13,000 in 2010), with any gifts in excess of the annual exemption being subject to a $1 million life-time exemption. Also be aware that if your total estate value might exceed the applicable federal and state estate exemptions in effect at the year of your death, the active child or children might be obligated to pay a significant estate tax attributed to illiquid business assets, which tax is due nine months after the date of your death. If there are insufficient liquid assets available to pay the estate taxes, your children might be left in a real bind. Life insurance might again prove invaluable in providing the liquidity necessary to pay the estate taxes without the need for a "fire sale" of less liquid assets such as business interests and real estate.

BUYING OR SELLING YOUR BUSINESS

What is involved in selling or purchasing a business?

The sale or purchase of a business incorporates a myriad of business, legal and accounting issues. When a business owner decides to put his or her business up for sale, he or she must decide upon a sale price. In most cases the business owner has only a vague idea of the value of the business, and will need expert guidance in determining an appropriate price.

For mid-to-large size businesses, an investment banking firm might be retained to determine an appropriate sales price and to find potential buyers. For smaller businesses (typically those worth less than ten million dollars), business brokers are often used to value and market the business. The primary difference between an investment bank and a business broker is that the former will be staffed with specialists having expertise in accounting, valuation and industry research, while business brokers would not typically have that depth of service. Also, investment banks will confidentially market the business directly to potential qualified buyers, while marketing by a business broker tends to be done through public sources such as in trade journals, newspapers and the internet.

Once a buyer has been found, each party will need to retain attorneys, accountants and possibly other professional advisors to assist with the transaction. The purchaser will need to conduct a "due diligence review" to ensure that he has all the relevant information needed to validate the purchase price for the business. The due diligence review will encompass such issues as:

- A market analysis of the ongoing demand for the business's products or service

- An evaluation of the capabilities of the existing employees, and whether additional employees will be required

- A review of the suitability of existing equipment and facilities

- A detailed review of the company's books (to be performed by an experienced accountant) to ensure that the purchase price is fair and reasonable

- A legal review that will include items such as (i) analysis of the company's organization documents such as bylaws, operating agreements, shareholder agreements, stock records and partnership agreements; (ii) review of the company's contracts and leases with third parties; (iii) a search of county and state records for liens, judgments and other public records affecting the company and its current owners; (iv) a review of any trademarks or copyrights being transferred; (v) analysis of any employment contracts and union agreements; and (vi) a review of the company's retirement plans to ensure adequate funding and record management.

Sometimes the purchaser will begin his due diligence review after the parties have executed a "letter of intent." In other circumstances the seller will insist that a contract of sale be executed before permitting the purchaser and his advisors access to company records. In either case, the parties and their representatives should sign a confidentiality and non-disclosure agreement protecting the seller's confidential information.

A significant issue is whether the sale will be structured as an "asset sale," or the sale of the company's ownership interests (for example, the shares of stock of a corporation or the membership interests of a limited liability company). In most cases the purchaser will prefer to purchase the company's assets rather than the seller's ownership interest. If the purchaser acquires the ownership interests, then he will be acquiring not only the company's actual assets, but will also be purchasing the company's liabilities. Also with a sale of the ownership interests, the purchaser will forfeit potentially favorable income tax advantages achieved through allocation of the purchase price among various asset types.

Whether signed before or after the due diligence review is completed, the contract of sale will include a number of standard provisions. These would include:

- the purchase price, including the amount of the down payment;
- whether the purchaser will be purchasing only business assets, or the seller's ownership interests;
- the amount to be financed, including the terms of any seller financing and collateral to be used as security;
- the allocation of purchase price among the various asset classes (i.e., real estate, machinery, goodwill, leasehold, covenant not to compete, inventory);
- the extent to which the purchaser will assume the seller's liabilities;
- representations and warranties for both seller and purchaser;
- the closing date;
- a list of assets to be conveyed;
- a statement of any existing or pending litigation for either party;
- any conditions to closing, such as governmental or bank approvals;
- seller's agreement to indemnify the purchaser against any unassumed liabilities.

After the contract is signed, the purchaser will need to complete any remaining due diligence items. If the purchaser is acquiring real estate as part of the deal, he will need to have a title search performed to ensure he is acquiring clear title. If bank financing is being used to finance part of the purchase price, the bank will go through its own due diligence procedure. Once all pre-closing items are completed, the closing will take place. If the full purchase price is being paid at closing, (either from the purchaser's own funds or through commercial financing), the seller will receive the full sale proceeds. More commonly, the seller will be taking back a note for a portion of the sale price.

At closing, the seller's attorney will prepare various documents that may include (1) bills of sale, (2) deeds (if real estate is involved), (3) assignments of equipment leases, (4) one or more promissory notes, (5) mortgages and security agreements, (6) employment agreements, (7) resolutions authorizing the sale of assets by the company, (8) equipment lists, (9) covenants not to compete, (10) assignments of phone numbers, websites, copyrights, trademarks and other intellectual property, (11) resignations of officers, (12) sales tax returns, (13) escrow agreements, (14) personal guarantees and (15) motor vehicle registrations.

If the seller is providing financing, after the closing the security agreement and UCC financing statements will be filed with the appropriate governing bodies to properly secure seller's interest in the business assets and any other collateral used to secure the purchaser's obligation to pay on the promissory note. These filings will ensure that the seller has "first position" to reclaim any of the collateral in the event that the purchaser defaults in any payments under the promissory note(s).

15 | Legacy Planning

A new trend in estate and financial planning has been growing over the past few years. It goes by many names, but is generally described as legacy planning. Legacy planning recognizes that you are much more than just your financial statement and a list of assets. More and more advisors are coming to the conclusion that comprehensive planning includes helping you pass on not only your wealth (financial assets), but also your wisdom (non-financial assets). That would include such things as your family values, life lessons, family stories, or your views on subjects as diverse as philanthropy, politics, or spiritual matters.

What exactly is legacy planning?

We are seeing a shift in Estate Planning, where clients are realizing that much more can be done with Estate Planning than simply passing on money and wealth. It is possible to create a Legacy.

Legacy Planning incorporates planning to pass on your core values and beliefs. Your core values include your fundamental beliefs about life, family, community, and the things you value that give life meaning. These core values translate into hopes and dreams you share for your loved ones and their future. Legacy Planning brings the "human element" to your estate plan.

In so doing, you are able to guide them with your wisdom, help them to understand more fully your beliefs, and set in motion your hopes and dreams for their future. It allows you to create an estate plan that uses your personal wealth as a means of accomplishing those long-term goals which define you. Through your estate plan, you can define yourself as a person and not just as a source of wealth.

You ensure that family traditions are carried on from one generation to the next. You can make your hopes and dreams for your loved ones become a reality, such as by providing opportunity for education to future generations. Your estate plan could also provide that the Trustee will match, dollar for dollar in tuition, any scholarship earned by a beneficiary in his or her chosen field of study.

You can stimulate hope and inspire dreams by encouraging entrepreneurship and a strong work ethic. You can strengthen family bonds and harmony by providing distributions that encourage family togetherness, such as regular family vacations. You can assist your child or grandchild to get a start in life by paying for their wedding and assisting them in purchasing their first home.

Perhaps your estate plan will inspire hard work by the beneficiary in his or her career, by providing distributions to match the beneficiary's annual income after a certain level has been attained. Or, you can provide distributions to a beneficiary who chooses to take up work in an occupation that has social value, even though the job may not pay very well in order to encourage social awareness.

If you have charitable goals, you can encourage your loved ones to further these goals and causes by creating a Charitable Foundation. A Charitable Foundation would allow your children to participate in making contributions to charities supporting your philanthropic goals. This would help encourage philanthropic awareness and behavior in your children.

In addition to motivating behavior, Legacy Planning can also discourage or prohibit unwanted behavior. For example, your trust could provide the Trustee is authorized to cut off distributions to a beneficiary who is on drugs or alcohol or has a gambling addiction. Such a provision could provide the Trustee is authorized to make distributions to pay for a rehabilitative program to treat the behavioral problem or addiction and, upon satisfactory rehabilitation, distributions would again continue for the benefit of the beneficiary. The Trustee may also be given the power to require future drug tests to assure the beneficiary has not had a relapse.

The opportunities to plan for your legacy are endless and limited only by your imagination, values, and ability to dream.

How do I pass my wisdom along with my wealth?

There are several options available to those who wish to pass their wisdom to succeeding generations.

The obvious first choice is through face-to-face personal contact on a daily basis. But often the pressures of daily life intrude, and the passing of wisdom never occurs.

A second method is to provide a written record. This can be done in a formal or informal manner. Simple notes, made as important ideas come to mind, can be collected in a special place, the location of which family members are notified in your estate planning documents. Sometimes people choose to write what is sometimes called an "ethical will," which is a letter expressing the writer's values, memories, experiences, and hopes and aspirations for the recipient of the letter.

On a more formal level, your estate plan can include instructions, distribution guidelines, and stories that reflect your core values and beliefs. For example, you may wish to include a Family Vision Statement or Philosophy with your estate plan. A Family Vision Statement can serve as a "blueprint" for living that reflects your core values and beliefs.

The Family Vision Statement can be used to craft provisions in the living trust that create incentives and guidelines to carry out your core values and beliefs. For example, if you value education, you can provide for distributions to be made to beneficiaries who graduate from college or maintain a minimum grade point average. Distributions may also be made if a beneficiary participates in community service or charity work in furtherance of your favorite causes and beliefs. By combining the Family Vision Statement with the living trust distribution guidelines, your beneficiaries are better able to understand your values and beliefs and work toward achieving your goals.

It may be relatively easy for individuals to decide how to allocate items of property, but some might find it difficult to express the things that mean the most to them in terms of values. To facilitate this, some advisors use the technique of allowing clients to express their values by encouraging the telling of stories which illustrate those values, rather than trying to define them. Some advisors use a series of questions designed to help the individual organize their thoughts, which they then record using a small digital recorder. This not only allows the advisor to better prepare the individual's plan, but also provides a permanent record of the conversation for future generations.

Is it really possible to put non-financial instructions in legal documents?

Yes, but it's important to remember that putting something into a legal document does not necessarily make it enforceable. If something is not enforceable by law or in incorrect form, a court will generally simply ignore it. Given that, there are certain non-financial instructions which are valid in legal documents, such as naming a guardian for a minor child. And it is possible that a court may rely on non-financial instructions to clarify the meaning of ambiguous language in otherwise enforceable portions of the document.

Perhaps the greatest advantage of including non-enforceable language in a legal document is that it confers a sense of importance upon the provisions. Even if the court will not enforce the provisions, those to whom the instructions are given will likely tend to give them more weight because of their inclusion in the document.

How can I discourage my child or grandchild from depending too much on his inheritance?

Your trust can provide that distributions will be made to your child on the condition that your child remains gainfully employed or, if unemployed, that your child is demonstrating steady progress toward becoming gainfully employed. You can also establish guidelines in your trust that provide that trust funds are to be used for funding non-luxury items, such as a used but safe car for transportation, and only if the beneficiary is able to pay for the ongoing maintenance and insurance of the car.

You can also carve out conservative distribution guidelines that allow the Trustee to make distributions solely based on demonstrated need. When combined with incentive provisions that allow the Trustee to pay for expenses that enhance a beneficiary's career, such as funding further education, a child's dependency over trust funds can be controlled.

How can a Family Mission Statement benefit my legacy planning?

Drafting a family mission statement can help affluent families articulate their core values and launch a discussion on the all-important topics of lifestyle, financial independence needs, inheritance and business succession. This can be a precursor to legacy planning.

Mission statements have been around a long time and have been used successfully by forward-looking companies that want to clarify their mission, vision, goals and objectives and to rally their board of director's management team and employee work force to their corporate purpose.

A mission statement can help affluent families address a host of questions about the importance of money or themselves, their families and their communities.

A well-crafted mission statement offers a clean cut basis for pondering the kinds of services and financial products and instruments, techniques, and tools their family will need as well as a benchmark against which these services and products can be measured.

Family mission statements can look quite different based upon each family's uniqueness. Some families prefer extremely short mission statements—one word, a sentence, a short paragraph supported by a more detailed operational strategic plan. Others prefer a more detailed family mission statement of one to five pages that includes the family values, heritage, goals, objectives, stewardship, family investment policy, established guidelines for charitable distributions and a system for family governance, etc.

What are the guidelines for developing a Family Mission Statement?

- Mission statements should be timeless.

- The best mission statements deal with both ends and means.

- Every member of the family should participate. Even if your children are younger, you can still start using this "family constitution" method. Just keep the mission simple and full of pictures.

- You do not invent your family mission. You detect it. You uncover it. Each family possesses special gifts, unique qualities and characteristics.

A family mission statement is an expression of strongly held beliefs that provide common purpose to all members of a family. It provides both the framework for familial cooperation and a standard for judging the growth and solidarity of the family.

What is a Family Council?

A family council is comprised of family members who come together as an organized group to address and manage an issue or a collection of issues.

The family council structure helps a family develop a system of family governance that includes a 100 year vision for the family, a code of conduct among members, a method for management and resolution of disputes and clarity of roles as heirs, trustee, beneficiary, and others.

It provides ongoing education regarding family assets and wealth preservation. It develops an inventory of the human intellectual capital of the family members. It makes each heir aware that the family wants him or her to utilize his or her full potential. It develops a process involving the entire family to have heirs achieve their own dreams and to learn to develop ways to protect growing children from the pitfalls of affluence.

The family council usually meets twice a year for a day or two with meetings held in a retreat setting and with an agenda that requires the work of the council along with family recreational activities.

What are some of the activities of a family council?

Some of the activities of a Family Council include:

- Communication workshops;
- Role definition;
- Identification of multiple roles each person may have;
- Responsibilities of beneficiaries;
- Responsibilities of trustees;
- Identification of individual uniqueness, giftedness and passions;
- Educational workshops on wealth management;
- Education funding;

- Tax law changes, etc.;
- Philanthropy;
- Family Foundation;
- The development of the human intellectual and financial balance sheets for all family members.

16 | After-Death Plan Administration

There is a common misconception that estate planning is an event or a transaction, while it is actually a process. Another common misconception is that once a plan is in place, there is nothing left to do—that somehow the plan will magically be carried out upon death. But the reality is that the work really begins when the plan is implemented after death. This chapter discusses all the things that must be accomplished after you're gone, or when you are in charge of administering the estate of a loved one.

What happens from an estate planning perspective when I die?

Depending on whether you've completed a will, a trust, or no plan at all, there are things to do when you die.

Typically, one of two things will take place. If you have no plan at all, or if you plan with a will, your estate will go through *probate*. If you plan with trusts, your estate will go through *trust administration*. These processes are described below, along with other issues and topics your family will need to consider.

What is involved in the Probate process?

Probate is a court process in which a part of your affairs are settled. The court proceeding applies to assets owned in your own name.

If there is no will, the process is called *intestate* probate. The State provides a statute to indicate how assets will be distributed. If you have a spouse, the spouse and children usually share in the estate assets in some way.

If there is a will, the process is called *testate* probate. The will tells the probate court how you want your assets distributed.

If there is a surviving spouse, and if no provision is made in your will for him or her, most state law provides that the surviving spouse may take *against* the will and may force a share to her or himself. In addition, surviving spouses may be given elections to take exempt property (often a cash substitute for personal property), homestead (also often a cash amount) and perhaps an amount for one year's living expenses. These are often referred to as *forced shares.*

The probate process is different in every state. In many states, the probate process looks like the following:

- A petition is filed with the court requesting a probate.
- The petition identifies people who would be intestate heirs and if there is a will, identifying those named in the will.
- These people are given notice of the proceeding.
- In many states, the person petitioning may request an informal or independent proceeding in which probate can be accomplished without court hearings.
- In these proceedings, those who wish to raise concerns may need to file their own petition requesting a court hearing on the concern.

After petition, a person is named to administer the estate. In some states, different names are used for this position if there is no will in contrast to those where there is a will. In those states, the person named is an *administrator* (male) or *administratrix* (female) if there is no will, and an *executor* or *executrix* if there is a will. In some states the term *personal representative* is used whether or not there is a will.

What does the personal representative do in probate?

The issues addressed in a normal probate proceed are similar:

1. Identify and collect assets;
2. Identify and pay legitimate bills and claims;
3. Pay taxes;
4. Distribute assets to those who should receive them.

What is involved in identifying and collecting assets?
Getting Organized

The process involves locating things such as bank accounts, safety deposit boxes, investment accounts, life insurance policies, cash, personal property, real estate, personal records, income tax returns, business documents such as buy/sell agreements, and other assets. Then, an inventory of those assets and their value is filed with the probate court, if required by state law. The inventory is eventually used in determining final distribution after payment of expenses, fees, and legitimate claims.

Administration is an asset by asset task. It will be helpful to create a spreadsheet which lists each asset, the asset's location, how title is held, the estimated value, plus a column for the verified value which will probably be filled in later. Each asset must be managed to preserve its value and provide for its proper disposition.

Record Keeping

It is best to keep one checking account. Everything goes into that one account and everything goes out of that account. If funds are received, they go into that account. If a bill is paid, it is paid from that account. If a cash distribution is made, it is made from that account.

If one account is used, required accountings will be far easier. All the data for cash transactions will be in one place.

Tax Identification Number and Income Tax Returns

When a person dies, that person's individual income tax stops. The estate then has income tax obligations. The Personal Representative must obtain a tax identification number. The deceased's final income tax return is due on April 15 in the year following death. The estate has options for choosing its tax year which should be discussed with a professional.

What if there aren't enough assets to pay expenses, fees, and claims?

If there are insufficient assets, a state statute usually provides for priority of payment. The following is a typical list of priorities for payment if there are insufficient funds to pay.

1. Administration costs and expenses;

2. Reasonable funeral and burial expenses;

3. Homestead allowance;

4. Family allowance;

5. Exempt property;

6. Debts and taxes with priority under federal law, including medical assistance payments such as Medicaid;

7. Reasonable and necessary medical and hospital expenses of the decedent's last illness, including compensation of persons attending the decedent;

8. Debts and taxes with priority under the law of the state;

9. All other claims.

What happens next after the bills and taxes are paid?

After assets are collected and bills and taxes paid, the person administering the estate usually files an accounting with the court. Things that are typically included in that report are:

1. The inventory of assets and values when the process began;

2. A list of income and other funds received as well as assets sold;

3. A list of the expenses, fees, and claims paid;

4. A record of changes in the value of the assets during the period of administration (which will typically take months);

5. A revised inventory of assets and values at the time of the report;

6. A proposal for how the assets will be distributed;

7. The proposal often requires acceptance before distribution can begin.

After everything else is administered, the personal representative distributes the assets to those who should receive them. The Court may require that a notice of estate completion be served on the interested parties, and after a stated period of time, the court may close the estate.

Are there any assets that transfer without having to go through probate?

Some assets may transfer without probate. These include:

1. Jointly held assets;

2. Accounts which are payable on death to a beneficiary other than your estate;

3. Assets such as life insurance, annuities, retirement plans, and IRAs, where the beneficiary is someone other than your estate.

There are many practical matters to take into consideration and these are covered in the description of the Trust Settlement Process.

Why is "title" important?

Title refers to how assets are owned, and there is a common expression among planners that "title equals results." In trust planning, for example, the assets must be titled to the trustee of the trust in order for the instructions in the trust to apply to those assets.

If the assets are titled solely in the name of the person who died, those assets are probated. There may be a will which provides instructions to the probate judge.

As mentioned previously, assets may transfer outside of trust and outside of probate if they are jointly owned or a contract beneficiary designation as part of an annuity, life insurance, or retirement account.

In every case, the title of ownership on the asset determines how it is handled after death.

What is Trust Settlement?

Instructions left in trusts and other planning documents usually make the administrative work easier, and can provide tax, asset, and other benefits. They also can make the settlement process less expensive. Nevertheless, there is work to be done and legal pitfalls to avoid.

I heard someone describe a Trustee as a "fiduciary." What does that mean?

The trustee holds the property of other people and has duties concerning preservation and investment of the trust property. In general, the trustee first has a duty to preserve the trust property.

Second, the trustee should try to make trust property as productive as is reasonable under the circumstances of the trust settlement. In other words, since trust settlement may require more liquidity and will terminate in a shorter time period than most ongoing trusts, the trustee should in most cases be more conservative in making investment decisions.

The fiduciary is generally personally liable to the extent of the value of the trust assets for the legitimate bills and taxes of the deceased.

Must the trustee(s) be identified?

After death, it is necessary to identify the trustee and make others aware of the trustee's authority. An affidavit of trust or a certificate of trust is used for this purpose. The affidavit or certificate is presented to people who deal with the trust assets so that they will know the identity of the person(s) in charge of management of the trust. Often it will be necessary for the new person taking over management, the successor trustee, to have a way to show persons doing business with the trust that a change in management has occurred.

If I'm serving as a trustee for a recently deceased loved one, what things should I consider first?

1. If a residence will be vacant for an extended time:
   a. Consider changing locks.
   b. Remove valuables from the residence, make a detailed inventory of them, and store them safely.
   c. Install an inexpensive security system which will dial out to a security firm if there is a break-in.
   d. In colder climates, consider a temperature alarm to prevent frozen water pipes, etc.
   e. Request Postmaster to forward mail.

    f. Decide whether to turn off some utilities (gas, electricity, telephone). This will be based in part on your decision about a security system, climate, etc.

    g. Stop newspaper deliveries.

    h. Advise the homeowner's insurance agent or company that the residence will be vacant and make appropriate arrangements for insurance. If title to the property is in the trust, the trust needs to be the named as the insured.

    i. If the property is a condominium or cooperative, arrangements must be made for payment of periodic fees, and the condominium or cooperative agreements must be reviewed so that the Trustee is aware as to what is required for compliance.

2. Determine immediate cash needs for any beneficiary and for immediate expenses, and identify accounts where cash is immediately available. (But do not make payments without discussing it first with the attorney who is assisting with administration.)

3. Cancel charge accounts, credit cards, and magazine subscriptions and ask for refunds, if applicable.

4. Make certain that property and casualty insurance coverage continues on personal effects, automobiles, real estate, and any goods in storage. If any of these items are titled in the name of Trust, make sure the Trust is the named as the insured.

5. If you have personal access or access as Trustee to a safe deposit box, do not remove the contents on your own. The box should be inventoried in the presence of a bank officer and only then should contents be removed.

6. Gather personal records, including checkbooks and statements for at least three years; obtain copies of income tax returns for the last three years.

7. Contact individuals who owe money to the deceased and arrange for continued collection.

8. Gather all life and accident insurance policies. Don't forget to check for policies issued by travel clubs, alumni associations, trade associations, and any other organizations that might make life insurance available to its members.

9. Contact the Social Security Administration and the Veterans Administration (if applicable) and advise them of the death.

10. Hold any Social Security or Pension check received *after* the date of death. If a direct deposit is made to an account after death, note the deposit and inform the attorney.

11. Decide about the employment of domestic help, security guards, or any other type of assistance that might be required for a dependent beneficiary.

12. Be prepared to demonstrate to third parties with whom you deal that you are in fact authorized to act on behalf of the Living Trust or Probate Estate. Your estate planning attorney can create an Affidavit of Trust that identifies your authority as Trustee. If there is a probate, your Letters of Authority identify you as Personal Representative.

13. Check to see if there are pets or other animals needing care.

14. Check to see if there are perishable items in the residence or in storage, and deal with them accordingly.

Are there things I should avoid during these early stages of administration?

- Avoid allowing someone to drive the vehicle titled in the name of the deceased until it is properly insured.

- Avoid distributing tangible personal property early unless it is specifically designated for a particular person, or unless all potential distributes agree on the distribution.

- Avoid being heavy-handed about your authority as trustee.

- Avoid deviating from the terms and instructions in the trust.

When do I provide information to a beneficiary?

The law of each state is different concerning the information given to beneficiaries and when the information must be provided. Professional help will probably be needed to obtain the requirements. As early as possible, the person who is the fiduciary should obtain information about beneficiaries and heirs. Beneficiaries are people named in a will, trust, retirement plan, pension plan, annuity, or life insurance contract designated to receive a benefit. Heirs are people who, in the absence of a different designation in a will or trust, will receive the estate and property of another upon that other person's death.

What about funeral arrangements?

Many trusts provide for the payment of funeral expenses. Some people who have made trusts may have made prepaid funeral arrangements or may have left memorial instructions. If those arrangements have not been made or if some want to enhance those arrangements, great sensitivity is in order. A heavy hand by the trustee at this stage is likely to result in lingering resentment throughout the rest of the trust administration.

What should I do about creditors?

Creditor claims fall into two categories: (1) those that arose before the loved one died and (2) those arising after death.

Claims Arising Before Death

Providing deadlines for creditors to collect is usually a good thing for the family. It provides certainty about the rest of the administration. Most probate procedures require publication of a notice to unknown creditors and actual notice to known creditors. The creditors then have a limited period of time—typically 4 to 6 months—to make their claims in writing or lose the claim. Where trusts are involved, some states permit a notice similar to that in probate. In other states where that procedure is not provided, practitioners sometimes open an empty probate and publish a notice to creditors in order to cut off potential creditor's claims.

Claims Arising After Death

Claims arising after death are usually referred to as expenses of administration. These bills may be for professional fees; expenses to manage, maintain and safeguard the assets; and personal representative and trustee fees and expenses.

How do I handle Social Security and pension payments?

A lump sum death benefit may be available from Social Security to the surviving spouse or child of the deceased. Check with the local Social Security Administration office.

The funeral director will generally help with stopping social security payments. If the deceased was receiving Social Security payments, the personal representative or trustee should verify this is done and if not done should give the notice to Social Security of the death. If payments are received to which the deceased was not entitled, they must be repaid.

Depending on the elections the deceased made during life, the right to receive pension payments may end. If there is a surviving spouse, the deceased may have made an election to have payments continue at the same or a lesser amount after his or her death. If payments are received to which the deceased was not entitled, they must be repaid.

Retirement plans and individual retirement accounts are different from pensions. They are like savings accounts with favorable income tax benefits. The beneficiary designation must be checked to determine how the account is to be paid. More details on handling retirement plans and IRAs are found in Chapter 10. Technical rules apply and professional help is usually needed.

If there is a surviving spouse, at age 60 that spouse may be able to claim monthly benefits on the social security account of the deceased. If there are minor children, social security benefits will likely be available and should be applied for.

What about annuities?

Fixed annuities are long term contracts with insurance companies. They usually have a beneficiary designation. The annuity may be inside a retirement plan or IRA or it may be a contract owned by the deceased or owned by the deceased's living trust. The annuity may have been treated like a savings account, building up value while deferring income taxes or the deceased may have exercised contracts rights to receive periodic regular payments. The annuity company should be contacted to determine what elections were made. If binding elections were not made, then the annuity contract should be reviewed to determine what elections' can be made now by the beneficiary of the annuity.

What do we do with life insurance policies?

Claims for life insurance should be made. Professional assistance is helpful because of the variety of options insurance companies provide for receipt of funds and because of the changes in name and entities which often happen between the time of policy purchase and claim.

Life insurance may have been offered as an incentive to open accounts or do business by credit unions, credit card companies, banks, automobile insurers, and others. The records of the deceased should be checked for these policies and it can pay off to check with those who might have provided the policies. These types of policies are usually in small amounts like $1,000 or $2,000. If a few are found, however, death benefits can total $5,000 to $10,000, making inquiry worthwhile.

What happens with minor or disabled beneficiaries?

Guardianship and/or Conservatorship may be necessary if there are minor or disabled beneficiaries. State laws differ, but guardianship typically describes who cares for the *person* of the beneficiary, and conservatorship describes who cares for the *finances (assets)* of the beneficiary.

Laws also differ on who can act on behalf of these beneficiaries. Disabled beneficiaries may have agents to manage their affairs under a durable power of attorney. For example, if a minor or an incompetent person is the beneficiary of a trust, will, or intestate estate, it may be necessary to appoint a guardian for that person. If a trust created during the life of the deceased is involved, there may be provisions in the trust which address this situation, and which make appointment of a guardian unnecessary.

TAX CONSIDERATIONS

What income tax issues should be considered?

There will eventually be a final income tax return prepared for the deceased for the year of death. You should consult your professional advisors for help with this step. A review of returns for the past three years will help identify income tax issues and, in addition, may alert the Personal Representative or Trustee to additional assets.

Will federal and state death taxes have to be paid?

Federal and state death taxes are not necessarily tied together in any logical fashion. Each state may have its own death tax pattern. Generally, a tax on the **transfer** of assets at death is called an "estate tax." The tax is usually calculated on the total value of the "estate" of the deceased person.

An "inheritance tax" is a tax on the **receipt** of assets by beneficiaries. Generally, the tax is calculated based on the amount the beneficiary receives and the amount exempt from tax. The tax rate may even vary depending on the relationship of the beneficiary to the deceased.

How are federal estate taxes handled?

If there is a federal estate tax, the value of the estate assets for federal estate tax purposes needs to be determined as quickly as possible.

If there is a federal estate tax, it applies to all assets owned by the deceased, including assets in his or her revocable trust. Assets not included in the deceased's probate estate are included in the deceased's estate for federal estate tax purposes. It includes real property, bank accounts, investments, insurance owned by the deceased, joint property for which the deceased paid, tangible personal property, retirement accounts, stock options, deferred compensation, and more.

If husband and wife planned, there may be a living trust or a trust in a will which divides the assets of the first to die into two (or more) trusts which are created after the death of the first spouse to die. One trust is used to preserve the exemption amount of the deceased person and the other is to obtain the marital deduction available because there is a surviving spouse. These techniques are discussed in greater detail in Chapters 4 and 5.

What do I do about the Generation Skipping Transfer Tax?

The generation skipping tax is an additional tax to the federal estate tax designed to discourage skipping generations as a means of avoiding federal estate tax. This tax is meant to preserve the federal estate tax by imposing an added tax when generations are skipped.

If assets are transferred to grandchildren, grandnieces and grandnephews, etc. or to persons 35 or more years younger than the deceased, there may be a generation skipping tax issue if the deceased transfers more than the amount allowed in total to people in these categories. This tax is discussed in greater detail in Chapter 4. If there is a question about the application of the generation skipping tax, contact a competent professional.

What things have the greatest potential to cause disputes?
Tangible Personal Property Including Pictures

Tangible personal property and pictures have value far beyond their economic value. When someone passes on, the tangible personal property and pictures bring back important memories and hold great sentimental value. Disputes may arise if not handled with sensitivity.

Other Disputes

There can be attacks on the documents. Was there undue influence, lack of capacity, or mistake? There may be actions to remove the trustee or to require additional accountings. There may be disagreements on the apportionment of taxes and expenses, and deciding who should bear the burden. Family businesses can be a source of great conflict, especially when some beneficiaries are involved in the business, and others are not. Previous chapters discuss how to plan to avoid disputes in the family business.

What happens in final distribution?

The final step in settlement of a trust or an estate is to distribute the assets to those who should receive them. The trust, will, or state statute will direct how the final distribution is to be made. Making a chart as to the sub-trust or person entitled to each asset's value will be very helpful.

The will or living trust may create sub-trusts or separate trusts. Those successor trusts will need to obtain their Tax Identification Numbers using IRS form SS-4 and should consider using IRS form 56 to notify the IRS that tax reporting is about to start.

If the administration follows the death of the first spouse, distribution may be to the surviving spouse or to sub-trusts created in the will or living trust of the deceased spouse. If outright distribution to a spouse or spouse and children is instructed, the distribution may not require extensive analysis. If distribution is to sub-trusts, the assistance of competent professionals is recommended so that the sub-trusts are properly established and so that assets are properly distributed to those trusts.

The Personal Representative or Trustee may wish to request that the beneficiaries consent to the proposed distribution. If a beneficiary does not consent, the personal representative or trustee may wish to request a court having jurisdiction to approve the proposed distribution. Assistance of competent professionals is advised.

APPENDIX A

Index of Contributing Authors

Authors Listed Alphabetically by Last Name

Robert M. Birgen, CPA (inactive), CFP®, CIMA
Abridge Partners, LLC
21700 E. Copley Drive
Suite 120
Diamond Bar, CA 91765
(909) 860-9992
www.abridgepartnersllc.com
rbirgen@abridgepartnersllc.com

T. Walton Dallas, J.D., LL.M.
Attorney at Law
T. Walton Dallas, P.A.
130 Riverview Drive
Suite A
Flowood, MS 39232
(601) 209-8327
www.estateplanning123.com
wdallas@estateplanning123.com

Michael A. Flanagan, CFP®, ChFC, CLU
Abridge Partners, LLC
6 Crawford Street
Middletown, DE 19709
(302) 378-1882
www.abridgepartnersllc.com
mflanagansr@abridgepartnersllc.com

Randy Fox
InKnowVision, LLC
1111 South Washington Street
Naperville, IL 60540
(630) 596-5090
www.InKnowVision.com
randy@InKnowVision.com

David Frisse, J.D.
Attorney at Law
Frisse & Brewster Law Offices, LLC
P.O. Box 430
307 West Wood Street
Paris, IL 61944
(217) 465-1234
www.frissebrewsterlaw.com
dave@frisselaw.com

Michael Glowacki, M.B.T.,
CPA, CFP®
President
The Glowacki Group
11400 West Olympic Boulevard
Suite 1500
Los Angeles, CA 90064
(310) 473-0100
www.glowackigroup.com
mg@glowackigroup.com

Suzanne M. Graves, J.D.
Attorney & Counselor at Law
1317 W. Foothill Boulevard
Suite 245
Upland, CA 91786
(909) 981-6177
www.SuzanneGraves.com
SGraves@SuzanneGraves.com

Scott Hamilton, J.D.
Attorney at Law
InKnowVision, LLC
1111 South Washington Street
Naperville, IL 60540
(630) 596-5090
www.InKnowVision.com
scott@InKnowVision.com

Frank W. Heers, J.D.
Attorney at Law
Heers & Heers
1450 Frankson Avenue
Saint Paul, MN 55108
www.selfsettledtrusts.com
heerslaw@comcast.net

N. Douglas Hostetler, CFP®,
ChFC, CLU
Hostetler & Church, LLC
6030 Daybreak Circle
Suite A150\106
Clarksville, MD 21029
(410) 740-3303
www.hostetlerchurchllc.com
dhostetler@hostetlerchurchllc.com

James D. Howard, Ph.D.,
CFP®, AEP®
Abridge Partners, LLC
421 W. Riverside Avenue
Suite 1700
Spokane, WA 99201
(509) 747-5101
www.abridgepartnersllc.com
jhoward@abridgepartnersllc.com

Jimmie L. Joe, J.D.
Attorney at Law
Law Offices of Jimmie L. Joe
A Professional Law Corporation
17700 Castleton Street
Suite 358
City of Industry, CA 91748
(626) 839-8980
www.theestateplanninglawyer.com
jjoe@theestateplanninglawyer.com

Joel Keeth, J.D., LL.M. (Tax)
Attorney at Law
Keeth-Scott Law Group, P.C.
1120 Lincoln Street
Suite 1511
Denver, CO 80203
(303) 914-1111 Denver
(970) 663-5206 Loveland
www.keeth-scott.com
joel@keeth-scott.com

J. David Kerr, J.D.
Attorney at Law
Kerr & Associates, PLLC
205 South Main Street
Mount Pleasant, MI 48858
(989) 773-7071
www.kerrandassociates.com
Estate-plan@lawyer.com

Bradley R. Konopaske, CFP®
Legacy by Design, LLC
Empire Asset Management Group,
   LLC
5 Clinton Square
Albany, NY 12207
(518) 465-6447
www.empireasset.com
brad@empireasset.com

Anthony Madonia, J.D.
Attorney at Law
Anthony J. Madonia & Associates,
   Ltd.
233 S. Wacker Drive
Suite 6825
Chicago, IL 60606
(312) 578-9300
www.madonia.com
tony@madonia.com

Bret A. Overdorf, CPA, CFP®
Bret A. Overdorf, CPA, PC
5952 Alexandria Pike
Anderson, IN 46012
(765) 642-9997
bret@overdorf.net

Scot Overdorf, JD, CPA
Attorney at Law
Law Offices of Scot W. Overdorf,
   P.C.
5913 Camelback Court
Indianapolis, Indiana 46250
(317) 845-5444
overdorf@comcast.net

Paul S. Paska, LUTCF
Legacy by Design, LLC
Empire Asset Management Group,
   LLC
5 Clinton Square
Albany, NY 12207
(518) 465-6447
www.empireasset.com
paul@empireasset.com

**Peter B. Scott, J.D., LL.M. (Tax),
CFP®**
Attorney at Law
Keeth-Scott Law Group, P.C.
1120 Lincoln Street
Suite 1511
Denver, CO 80203
(303) 914-1111 Denver
(970) 663-5206 Loveland
www.keeth-scott.com
peter@keeth-scott.com

Richard Shapiro, J.D.
Blustein, Shapiro, Rich & Barone,
   LLP
10 Matthews Street
Goshen, New York 10924
(845) 291-0011
(866) 692-0011 (toll free)
http://www.mid-hudsonlaw.com
rshapiro@mid-hudsonlaw.com

Andrew Sigerson, J.D.
Andrew C. Sigerson, P.C. LLO
Legacy Design Strategies, LLC
13750 Millard Avenue
Suite 200
Omaha, NE 68137
(402) 505-5400
www.ldstrategies.com
andrew@ldstrategies.com

Ronald E. Stutes, J.D.
Attorney & Counselor at Law
The Stutes Law Group, LLC
2900 Westfork Drive
Suite 200
Baton Rouge, LA 70827
(225) 295-5654
www.stuteslawgroup.com
stuteslawgroup@aol.com

Joel S. Williams, Ph.D., CFP®, IMCA
President
JSW | An Alliance of Wealth
    Advisors
1995 S. Main Street
Suite 903
Blacksburg, VA 24060
(888) 553-2211, ext. 540
www.JoelSWilliams.com
joelw@JoelSWilliams.com

Index